Freedom For Catalonia?

Catalan Nationalism, Spanish Ident...
Barcelona Olympic Games

Although the fight for independence by national minorities has received much attention recently, there is no study of how globalised sport in its most advanced form can help to stimulate it. This book shows how the 1992 Olympic Games raised the tension that already existed between Catalonia and Spain, from the time they were awarded to Barcelona until they opened. John Hargreaves analyses and explains the way in which the conflict developed and was eventually resolved in terms of the special characteristics of Catalan nationalism, the nature of the new Spanish democracy and the special role played by the International Olympic Committee.

This book will be relevant to academics, researchers and postgraduates specialising in nationalism and Catalan nationalism, as well as being of interest to teachers, researchers and students of political sociology, cultural studies and sports studies, and professionals working in the fields of culture, sport, recreation and leisure.

JOHN HARGREAVES is Visiting Professor at the Chelsea School Research Centre, University of Brighton. He is the author of *Sport, Power and Culture*, and has published articles in *Nations and Nationalism* as well as writing numerous articles on the sociological analysis of both sport and nationalism.

Freedom For Catalonia?

Catalan Nationalism, Spanish Identity and the Barcelona Olympic Games

John Hargreaves

University of Brighton

PUBLISHED BY THE PRESS SYNDICATE OF THE UNIVERSITY OF CAMBRIDGE
The Pitt Building, Trumpington Street, Cambridge, United Kingdom

CAMBRIDGE UNIVERSITY PRESS
The Edinburgh Building, Cambridge CB2 2RU, UK   www.cup.cam.ac.uk
40 West 20th Street, New York, NY 10011–4211, USA   www.cup.org
10 Stamford Road, Oakleigh, Melbourne 3166, Australia
Ruiz de Alarcón 13, 28014 Madrid, Spain

First published 2000

Printed in the United Kingdom at the University Press, Cambridge

Typeset in Plantin 10/12 pt in QuarkXPress™   [SE]

A catalogue record for this book is available from the British Library

Library of Congress Cataloguing in Publication data

Hargreaves, John (John E. R.)
Freedom for Catalonia? Catalan Nationalism, Spanish Identity,
and the Barcelona Olympic Games/John Hargreaves.
    p.   cm.
Includes bibliographical references.
ISBN 0 521 58426 4 (hb). – ISBN 0 521 58615 1 (pb)
1. Nationalism – Spain – Catalonia – History – 20th Century.
2. Catalonia (Spain) – Politics and government – 20th century.
3. Olympic Games (25th: 1992: Barcelona, Spain) – Political
aspects.   4. Nationalism and sports – Spain – Catalonia – History – 20th
century.   I. Title.
DP302.C69H37   2000
320.54'0946'70904–dc21   99–36186   CIP

ISBN 0 521 58426 4 hardback
ISBN 0 521 58615 1 paperback

Contents

Tables

Acknowledgements

The fieldwork for this book was carried out in Catalonia, mainly in Barcelona, in the months running up to the Games and in their aftermath. I should like to express my gratitude to the Economic and Social Research Council for their award (R.-000.-23.-3970) and to the Leverhulme Foundation for giving me a Fellowship, without which the fieldwork would not have been accomplished.

It is hardly possible to mention all the people, many of whom became good friends during my stays in Barcelona, whose kind help and cooperation made this research possible, but I would like to record my thanks especially to the following: Miquel de Moragas, director of the Centre d'Estudis Olímpics at the Autonomous University of Barcelona; Rafel Llusà, Jefe de Gabinete of the Town Hall Sports and Olympic Games Directorate; Albert Mújica, of the Catalan government Directorate of Sport; Alfred Bosch, personal assistant to the director general of the Barcelona Olympic Games Organising Committee (COOB); Josep Roca, Ceremonies and Torch Project Manager at COOB; Jordi Sánchez of La Crida; Marc Puig of Acció Olímpica; and Xavier Vinyals of the Catalan Olympic Committee. For what amounted to many stimulating hours of discussion, much helpful advice and congenial company I should like to thank, especially, the following colleagues at the Autonomous University of Barcelona: Antoni Estradé, Lluis Flaquer, Salvador Cardús, Jordi Busquet, Ferran Brunet, Joan Botella, Geroni Sureda; and, at the University of Barcelona, Angel Zaragoza. I owe much also to Nuria Puig of the National Physical Education Institute of Catalonia for her constant help. My thanks must also go to two colleagues with whom I have been fortunate enough to mull over Catalan and Spanish politics and whose stimulating influence I have felt over the last few years – Manuel García Ferrando of the University of Valencia and Josep Llobera of University College, London. I alone am responsible, however, for the account that follows.

Abbreviations

ABC	American Broadcasting Company
COC	Comitè Olímpic de Catalunya (Catalan Olympic Committee)
CIS	Centro de Investigaciones Sociológicas (Centre for Sociological Research)
COOB	Comité Organizador Olímpico de Barcelona (Organising Committee of the Barcelona Olympic Games)
COE	Comité Olímpico Español (Spanish Olympic Committee)
CDC	Convergencia Democràtica de Catalunya (Democratic Convergence Party of Catalonia) – nationalist party led by Pujol and one of the two constitutent parties of CiU (see below)
CiU	Convergencia i Unió (Convergence and Union Party) – the main nationalist party forming the government of Catalonia
CCOO	Comissiones Obreras (Workers' Commissions) – Communist trade union
ERC	Esquerra Republicana de Catalunya (Republican Left of Catalonia) – the main separatist party
ETA	Euskadi ta Askatusuna (Basque Homeland and Liberty) – Basque separatist terrorist organisation
FIFA	International Federation of Football Associations
IAAF	International Amateur Athletic Federation
IC	Iniciativa de Catalunya (Catalan Communist Party)
IOC	International Olympic Committee
ISL	International Sport and Leisure – the major international sports promotion agency
IU	Izquierda Unida (Spanish Communist Party)
JERC	Joventuts d' Esquerra Republicana de Catalunya (Republican Left Youth of Catalonia) – ERC youth organisation
JNC	Joventut Nacionalista de Catalunya (Nationalist Youth of Catalonia) – CDC youth organisation
NBC	National Broadcasting Company
NOC	National Olympic Committee
OCA	Olympic Council for Asia
PP	Partido Popular (Spanish Conservative Party)
PRC	People's Republic of China
PSC	Partit Socialista de Catalunya (Catalan Socialist Party) – affiliate of PSOE (see below)
PSOE	Partido Socialista Obrero Español (Spanish Socialist Workers Party)
TOP	The Olympic Sponsorship Programme
UDC	Unió Democràtico Cristiano (Christian Democratic Union) – one of the two constituent parties of CiU (see above)
UGT	Union General de Trabajadores – trade union linked to PSOE (see above)

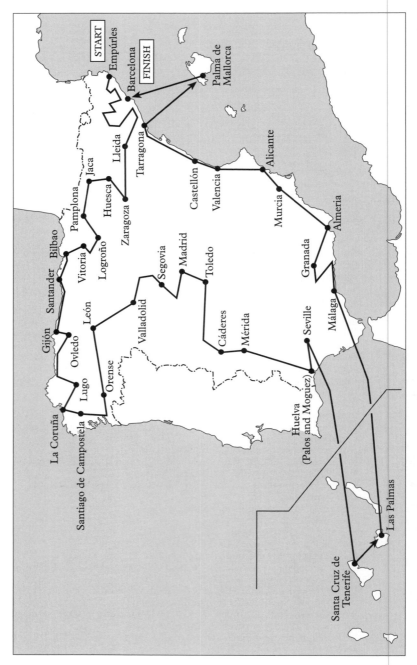

Map 1 The Olympic torch: its journey around Spain

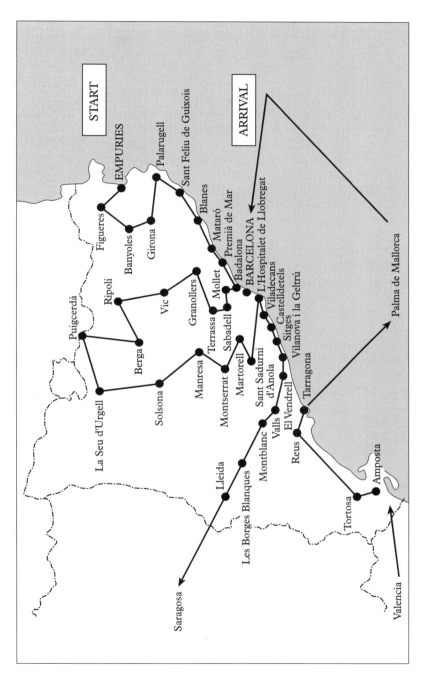

Map 2 The Olympic torch: its journey around Catalonia

Introduction

One of the most intriguing developments of recent years has been the strengthening of local, regional and national identities in the context of the activities of supra-national structures such as the European Union and multinational business corporations, processes of globalisation, and the emergence of a 'new world order' with the collapse of the USSR. The problem of the resurgence of nationalism in the modern world has attracted much scholarly, as well as public interest, but relatively little attention has been paid to the role of sport in this connection and to the role of the Olympic movement in particular, which is a quintessentially global phenomenon. There is no specifically sociological monograph on this problem.

It is abundantly clear that the Olympic ideal of a non-political Games contributing to international understanding cannot be taken at face value, given the extent to which the Olympic movement, in reality, is subject to the play of political, economic and cultural forces. In particular, symbols of the nation and the state and ritual practices celebrating national identities are at the core of the Olympic Games. However, it is certainly a moot point as to whether Olympism merely reflects the influence of such forces, or whether it exists in a much more complex dynamic relationship with them.

The 1992 Barcelona Olympic Games presented an excellent opportunity to examine the relationship between Olympism and nationalism in the form of a case study. The host city is not only an important industrial metropolis within the Spanish state: it is also the capital of Catalonia, a historic nation with a strong sense of cultural identity. Given the past animosities between Madrid and Barcelona – not least during the civil war when Catalonia fought against Franco on the Republican side and suffered his 'politics of revenge' as a result – and given all that was at stake for Spain and for Catalonia economically, politically and culturally as a result of Barcelona's successful bid for the Games, there were bound to be tensions if not outright conflict between them, in which Catalan nationalism would play a major part.

What follows is an analysis of a specific conjuncture: Olympism had reached its apogee as a global cultural phenomenon and Catalan nationalism was flexing its muscles as part of a contemporary resurgence of ethnic nationalism. Of course, these Games had their own specific features, but hopefully an in-depth examination reveals something of the character of modern nationalism as well as of Olympism.

Chapter 1 analyses the relationship between sport and nationalism in general terms with reference to a range of instances. Particular attention is paid to the need to employ a more rigorous conception of the nation and nationalism than in the past in this connection, to the character of sport as a cultural form, and to the part played by symbols in the relationship between sport and nationalism.

Chapter 2 adumbrates further the conceptual framework for understanding nationalism introduced in chapter 1, and sets the relationship between Catalonia and Spain in a socio-historical context, showing how nationalism became a dominant force in Catalan political life. Thus it sets the scene for the conflict that was occasioned by the Olympics.

Chapter 3 examines the structure of Olympism as a global cultural phenomenon, the political, economic and cultural dimensions of its activities, and its relationship to nationalism.

Chapter 4 gives a detailed account of the nationalists' campaign to Catalanise the Games and how conflict developed between the Catalan nationalists and their opponents in the period between when the Games were awarded to Barcelona and when they actually opened.

Chapter 5 compares the extent to which the Games as a mode of cultural performance were, on the one hand, Catalanised and, on the other, Españolised, in terms of the elaborate, complex symbolic work that went on throughout the length of the Games.

Chapter 6 examines Olympic internationalist ideology and shows how it, together with Europeanisation, Americanisation and globalisation interacted with the process of Catalanisation.

Chapter 7 adduces the factors responsible for the outcome of the conflict between the competing interests that were mobilised around the Games, with particular reference to the strategies adopted by the different agents, the gains they made, and the nature of the political culture that they shared.

Chapter 8 summarises the findings, assesses the significance of the outcome for relations between Spain and Catalonia in the future, and what this indicates about the extent to which the viability of pluralist states is challenged by ethnic nationalism.

1   Sport and nationalism

Introduction

While specialists in nationalism have paid a good deal of attention to central aspects of culture such as language and religion, they have paid remarkably little attention to that other aspect of culture around which nationalism so often coheres in the modern world, namely, sport. Analysis of the relationship has suffered from inadequate conceptualisation as well as ideological bias. There is also an unfortunate tendency in the literature on this question to treat sport as a mere reflection of politics.

In realist international relations theory, if nationalism permeates international relations, then we should expect the conduct of sport at the international level automatically to reflect this state of affairs (Kanin, 1981). From Marxisant perspectives sport provides a ready vehicle for diffusing nationalist ideology to the masses and diverting them from their true interests. Thus the celebration of the American nation in the 1984 Los Angeles Games has been interpreted as promoting American ideals and values in a nationalist mode that helped to conceal and mitigate the effects of major divisions in American society (Lawrence and Rowe, 1986). References to sport and the nation in the British mass media are taken to represent the hegemony of 'banal nationalism' (Billig, 1995) and successive Conservative governments in Britain are held to have used sport for 'nationalistic purposes' (Houlihan, 1997). Globalised sport is said to have legitimised British imperialism and nationalism in the late nineteenth and early twentieth centuries (Holt, 1995) and to be helping to foist Western rationality and values on the non-West today (MacAloon, 1996; Houlihan, 1994). Such accounts are deficient, not only because they have little if any conception of sport as an autonomous cultural form, but also because they have no clear conception of nationalism.

The prevalence of loose conceptions of nationalism where sport is concerned is a major source of confusion. The term has come to signify ideas, sentiments and policies, including state policy, international conflicts and supportive public opinion. Often it means no more than an irrational, atavistic form of politics, or obnoxious and aggressive policies pursued by governments. If all policies that states and nations adopt and their consequent actions in pursuit of what they conceive to be 'the national interest' are regarded as nationalist, then the use of the term is emptied of any specific meaning and it is rendered useless as an analytical tool (Breuilly, 1993). The nub of the confusion is a common failure to distinguish nationalist politics from other forms of politics, and this stems from the propensity to equate the state with the nation, and nationalism with the behaviour of the 'nation-state'. A vast diversity of cases of sport supposedly getting tied up with nationalism can thus be adduced, making it difficult, if not impossible, to formulate a theory which would encompass all of them, and indeed making it difficult not to find a connection between sport and nationalism. When it is claimed that cases as diverse as the role played by gymnastics clubs in the process of German unification in the nineteenth century, the nineteenth-century British cult of athleticism, hooliganism among English football supporters today, the Nazi-organised Berlin Olympics of 1936, Olympic politicking between the US and the USSR during the cold war, and public references to cricket by the last conservative prime minister, John Major, all reveal the machinations of nationalism at work in sport, there is plainly a need to be clear about what is meant by nationalism.

Nationalism is a specific type of politics generated where political movements seeking or exercising state power justify their action by attributing a specifically nationalist meaning to the symbol 'nation' (Brubaker, 1996). Essentially, nationalist ideology takes the form of a claim that there exists a nation with an explicit and peculiar character, one of a world of nations, each with its own individuality, history and destiny. The nation is the source of all political power: loyalty to it overrides all other allegiances and its interests take priority over all other interests and values. Human beings must identify with the nation if they want to be free and realise their potential. If the nation is to be free and secure it must have sovereignty: that is to say the nation must possess its own state so that state and nation coincide (Breuilly, 1993; Smith, 1991). The idea of the peculiar nation is the explicit foundation of nationalists' political claims: statements in these terms, often incorporating the idea that the nation is seriously threatened, constitute the central ideological assertions deployed by nationalist movements and organisations.

Confusion about nationalism results when the elementary analytical distinction between the state and the nation is ignored and the two entities are elided. The concept of the state refers to the institution which successfully claims the monopoly of the legitimate use of force within a given territory (Weber, 1948). Nations, on the other hand, are population groups held together by a particular kind of enduring identity which encompasses common myths of origin, historical memories, a common culture, conceptions of common rights, duties and economic opportunities and, above all, attachment to a given territory.[1] Modern states attempt to minimise and overcome internal divisions by fostering a sense of national identity, and governments typically claim to act in the national interest. Consequently, the two terms, 'state' and 'nation' are taken to be synonymous, as in the tendency to refer to the modern polity as the 'nation-state'. It should be clear, however, that it is possible for nations to emerge and exist for long periods without having states of their own. And the corollary of this is that many modern states – in fact the majority of them today – despite their nation-building ambitions, are multinational, rather than one-nation states. Of course, states and nations are often nationalistic, but they are not necessarily so, for nationalist movements emerge and nationalist strategies are adopted only in certain conditions and these vary tremendously.

Lastly, it should be clear that nationalism may function in support of or against the state. States may encourage nationalism in response to perceived internal or external threats, or they may be taken over by nationalist movements emanating from below. Alternatively, a nationalist movement may be generated among a national minority seeking to enhance its position within, or gain its independence from, its host state.

Nationalist and non-nationalist constructions of sport distinguished

Having cleared the ground conceptually as to the specificity of nationalist politics, it is possible to determine which kinds of cases can be classified as genuinely nationalist constructions of sport and which cannot. Let us first take the case of gymnastics and German nationalism. In the early nineteenth century, Johann Friedrich Jahn invented *Turnen*, from which German gymnastics, the modern form of competitive gymnastics, developed as a means of strengthening and directing the German national will

---

[1] The attempt to define the nation and use it as an analytical category is challenged by Rogers Brubaker (1996) on the grounds that to treat nations as 'real' substantial entities is to mistake a category of practice for a category of analysis. It is to reify a category that is a constructed, ideologically manipulated, fluid and continually changing aspect of political practice. In his opinion we would be better off referring to 'nationhood' or 'nationness'. Defining the nation is undoubtedly difficult and full of traps, but without a definition one cannot get anywhere and, as he admits, most commentators recognise that nations are not fixed entities. Of course, the same objection could be made with respect to the state, and he is inconsistent in not doing so. Also, in any case, the same objection could surely be applied to 'nationhood' and 'nationness'.

in the cause of German unification. The *Turnen* movement advocated the superiority of everything German over the foreign. Immensely successful in creating a network of clubs throughout Germany, *Turnen* became a pillar of German nationalism – so much so that when football spread to the continent from Britain it was denounced in Germany as 'the English disease', as un-German, a symptom of Anglo-Saxon superficiality and materialism, the product of a land without music or metaphysics. English games were considered rational, international and semitic, lacking 'higher values' such as reference to *Volk* and *Vaterland* (Dixon, 1986). Here we have an unequivocal case of sport being used to mobilise nationalist forces against the existing state structures and helping to produce a new, modern and highly nationalistic German state.

Contrast this with the cult of athleticism in Britain at the time. In Britain, it was to a significant extent through the cult of athleticism promoted in the public schools as the second half of the nineteenth century wore on, as the empire grew, and Britain came close to achieving global hegemony, that a sense of national superiority, tinged later with jingoistic sentiment, was diffused, especially among the dominant classes (Hargreaves, 1986). An important cultural aspect of the expansion of Britain's power was the export of sport to large areas of the world and especially to the empire, where it provided a source of social solidarity for the British in an alien environment and a means of enculturing their subjects.

It has been argued that British nationalism thus concealed itself under the cloak of racist imperialism which, it is claimed, was a prominent feature of the cult of athleticism (Holt, 1995). The cult of athleticism as a child of its times was, no doubt, permeated by imperialist sentiment, but the claim that it was racist–nationalist is based largely on the fact that social Darwinist notions of racial superiority were currently in fashion. However, British imperialism was not a unitary phenomenon: it was driven as well by a variety of other ideal and material interests, from religious conviction, strategic considerations, economic advantage and philanthropic motives to liberal and progressive ideas. Even if we were to accept that racist imperialism inspired the cult of athleticism and that racism and imperialism could be equated with nationalism, there would still be a problem. The cult of athleticism was largely restricted to the elite's sports, and so could not possibly have been used to help mobilise a mass nationalist movement.

The promotion of sport in Britain differed fundamentally from the pattern in comparable countries like Germany and France at the time. There was no centralised state direction of sport, or any ambition to encompass the whole population, let alone a concerted drive to promote sport for military preparation and national unity. Those who favoured such policies in ruling circles were a small minority who failed to obtain the requisite support for their programme (Hargreaves, 1986; Kruger, 1996). Sport was, in the main, firmly in the hands of elements within civil society – the public schools, the churches, and the voluntary associations – whose efforts to spread a suitably modified version of the cult of athleticism, through the rational recreation movement, were limited to targeting only certain sections of the population deemed to be in need of social order and discipline. Sporting activity in Britain before 1914 may often have had patriotic overtones but it hardly amounted to the kind of nationalistic mobilisation we see at the time in Germany and France.

Today, great national sporting events like the FA Cup Final, enveloped in rather elaborate ritual and ceremonial activity, deploy powerful symbols of the nation – the presence of royalty, flying the Union Jack, playing the national anthem, singing 'Abide with me', etc. – and thereby celebrate national unity, but this is far from constituting a mobilisation of nationalist sentiment as such. It is true that English football hooliganism today is tinged with xenophobia and ethnocentrism, but this involves only a minority of supporters and hardly amounts to the significant manifestation of English ethnic nationalism that some commentators are wont to detect. Nor should the vociferous support given by immigrant groups to visiting cricket teams from their countries of origin, when they play against England, be necessarily taken as expressions of anti-British nationalist sentiment, although clearly questions of ethnic and national identity are involved here (Werbner, 1996).

In fact, paradoxically, the way that indigenous nationalism manifests itself in sport in Britain is predominantly in the form of minority, peripheral nationalism directed against the British state. Apart from Welsh and Scottish nationalism, which tends to be given vent in football and rugby matches against England, and which is of limited political significance (Jarvie and Walker, 1994), easily the most important nationalist construction of sport within the British state concerns Irish nationalism. The thinking of leading Irish nationalists like Archbishop Croke lay behind the foundation in 1884 of the Gaelic Athletic Association. He complained of 'the ugly and irritating fact that we are daily importing from England not only her manufactured goods . . . but her fashions, her accents, her vicious literature, her dances and her pastimes to the utter discredit of our grand national sports, and to the sore humiliation, as I believe, of every son and daughter of the old land' (Holt, 1995: 45). The Gaelic Athletic Association established itself as the most important sporting body in Ireland in the struggle for Irish independence that culminated in the formation of the Irish Republic in 1921. It pursued a policy of promoting exclusively Irish sports, like hurling and Gaelic football, and refused to play English sports on the grounds that they undermined Irish culture. It plays a prominent part in the Irish republican, nationalist movement in Northern Ireland today (Sugden and Bairner, 1986; 1993). Indeed, sport is one of the most important ways in which divisions between the Catholic nationalist and Protestant unionist communities are maintained. Although rugby, cricket and hockey are organised on an all-Ireland basis, i.e. their governing bodies embrace the British North of Ireland and the Republic of Ireland (with which Irish nationalists north of the border want to unite), these particular games are played mainly by members of the Protestant unionist community. The most popular game in both communities – soccer (football) – despite much governmental effort to make it function in a way that breaks down communal barriers, divides the two communities, since clubs increasingly tend to be exclusively identified with one or other community (Sugden and Bairner, 1993; Bairner and Darby, 1999).

There are many other instances of stateless nations and peoples systematically cohering around sport against their host states, including Quebec nationalism against Anglophone Canada (Harvey, 1999), Norwegian nationalism directed at Sweden before the two countries separated (Goksøyr, 1996), Flemish nationalism against Francophone Belgium (Vanreusal *et al.*, 1999), the Finns against Tsarist domination, the Slav nationalist Sokol movement against their Austro-Hungarian, Tsarist and Ottoman oppressors in the later nineteenth and early twentieth centuries (Guttmann, 1994), and independence movements among the many peoples emerging from colonial rule in Asia and Africa in the twentieth century, such as South Africa, India and the West Indies (Guelke, 1993; Guelke and Sugden, 1999; Appadurai 1990; James, 1976; Monnington, 1986; Stuart, 1996).

Sport has played an important part in the development of African nationalism and one of the most striking, and in some ways unusual, cases is that of the emergence of the new South Africa (Guelke, 1993). Under the apartheid regime the sense of identity of the white community, and in particular the Afrikaners, cohered to a considerable extent around a fanatical attachment to sports, especially to rugby and cricket. Tolerance of the regime in international circles was achieved to a significant extent through its international sporting contacts. Consequently, the international sports boycott of South Africa from the 1970s onwards proved to be a potent weapon in the hands of the anti-apartheid movement: it reinforced black nationalism and pan-Africanism, helped to demoralise the whites, and was a major factor in the demise of the regime.

The fact that South Africa was so heavily implicated in, and reliant upon, the globalised sports system was absolutely fundamental to the successful outcome of the anti-apartheid struggle. Every international sports body, from the IOC and FIFA to individual international sports federations and virtually every government, was persuaded through an extensive world-wide campaign lasting for thirty years to boycott South African sport. Campaigns around globalised sports like rugby and cricket, and around the Olympics, possibly did more damage to the South African apartheid regime in propaganda terms and did more to mobilise opposition to apartheid world-wide than any other form of action. That regime collapsed, not primarily from internal opposition which, important as it was, was relatively ineffective against South Africa's formidable security apparatus, but from globally organised pressure in the political, economic and cultural spheres, and global sport proved to be, in many ways, South Africa's Achilles' heel.

The African National Congress (ANC) government now in power regards sport as one of the main instruments for building a multiethnic nation, although there is little concrete evidence that it actually performs that function, given the enormous divisions between the different racial groups (Guelke and Sugden, 1999).

Nationalism has been the ideological bedrock of fascist and quasi-fascist regimes and they provide some of the most outstanding examples of the subordination of sport to state nationalism. Mussolini's Italy pioneered the process whereby sport and leisure institutions for the mass of the population were thoroughly integrated into the corporate state (De Grazia, 1981), and top-level sport was systematically developed with the objective of producing successful national teams for the greater glory of the fascist nation-state. Thus the international prestige of Italy was enhanced when it took second place in overall terms in the Los Angeles Olympics of 1932 and when it won the FIFA World Cup in 1934 and 1938 (Kruger, 1996).

Although Franco's Spain cannot be classified unequivocally as a fascist regime, its overall character places it closer to that type of political system than any other. Sport, and in particular football, was made to serve the cause of *franquista* nationalism in the most thorough attempt in Spanish history to create a centralised, homogeneous Spanish nation (Shaw, 1987; Burns, 1999; Duke and Crolley, 1996). The Spanish League clubs were taken over and administered by Franco's placemen with the intention of transforming the football stadium into a kind of nationalist church where the nation and its values could be celebrated through nationalist propaganda, ritual and symbol.

Japanese fascism lacked the degree of coordination and a mass-based party that characterised Italian and German fascism, but like them it was virulently nationalist. Sport was accordingly structured with the aim of producing a fit and healthy population ready for war, and elite sport was generously supported by the state with the objective of enhancing Japan's prestige through success in international competition (Abe, Kiyohara and Nakajima, 1992).

German nationalism was at the root of national socialism, and in terms of planning, organisation, political control, ideological content, techniques of presentation (particularly the use of the media) and financing, the manner in which the Nazi regime staged the Berlin Olympics of 1936 probably represents a watershed in the relationship between sport and nationalism, in that it revealed how effectively international sport could be used by a ruthless state nationalist machine (Mandell, 1971). One aspect among many that exemplified the Nazis' mastery of sport for nationalistic purposes was the Olympic torch relay, now a standard feature of every Games. Invented by the 1936 Olympic Games organiser and classical scholar Carl Diem, like these Games as a whole it was designed to mobilise German nationalist sentiment in the most unprecedented, spectacular way. For the first time the sacred Olympic flame was conveyed by a torch lit at Olympia, the birthplace of the ancient Games in Greece, and carried by a relay of hundreds of athletes through the intervening countries to the host city, Berlin. Mythology, classical scholarship, costume, architecture, dance, music, images of the countryside, sport and recreation, were all integrated into an elaborately staged exercise, involving complex ceremonies and ritual practices, which was intended to symbolise the supposed links between the Nazi state, German culture and the origins of European civilisation. The exercise was brilliantly filmed for propaganda purposes by Hitler's favourite filmmaker, Lenni Riefenstahl. In this context the torch relay functioned as a symbol of Germany's greatness and her role as a leader of European civilisation. In subsequent Olympic Games it would come to signify quite different things.

In common with national socialism, communist forms of totalitarianism attempt to obliterate civil society and thoroughly to incorporate sport into the service of the state. Although the former German Democratic Republic, the Soviet Union and, today, Cuba have been enormously successful in using sport to represent them favourably on the world stage, it would be a mistake in most cases to assimilate fascist and communist uses of sport to the same nationalist category. With the exception of Cuba, which is a rather special case,[2] the meaning of the nation is different in

---

[2] Arguably, the nationalist element in Cuban communism is at least as important, if not more important, than socialism. The official slogan *Patria o Muerte* ('Homeland or Death') is one indication of the regime's strength of commitment to the politics of nationalism.

these instances: clearly, the symbols that communist regimes deploy signify specific nations, but in most cases the ideological underpinning is state socialist and internationalist rather than nationalist. Therefore the fact that sport is so thoroughly integrated into the diplomatic armoury of these regimes is best understood in terms of international relations theory, such as it is, rather than theories of nationalism.

The same is true of much of the functioning of sporting activity in the modern state system. In the cold war conflict between the two superpowers that developed around the Olympic Games from 1952, when the Soviet Union entered the competition for the first time, success in the medal table supposedly demonstrated the superiority of American capitalism or Russian communism. The culmination of this policy was the US boycott of the Moscow Olympics in 1980, in response to the Soviet Union's invasion of Afghanistan, and it was followed by the Soviet Union's boycott of the next Games in Los Angeles, in retaliation.

The superpowers in this instance, like many states, favoured the use of sport as an instrument of foreign policy in pursuit of their perceived 'national interests', largely because it is cheap and relatively risk-free, and they implemented their policy with regard to sport in a realist and pragmatic mode that had little if anything to do with nationalism. The objective may be to gain legitimacy internationally: for example, when Mexico's one-party state staged the Olympics in 1968 and Argentina's military regime staged the World Cup in 1978 – occasions that were used to create an impression of political stability, whereas in reality the opposition was being violently repressed. The motivation may be, partly, to wrongfoot an opponent, as when South Korea used the Seoul Olympics in 1988 to make an invidious comparison between itself and the communist North. Or it may be for a mixture of reasons, including nationalist sentiment. Smaller, weaker countries, like Kenya with its excellent record in distance running, can put themselves on the map through success in international sport, and this is often part of their 'nation-building' strategy.

Explaining the linkage between sport and nationalism

It is unlikely at this stage that any single theory of nationalism can satisfactorily explain all the aforementioned instances, let alone the many more that exist. Realistically, the most that can be expected is that a framework or approach at a relatively high level of generality can be formulated which can be appropriately modified and refined, as required, for the analysis of a given case or cases. Such an approach would require at the very least a synthesis of perennialist and modernist approaches to theorising nationalism, as well as an adequate notion of sport as a modern cultural form.

A synthesis of the two major kinds of approach to nationalism, the perennialist and the modernist, is required because exclusive reliance on either one of them has its dangers: the perennialists tend to downplay the importance of structural bases of nationalism, and modernists to downplay the significance of its cultural antecedents. Perennialism stresses the ethnic origins of nations and the importance of cultural tradition and of cultural nationalism as a foundation of nationalism. Nations cannot be constructed, invented or imagined out of thin air, as modernists and postmodernists seem to imagine (Smith, 1986, 1991; Armstrong, 1982; Hastings, 1997; Llobera, 1994). Modernists, on the other hand, stress that nationalism is a response to increasing state centralisation, capitalist economic development, and an associated tendency to cultural homogenisation in societies undergoing modernisation, and that the cultural and political traditions that nationalists are so often willing to defend with their lives are, in fact, relatively recent concomitant inventions (Gellner, 1983; Hobsbawm, 1990; Anderson, 1983; Breuilly, 1993).

Sport and nationalism are interrelated through their anchorage in common cultural traditions that may undergo sharp transformations as modernisation occurs. Sport functions as a point of coherence for national movements to the extent that it is central to the culture, or can be made so by a nationalist movement. Seen from a perennialist perspective, just as nationalism has pre-modern origins, so sport has its pre-modern origins in games, physical recreations and pastimes of all kinds that are an important part of the cultural life of all pre-modern societies. That is why sports so often have associations with rural life. A people's identity forms around such pursuits as an integral part of its attachment to place, territory or homeland, its myths of origin, its customs, its art and literature, its language and religion, its memories of great events in the past, or whatever. Where civil society is very well developed, as in the case of pre-industrial England and some other parts of Britain, participation in a rich variety of popular sporting recreations was well institutionalised – folk football and cricket, horse racing, cruel sports involving animals, pugilism and wrestling, bowling, footracing, forms of golf and so on – and sports more exclusive to the elite such as tennis, shooting, fencing and hunting flourished as well.

The sports we play and watch today, in contrast, are the result of modernisation processes in which such traditional recreational forms were reformed and restructured, and thereby their meanings were transformed. They were 'nationalised' in the sense that they largely lost their original local and social class associations as they were diffused in homogenised or standardised forms throughout the country; indeed they were universalised, in so far as Britain exported much of its sporting tradition to the rest of the world. In this modernisation process sports came to occupy a central position in the popular culture of very different kinds of societies. Concomitantly, a sense of national identity cohered around popular sporting forms like football in Europe and in Latin America, and around other sports like cricket in the white dominions, the Caribbean and the Indian sub-continent. In this country this process occurred to some extent spontaneously, but increasingly it occurred at the behest of the urban gentry, sections of the intelligentsia and astute politicians, who consciously attempted to engineer a national identity (Hargreaves, 1986). In Britain sport became part of the mythology of national identity to the extent that love of sports, and the values of fair play that they are supposed to inculcate, are still thought to differentiate the British from other nations. Sport could not have acquired such status in the national consciousness had it not been so deeply rooted in the culture of premodern Britain, but also, had it not been thoroughly modernised in the nineteenth and twentieth centuries. On the whole, though, sport was not imbued with nationalist meanings as such in this particular case. Elsewhere it clearly was, as some of our examples show, and the reasons why depend on the particular circumstances of each case. With more comparative work we should be in a better position to begin to formulate the necessary and sufficient conditions in which nationalism and sport become linked.

Any aspect of culture – music, literature, religion, architecture, etc. – may, in principle, be given a nationalist inflection, depending upon its specific features and the political context. There are certain features of sport, however, which enable it readily to represent the nation and function well as an adjunct of nationalist politics in given circumstances. At the most basic primordial level, sport gratifies the play instinct by providing opportunities for acquiring and exhibiting valued physical qualities connecting man to nature and which for most of our history have been necessary for physical survival – skill, endurance, strength, speed, etc. Crucially, it provides opportunities to acquire and display moral qualities – courage, aggression, leadership, self-control, initiative, willpower, steadfastness in adversity, self-sacrifice, loyalty – qualities commonly perceived as essential for cultural and for national survival.

The contest element in sport is especially significant because it allows opposition, conflict and struggle to be experienced and represented in extremely dramatic and spectacular ways, whereby sports can be made to map national struggles. Sporting contests are liminal: they are conducted according to rules that suspend reality by equalising contestants' chances of winning. If, on the whole, there are no such rules ensuring equal competition between states and nations in the real world, the laws of sport allow them to compete equally by proxy, and in doing so a potential is generated which facilitates the articulation of nationalist sentiment. The ritual activity which now envelops the great sporting contests – dramatic openings and closings, victory ceremonies, etc., in which national symbols are prominently deployed – does, to one extent or other, draw on national cultural tradition, but what we witness in sport as a result is a representation of the nation that is quintessentially modern. The increasing elaboration of rules and regulations, the application of science and technology to enhance participants' performances, state intervention and control, mass marketing, spectacularisation and the globalisation of sport are aspects of a universal modernising process. Far from eroding nationalism, the modernisation of sport may provide it with new opportunities to mobilise support, given the right conditions. Once sport is harnessed to nationalism, it constitutes a powerful cultural resource in its service. Through sport, highly condensed and instantly effective images of the nation can be diffused to mobilise the potential nationalist constituency and to legitimate the movement externally. The power of such images resides in their impact, not only at the cognitive level, but above all at the emotional level, and in their appeal to the aesthetic senses.

The most potent and decisive way nationalist ideology is communicated and nationalist mass movements are generated and sustained is through the language and symbolism of nationalism. Modern nationalism is a complex ideology incorporating abstract ideas about autonomy, identity, national genius, authenticity, unity and fraternity, in terms of which given populations are characterised by a significant proportion of their members (most importantly by nationalist intellectuals and the intelligentsia) as actual or potential nations (Smith, 1991). Language and symbolism, rite and ceremonial play a crucial part in demarcating boundaries between communities. Nationalist language, symbolism, rite and ceremonial connect nationalist ideology to the culture of wider segments of the population, that is, to popular or mass ideas and beliefs, sentiments, customs, styles, mores and ways of acting and feeling shared by members of a community of historic culture, so that the nation and national identity become a 'natural' part of the culture. Sporting occasions, big and small, provide almost limitless possibilities for deploying the language and symbolism of the nation – flags, anthems, parades, oaths, folk costumes, national recreations, spectacular cultural performances incorporating mythology, the arts, music, poetry, song, dance, design and so on –

symbols which, in certain circumstances, may be manipulated by a political movement and attributed with a nationalist meaning. As we have seen in the case of the *Turnen* movement, an entire sport may even be invented in the service of a nationalist project.

Nationalism can be understood as a form of civil religion. In his sociology of religion Durkheim noted the power of symbols and ceremonies to evoke intense emotional identification with the collectivity (Durkheim, 1982). But it is not simply a question of emotional response: the sacred aura with which nationalist symbols are endowed means that they can exert an especially powerful impact, not only at the emotional level but also at the cognitive and aesthetic levels simultaneously. Ritual and ceremonial activity are rule-governed forms of behaviour of a symbolic character that draw the attention of participants and onlookers to objects of thought and feeling which are held to be of special significance (Lukes, 1975). Ritual symbols 'condense many referents uniting them in a single cognitive and affective field. Each has a "fan" or spectrum of referents which tend to be interlinked by what is usually a simple mode of association, its very simplicity enabling it to interconnect a wide variety of signification' (Turner, 1970). Ritual symbols may very powerfully connote, as well as denote, what is important; and what they connote – that is, what they covertly convey – is often more important. Nowhere is all this more apparent than in the case of nationalist symbols and ceremonies. They embody nationalism's basic concepts, making them visible and distinct for every member, communicating the tenets of an abstract ideology in palpable, concrete terms that evoke an instant emotional, cognitive and aesthetic response from all strata of the community (Smith, 1991: 77). Durkheim characterised religious ritual as, in reality, a celebration of society. Similarly, nationalism could be characterised as the community self-consciously worshipping itself as the nation. In many ways the ceremonial and symbolic aspect is the most decisive in the success and durability of national identity because it is the area in which individual identity is most closely bound up with collective identity. Today the chief reason why the symbolic and ritual aspects of nationalism impinge so directly on the sense of individual identity lies in the revival of ethnic ties and ethnic identification.

As we shall see, the Olympic Games is especially rich in symbol and ceremonial, and these points apply particularly to the Barcelona Olympics because they were permeated by the language and symbolism of Catalan nationalism. We will focus later on how these key symbols were deployed.

2   Catalan nationalism

Introduction

In order to understand the political context in which the Barcelona Games took place it is necessary to provide a sketch of the way relations developed between Spain and Catalonia and of the ensuing character of Catalan nationalism. It should be stressed that this is a sketch and not a comprehensive account. Catalans constitute a very important historic national minority within their host state, Spain, against which they have generated a highly effective nationalist movement. There is no general theory of nationalism that will definitively unravel the complexities of Catalan nationalism (Llobera, 1989), but the distinction between civic and ethnic nationalism as a taxonomic device, and judicious use of ideas derived from both perennialist and modernist approaches, referred to briefly in the last chapter, offer effective insights and, hopefully, an appropriate framework of explanation.

It is useful to distinguish in analytical terms two different models of nationalism. Nations and national identities are necessarily exclusive, in that they involve the enforcement of boundary-maintaining processes differentiating one population from another. However, the ethnic model, in contrast to the civic, tends to draw the boundaries more exclusively, in the sense that to be accepted as a legitimate member of the national community, individuals are required to possess certain cultural attributes. Civic conceptions, on the other hand, extend membership on a legal–rational basis to the total population of the territory in question, irrespective of ethnic attributes. The historical origins of the two models are different. State-induced 'nation-building' in the West, the classical examples being Britain, France and the United States, was carried out under the influence of universalist Enlightenment ideas concerning liberty, equality and natural rights (Tilly, 1975). A sense of membership of a national community and loyalty to the emergent state-nation was successfully inculcated in their populations through the extension of citizenship rights. The civic nation's criteria of membership are primarily universalistic – allegiance to and equality before the laws governing a given territory. Cultural criteria are secondary. In contrast, other states in central, eastern and southern Europe emerged as 'nation-states' later, in the nineteenth century, inspired by romantic nationalist notions such as those of Herder, who saw the nation as an eternal and unique community united by the spirit of its people, which is expressed in their culture and, above all, in their language. One's membership of the national community, therefore, if it is not prescribed by ancestry (and this is often an explicit requirement in given cases) is prescribed by immersion in the demotic culture. The ethnic nation's criteria of membership are primarily particularistic – whatever the territorial location, one belongs by descent and/or presumed common cultural characteristics, such as language, customs and religion. It was this conception of the nation that had a profound influence on early Catalanist thought and the Catalan nationalist movement when the latter emerged in the late nineteenth century (Llobera, 1983).

In saying that nations and nationalism may take a civic or ethnic form it should be clear that we are making an analytical distinction – that is, these are contrasting ideal types which have been widely employed in the analysis of nationalism (Greenfeld, 1992; Smith, 1991). In fact, some mixture of the two types is usually present with one or other type predominating in given instances.

The distinction between ethnic and civic models has been criticised on the grounds that 'ethnic' in this connection is too diffuse a category. It subsumes both ascriptive criteria of membership, notably ancestry and race, as well as cultural, i.e. acquired criteria of membership, such as language and religion. Also, civic countries like France enforce ethnic criteria of membership, such as language and culture (Nieguth, 1999; Brown, 1999). While these observations are correct, it does not necessarily follow that the distinction is invalid. The kind of nationalism that is based upon race and ancestry can be distinguished from that which is based upon cultural criteria and it can be categorised as a separate type of ethnic nationalism, Nazi Germany being the prime example. The enforcement of ethnic criteria of membership in civic cases varies, but even where such enforcement is relatively rigorous, as in France, ethnic criteria, in the long run, have not overridden the predominant conception that the French nation consists of a legal and political community of equal citizens and that France is their historic homeland (Smith, 1991: 13–14).

With regard to Catalan nationalism, the fact of the matter is that it was generated by the pressures of modernisation, but it also had its roots and origins in the pre-modern 'ethnonation' (Llobera, 1989; 1994). That nationalists will readily attempt to construct or invent the character of the nation with any materials at their disposal has led some influential theorists of nationalism to argue that nations are merely a modern 'invention' (Anderson, 1983; Hobsbawm, 1990; Gellner, 1983). While it is important to recognise the extent to which nations and nationalism are creatures of modernity, it is also important to recognise that nations and nation-states cannot simply be invented out of nothing. They require among other things, including luck, a strong 'ethnonational' potential, that is to say, a strong pre-existing sense in a given population that it possesses highly valued elements in common which are deeply rooted in the past.

Catalonia in the pre-modern era

A long-lasting polity and its loss

From the mid-twelfth century Catalonia had been an equal partner in a confederal union with Aragon, and it provided the reigning dynasty of the crown of Aragon at key periods. Through dynastic union or conquest, Catalonia expanded its territory to become the dominant military and trading power in much of the Mediterranean from the thirteenth to the fifteenth centuries, ruling at various times Languedoc, Majorca, the kingdom of Valencia, Sicily, Sardinia, Naples and territory in Greece. At the hub of the most advanced part of Europe in the Middle Ages, Catalonia functioned as a conduit for economic, political and cultural exchange between Europe and the Iberian Peninsula. Catalonia had one of the earliest parliaments in Europe, the Corts, and a written constitution, the Usatges (usages) codifying established customs and practices (Balcells, 1996). Relations between everyone – nobles, burghers, peasants and clerics, as well as between the king and his Catalan subjects – were seen as being based upon negotiation. The king could not revoke laws without the Corts' permission, and was not considered legitimate until he had sworn to respect the basic law of the land in the presence of the Corts. It became the task of the Generalitat, a standing committee of the Corts, to defend the laws, to negotiate grants of money to the king and to manage taxation. Feudalism in Catalonia, in marked contrast to Castile, which was not, properly speaking, a feudal state, is thus the origin of the Catalan practice of political negotiation, of contractualism and of pactism, a tradition which continued long after the union with Castile (Giner, 1984).

At the time of the dynastic union between the kingdoms of Aragon and Castile (1469) to form the new powerful, emerging state of Spain, Catalonia was suffering from a long period of demographic and economic decline, brought about by plague and civil war. While it retained its own independent institutions, currency, customs and tax system – the Spanish crown could not raise taxes without the permission of the Corts – and Catalan remained the official language, it was politically subordinated to Castile, the Corts met much less frequently, and it was economically weakened. Catalan merchants were excluded from trade from their ports with the Spanish colonies until the late eighteenth century, so Catalonia did not benefit commercially from Spain's vast empire in the new world, at the very time when western Mediterranean trade had collapsed due to the expansion of the Ottoman empire. Catalonia experienced economic stagnation, political immobility and a loss of cultural vitality as a result (Balcells, 1996).

In the war between France and Spain in 1640 the Catalan peasantry revolted and the Generalitat, under the leadership of Pau Claris, followed suit, supported by France, and declared Catalonia's independence. Catalonia was eventually defeated and, ironically, lost its northern provinces across the Pyrenees to its erstwhile ally, France. Although its system of self-government was not dismantled, it was whittled away and weakened. The Spanish king acquired control over nominations to the Barcelona City Council (Consell de Cent), and the Corts, no longing controlling the Generalitat, did not meet again until 1701.

The catastrophic loss of autonomy came in 1714 as a result of the War of the Spanish Succession, between Britain and its allies against France and Spain. Catalonia took the opportunity to revolt again and took the side of Spain's enemies. Deserted ultimately by the latter, Catalonia was eventually crushed. Under the Decree of Nueva Planta all Catalan political institutions were abolished and Castilian laws, absolutism and centralism were imposed; public use of the Catalan language was prohibited shortly afterwards, and the region was subjected to a heavy burden of taxation (Balcells, 1996). The anniversary of the date of the surrender of Barcelona to Spanish and French troops, 11 September, is celebrated as the Catalan national day (La Diada). Choosing this, of all days, as the national day, might seem to be rather bizarre and perverse, and it is a source of amusement to some in the rest of Spain. Nevertheless, it is an effective way of preserving the memory of Catalonia's subjugation and of rekindling the desire to recover her lost autonomy; and it reflects the sense of irony for which Catalans are well known.

The Catalan language

Catalonia, together with the Midi, developed similar dialects of Latin, the *langues d'oc*, which were spoken over a wide area of the western

Mediterranean. Catalan was a literary language in the Middle Ages, when it flowered in the *œuvre* of the intellectual genius of his time, the Mallorcan philosopher, poet, missionary and mystic, Ramon Llull (1235–1316). It rivalled Provençal as the language of troubadour poetry in the fourteenth century, and Dante, Petrarch, Boccaccio and other Italian humanists were translated into Catalan early in the fifteenth century (Hughes, 1992). Catalan declined as a language of culture after the fifteenth century and declined even further when its public use was prohibited after 1714. Nevertheless, by the nineteenth century it was still the language of the people (Llobera, 1989) and with the general revival of Catalan culture at that time it recovered its previous status.

The strong attachment to the language and its identification with being Catalan has made it the single most important rallying point of Catalan nationalism. Severely threatened and weakened by Franco's policy of suppressing its usage, it was nevertheless preserved in the family and protected within the institutions of Catalan civil society. It is commonly said that no one can really be called a Catalan who does not speak the language and that language plus 'national character' make up the *fet diferrential* (that which differentiates the Catalans from others) as the poet Joan Maragall called it (Hughes, 1992). This notion of difference is an important part of Catalan identity: it is part of a historic culture, in the wider sociological sense, of a body of ideas, values, beliefs, practices and norms, and a sense of historical destiny spanning the pre-modern period and the modern periods. We will return to the popular notion of Catalan national character in a moment. Beforehand, we need to discuss two other features of Catalan culture: pactism and associationism.

Pactism

The pactist notion that rules are made by free agents entering into contracts of their own accord and that social life is based upon bargaining and negotiation between them, and not upon unilateral violence and imposition, became deeply ingrained in Catalan political culture, and contractualism became an essential component of the Catalan way of life. It was linked to the patrimonial concept of property as embodied in the *masia*, or manor. The *mas*, the traditional economic and family unit of rural Catalonia, based on patriarchal law and traditions – the *dret pairal* – was the backbone of the Catalan pre-industrial world. Contractualism survived through Catalan civil law, which even managed to remain substantially intact through the Franco era (Giner, 1984).

Catalonia's relatively small size and demographic weight and her experience of subordination within a powerful unified state, which it could not lead or dominate as, for example, Piedmont and Lombardy were able to do in the case of Italy, meant that the Catalans had to fall back on diplomacy, cunning, patience, manoeuvring, compromise, accommodation and appeasement. This structural condition is, above all, what reinforced the pactist stance.

There is a danger of exaggerating the role of pactism in Catalan life – of seeing the past and present as timeless and pactism as an essential feature of the Catalan 'national character' (Llobera, 1989; Sobrequés, 1982). Contractualism – the propensity to bargain realistically and to form coalitions – is not restricted to Catalonia. Furthermore, it has broken down in times of crisis – during the fifteenth century when open class warfare and civil war in Barcelona accelerated its decline as a maritime power and commercial emporium, during the *Setmana Tràgica* in 1909 when insurrection and atrocity disfigured the city and also, of course, under the Second Republic when civil war engulfed Catalonia and the whole of Spain (Brennan, 1962). Nevertheless, it is a stance which distinguishes the behaviour of Catalans from that of the rest of Spain, where it is well recognised, not without some irritation on the part of those who interpret it as Catalan wiliness. Compared with the rest of Spain then, there is a recognisably contractualist stance in certain key Catalan institutions and the frequently contractualist, bargaining attitude of Catalan interests to this day is easily noticeable (Giner, 1984); it is a feature of both Catalan politics and of Catalan civil society. As a relatively stable cultural pattern it is a useful way of understanding the way conflict is managed in Catalonia down to the present day, the strategies that are adopted and the processes of accommodation that occur; and this is especially important when examining the way Catalan elites deal with each other and with the central powers. This pattern was strongly in evidence, as we will demonstrate, in the conflict between nationalists and their opponents generated by the Olympic Games.

Associationism

Catalans have found their collective identity by habitually falling back on the institutions of civil society. One of the results is that Catalonia today is exceptional in having been able to maintain traditional festivities, dances and games as an integral part of popular culture, rather than preserving them, as elsewhere in advanced societies, merely as folkloric relics. Such aspects of Catalan popular culture as their national dance, the *sardana*, functioned as forms of political affirmation at times when Catalonia was struggling against repression and they have done so right into the modern era. During the Franco regime they were especially important in this respect, and they have functioned as points of mobilisation for the nationalist cause ever since, as we will demonstrate later with respect to the Barcelona Games.

The intense private associationism of Catalan society and the proliferation of voluntary associations, many of them devoted to the maintenance of such traditions, rituals, games, dances and festivities, is a key feature of Catalan culture. The high number of voluntary associations and the wide scope of their activities put one in mind of similar patterns in the development of civil society elsewhere in Europe, such Flanders and England. The same intense associationist impulse that produced the choirs, mountaineering clubs, pigeon-fancying clubs, privately funded public libraries, the *ateneus* (self-improvement associations), cooperatives of all sorts, philatelic associations, theatrical societies, local and civic action groups, amateur geographical and astronomical clubs, etc., that characterised Catalan civil society from the nineteenth century, goes back in an unbroken line to the period of the ancient guilds and civic trade centres (Giner, 1984).

The 'national character'

The *fet differential* is a set of popular beliefs as to what constitutes the Catalan character which have been assiduously propagated by Catalan intellectuals. Some have tried to present what specifically differentiates the Catalan character in ideal typical terms (Ferreter i Mora, 1960; Vicens Vives, 1954), but the difficulty here is in knowing where popular prejudice and ideology end and scientific analysis begins. As with all forms of cultural identity, Catalan identity involves to some degree a stereotype of the 'other', and that other is the Castilian. Catalans tend to pride themselves on their four virtues: *continuitat* (working steadfastly over the long term to achieve objectives), *mesura* (taking a measured, balanced view of things), *ironia* (an ironic outlook on life), and *seny* (a rational attitude characterised by good, practical commonsense) (Flaquer and Giner, 1991a; Flaquer and Giner, 1991b). *Rauxa* is the other side of the coin to *seny* – a propensity to seek relief, on occasion, from social constraint by indulging in uncontrollable emotion and outbursts of irrational behaviour: from getting drunk and fornicating to burning churches and convents. Catalans are supposed to have a liking for hard work, to be frugal and efficient, to possess a certain genius for innovation and to love their country. They do not readily open themselves to outsiders but when they do the resulting relationships are lasting and profound. Whether this is an objective picture or not is difficult to establish. These qualities which are thought to differentiate Catalans are, in the main, those which we associate with the growth of capitalism and the industrial revolution, and of the regions of Spain it was Catalonia that first witnessed the growth of mercantile and industrial capitalism, so there is some objective support for popular belief. Catalonia, then, has often been seen as a very 'bourgeois' society with some justification.

What becomes more difficult, if impossible, to substantiate is the corollary – that the Catalan virtues are not shared by Castilians who, in contrast, are held to be inclined to over-indulge their emotions, to live for the moment, to be prone to indolence, and to have a morbid, effete side to their character and a taste for oppressing and exploiting people like the Catalans. Castilians, returning the compliment, are prone to see Catalans as rather dull and materialistic: as a pedantic, mean and unimaginative nation of shopkeepers (Hughes, 1992).

Self-styled 'real Catalans' – *Catalans de sempre* as they are called – can be xenophobic. The pejorative epithet *xarnego*, a term once applied in rural localities to outsiders and then in wider usage to refer to foreigners, is sometimes applied to working-class immigrants from the south of Spain, with something like the connotations of the term 'nigger' (Hughes, 1992: 30; Conversi, 1997: 209). The more rural the location the more strongly these contrasting stereotypes tend to be held.

Of course the stereotype of the eternal Catalan character is, from an analytical point of view, a naïve essentialist notion, but what matters is not so much whether this is an objective description of the Catalan character (although there are elements that ring true with dispassionate observers), but that many Catalans adhere firmly to such beliefs about themselves and differentiate themselves from Castilians in something like these terms, and that such discourse is ideologically manipulable.

The failure to modernise Spain successfully

Bourgeois civil society and industrialisation

Catalonia's economic prosperity burgeoned in the eighteenth century. Trade with Spain's overseas empire was no longer restricted and a markedly bourgeois civil society thrived. Catalonia was the only area in southern Europe, apart from Lombardy, to experience the industrial revolution at roughly the same time as north-western Europe. It stepped into the vanguard of Spanish industrialisation and modernisation in the nineteenth century, when Spain, compared with its main rivals in Western Europe, was a byword for backwardness (Solé Tura, 1974). Catalan industrialisation was autochthonous, based on the textile and consumer goods industries – sectors that were small-scale and more competitive than the big banking and heavy industry monopolies that emerged later in the Basque Country under the control of Madrid, and that heavily depended on foreign capital. The Catalan bourgeoisie, unlike the Basque oligarchy, was not integrated into the politico-economic regime at the centre, from which it remained alienated (Diez Medrano, 1995). This was a cultivated, forward-looking, modern bourgeoisie in every sense. The growth of industrial capitalism in Catalonia and the exceptionally severe class polarisation it entailed, generated a social structure which diverged radically from that of the rest of Spain, where a pre-industrial landed oligarchy was entrenched in power both in countryside and town.

The Renaixença and romantic nationalism

The growth of bourgeois civil society in the eighteenth century and industrial development in the nineteenth century were, no doubt, complexly related to a major revival in Catalan culture from the 1830s, the *Renaixença*. Catalan intellectuals – writers, historians, professors and, above all, poets – inspired by the romantic movement, romantic historiography and ethnic nationalism emanating from other parts of Europe, began to idealise the Catalan past, searching ancient peasant traditions, folklore and folk culture, popular language and Romanesque–Gothic architecture for what was authentically Catalan, to recover Catalonia's former glory and distinct stature. The middle decades of the century witnessed a crusade to revitalise the culture and the language and, in contrast with the lethargy of the rest of Spain, a wave of creative activity swept every sector of society, touching all fields of the humanities (Conversi, 1997). The richness of modern Catalan literature, for example, dates from the 1840s. The revival of the *Jocs Florals* in 1859, ancient poetry contests and historic pageants comparable to the Welsh eisteddfods, was a notable example of the kind of activity aimed at re-establishing the prestige of Catalan. In these decades the *Renaixença*, an urban phenomenon originally, penetrated the more backward and conservative rural hinterland and was one of the factors that later helped to shift the allegiance of the rural population from Carlism to Catalanism. Catalan cultural nationalism became a major force in Catalan life – a programme consciously differentiating the region from the rest of Spain and serving as a platform for the emergence of political nationalism in the 1880s (Conversi, 1997).

The influence of religion

The Catholic church in Catalonia was not the driving force of nationalism that it has been in the Basque Country, Poland and Ireland; indeed, there is a strong anti-clerical tradition there. However, clerics were often at the forefront of resistance to Castilian encroachment in the eighteenth century and, despite their bishops, many parish priests stubbornly persisted with the use of the vernacular (Llobera, 1994: 141). The fact that religion never played a central role in Catalan nationalism, and that the church was immersed in a secular society, seems to have made it more tolerant and enlightened than it was in the rest of Spain (Giner, 1984; Conversi, 1997). The main connection between the church and early Catalanism was through *pairalisme*, a conservative, anti-urban, anti-modern, bucolic ideology identifying the Catalan spirit with Catholicism and with the traditional Catalan rural way of life. *Pairalisme* found much in the *Renaixença*'s nostalgia for an idealised mediaeval past to sustain it. Individual clerics, notably Balmes earlier in the nineteenth century and Torres i Bagès towards the end of the century, were important in helping to put Catalanism on a conservative path which it took up to the 1920s. For Torres i Bagès the patriarchal family of the *casa pairal* was the model for Catalan society. He argued for an organic, traditional state whose value system was the same throughout at individual, family, town, church and government levels. Catalonia, he contended, is 'pre-eminent among Iberic peoples' . . . because of 'her ancient seeds hidden in the earth, in the Catalan humus made of our tradition . . . love and steady work, modesty of life, a practical and alert spirit not given to phantasy, a respect for family hierarchy.' The source of all this is family life: 'Love for the homestead, the *casa pairal*, the desire to conserve the patrimony, the order of the family hierarchy . . . all is superior where regional life has been maintained . . . as opposed to those areas which are confused with the great mass, the nation.' The church is the sole guarantor of Catalan heritage: 'Catalonia and Church are two things in our past history which cannot be separated . . . if anyone wishes to reject the Church, have no doubt that at the same time he must reject the Fatherland along with it' (Hughes, 1992: 318–19).

With the exception of the Basque Country and Catalonia, during Franco's dictatorship until the 1960s the church remained an accomplice of the regime. In Catalonia it was virtually the only major institution that was in a position, and willing in limited ways, to publicly defend Catalan culture and the language against the repression. The Benedictine national shrine of Montserrat, in particular, was at the forefront of this limited resistance. A form of Christian democrat Catalanism was tacitly allowed to emerge, shielded by the church and fostered in church-related organisations. The future leaders of the main nationalist party and of the socialist party came out of such a background (Balcells, 1996).

A weak, ineffective state

The manner in which the state acts *vis-à-vis* potential or actual opposition in its attempts to manage the modernisation process is a particularly

important factor in stimulating and provoking the emergence of nationalist movements (Breuilly, 1993). The Spanish state was exceptionally
advanced and powerful in the sixteenth century and it remained relatively
powerful during the seventeenth and eighteenth centuries. A certain
sense of Spanish patriotism and identity had been stimulated in the struggle against French occupation during the Napoleonic Wars (Junco,
1996), and Spain joined in the general process of state centralisation and
homogenisation that was accelerating in Europe in the early nineteenth
century. But as it was increasingly confronted by the need to modernise,
the shortcomings of the Spanish state were revealed.

The requisite finances, administrative framework and managerial
capacity were lacking, so state centralisation measures were clumsy and
inefficient and the country, apart from Catalonia, failed to modernise
economically and politically (or, for that matter, culturally) and regional
variations were much more pronounced than in comparable parts of
Western Europe. Moves from the centre to deal with this now ran into the
mounting obstacle of Catalan interests. Catalan industrialists wanted
their markets to be protected from foreign competition and Catalan elites
wanted a bigger say in the direction the country was to take. The centre's
movement towards free trade was successfully halted, but it would not
otherwise accommodate Catalan industrial interests and could not
understand Catalan resentment. Catalans did not obtain the kinds of
benefits, for example, that Scotland acquired from being part of the successful British state. Ireland's experience of the host state was different
and it was precisely there that ethnic nationalism against the British
erupted, only in that case minority nationalism was associated with
underdevelopment. Catalonia, in comparison, was the most developed
part of Spain and felt aggrieved at being held back by an inefficient state
(Linz, 1973).

The emergence of political nationalism

An ethnically based nationalist movement is likely to develop in these
kinds of circumstances, that is, where there is uneven development at the
periphery. A segmental division of labour between centre and periphery
concomitantly develops, and peripheral elites monopolise valued niches
in the occupational structure and in key institutional spheres (Hechter
and Levi, 1994). Uneven development cannot by itself explain the nature
of an individual case like Catalonia, however, since peripheral nationalisms can exhibit very different characteristics: for example, in their pro-
pensities to violence. To explain the Catalan case it is necessary to focus
on the specific nature of the relationship between central and Catalan

elites and, secondly, on the specific nature of political competition in the periphery. Now, whether central and peripheral elites are strongly integrated economically and politically has a strong bearing on the structure of political competition in the periphery as well, and hence on the character of peripheral nationalism. Where they are not integrated with central elites, peripheral elites are likely to be more involved in nationalist movements and these movements are consequently likely to be more variegated (Diez Medrano, 1995). Where the national minority, in addition, is culturally confident and possesses its own political culture and civic institutions, the nationalists are likely to be more flexible in their dealings with the host state (Conversi, 1997). Catalan elites were not only not integrated with central elites, they were also very confident about their culture. They actually went to some lengths to try to work with elites at the centre, not least because the growing power and militancy of their own working class alarmed them, and they needed the state to protect them. From their point of view they met with little reward for their efforts and, accordingly, increasingly turned in a nationalist direction.

Nationalism also came out of political movements that had taken a hold in Catalonia before the 1880s. Rural Catalonia, together with the Basque Country, Navarre and Aragon, was a stronghold of Carlism, a deeply conservative, Catholic movement which launched three wars against state centralisation between 1833 and 1872 (Brennan, 1962). Given Catalonia's history, it is not surprising that federalism and republicanism, which played an important part in Spanish politics as the century advanced, also took hold in Catalonia. As self-conscious modernisers, Catalan elites increasingly felt themselves to be hamstrung by an inefficient, backward, parasitical centre that did not recognise their region's unique qualities or represent its interests. The last straw came with the crisis of 1898, when Spain, as if to confirm its decrepitude, suffered defeat in the war with the United States and lost the only economically important parts of the empire that were left: Cuba, Puerto Rico and the Philippines. From the 1880s these forces – a politically conservative but modernising bourgeoisie, the cultural elite and elements of the intelligentsia with an investment in the *Renaixença*, and the Carlists, Federalists and Republicans – tended to coalesce, and an increasingly well-organised nationalist movement came to dominate Catalan politics by the turn of the century.

Under pressure from the nationalists, the centre conceded a limited form of regional government to Catalonia in 1914 (the Mancomunitat) headed by Prat de la Riba, the leader of the nationalist party, the Lliga Regionalista. Its most important achievement was to foster Catalan culture by carrying on the work started when Prat de la Riba became president of the Diputació de Barcelona in 1907. The Institut d'Estudis Catalans (Institute of Catalan Studies) was created, where the linguist, Pompeu Fabra, carried out a programme of linguistic reform, culminating in a unified standard language. Now the new framework of government, the education system and the newly created National Library were used to implement his programme (Conversi, 1997).

The Mancomunitat's cultural cadres were the *Noucentistas*. *Noucentisme* (the New Century Movement) was a Catalanist movement dedicated to reforming Catalan society and reshaping its culture through a synthesis of classicism and an elitist, modern managerialist vision of the new order. Its high priest, Eugeni D'Ors, later a Franco supporter, was vehemently opposed to *Renaixença* romanticism, the modernism of Gaudí, and the cosmopolitan rationalism of the avant-garde (Hughes, 1992; Vázquez Montalbán, 1992). The nationalists used the new framework of regional government to such effect that it was abolished, and the nationalist movement was repressed as a danger to Spain's national integrity when Primo de Rivera's dictatorship was installed in 1923.

Catalan nationalism took a left turn from thereon and Spain's chronic political instability did not permit the dictatorship or the monarchy to survive long. With their fall and with the left initially in the ascendancy, the nationalist ambition for autonomy was realised when the Generalitat was restored under the Second Republic (1932–9).

The Franco regime

Unfortunately for Catalonia, the right rebelled against the Second Republic under the leadership of General Franco and brought it down in the civil war of 1936 to 1939 (Thomas, 1965). Franco's quasi-fascist nationalising state, in contrast to its predecessors, was strong and effective. It promptly instituted the most thorough attempt in the history of Spain to subordinate the country to central control, and Catalonia was singled out for treatment as having constituted an especially serious threat to the state's integrity. Thousands were executed or imprisoned or forced into exile; the region's autonomous form of government, the Generalitat, was abolished and replaced by virtually total control from the centre. A policy of cultural genocide was implemented: the Catalan language and key symbols of Catalan independent identity and nationhood, such as the flag (the *senyera*), the national hymn ('Els Segadors') and the national dance (the *sardana*), were proscribed. Any sign of independence or opposition, in fact, was brutally suppressed. Catalan identity and consequently the Catalan nation were threatened with extinction.

Yet although Catalan culture and identity were weakened by the regime's onslaught, they managed to survive somehow, at least in the private sphere, due to a great extent to the stubborn efforts of a relatively small number of dedicated members of the intelligentsia (Llobera, 1989). As in so many other cases where attempts have been made to destroy a nation, the experience of Franco's 'politics of revenge' (Preston, 1990) ultimately proved to be the strongest factor responsible for the salience of Catalan nationalism today and for the tension that still exists between Catalonia and the Spanish state in the new democratic Spain.

The second most important factor in stimulating Catalan nationalism was the rapid economic modernisation of Spain that Franco belatedly, yet very successfully, undertook in the late 1950s and early 1960s. Spain fell into a pattern of late modernisation more characteristic of southern Europe, where there has been a tendency for it to be carried out, with varying degrees of success, under the aegis of autocratic regimes (Giner, 1986; Kurth and Petras, 1993). Catalonia, as the most economically advanced region, along with the Basque Country, was in the vanguard of this modernisation and attracted a large influx of Castilian-speaking immigrants, particularly from the more backward south of the country, where standards of living were almost on a par with North Africa at the time, or so it seemed to many Catalans. By the 1970s the immigrant population constituted approximately 50 per cent of the population of Catalonia and some working-class districts of Barcelona were more or less exclusively immigrant and Castilian-speaking. This posed a threat, particularly to the survival of the Catalan language, the linchpin of Catalan identity, as well as a general threat of cultural homogenisation. It created a major division in Catalonia between two societies in which ethnic and class divisions coincided, for the indigenous Catalans tended to be more middle class and the immigrants working class. Also, the rapid modernisation process had, by the time of the transition to the democratic regime, considerably evened up the economic differences between Catalonia and the rest of Spain, so that modernity was more generalised and Catalonia has lost, to a significant extent, the basis for its distinctiveness. The politics of nationalism thus met the need among the indigenous Catalan population for a secure sense of identity in circumstances that were rapidly changing and seriously threatening their cultural identity.

National identity in the new democratic Spain

In the transition to liberal democracy after Franco's death (Perez Díaz, 1993; Linz and Stepan, 1996), Catalan nationalism asserted itself vigorously and the 1978 Spanish constitution paved the way for the 1982

Statute of Autonomy for Catalonia, restoring the Generalitat and parliament (Balcells, 1996). Since the first elections for the Catalan government in 1982 it has been in the hands of the main nationalist party (Pallarés, 1994). Historically, the behaviour of the Spanish state towards Catalonia has been, and still is today, the most significant factor determining the character of Catalan nationalism; and today's democratic state is still associated in the minds of Catalan nationalists with centrism and repression. However, Catalan nationalism is not simply a function of the interaction between the Spanish state and Catalonia, but of the structure of Catalan politics as well.

Where nationalism against the state is concerned, there are in fact two foci of conflict: between the 'nationalising' or host state and the national minority, on the one hand, and within the national minority, on the other. The structure of political competition within the national minority is a crucial factor in determining the nature of its reaction to the central state, which may range from non-cooperation, separatism and violence to cooperation, flexibility and participation in coalition governments. Nationalist movements may stop short of demanding complete independence because they perceive the balance of costs and benefits to be unfavourable. In other words, they may be inclusive in the sense of wanting more autonomy, but not complete independence, or they may be exclusive, that is to say, their aim is separation and complete independence from the host state (García Ferrando et al., 1994).

Within the national minority the different organisations, parties, movements or individual political entrepreneurs each seek to represent the minority to its putative members, to the host state, or to the outside world, while trying to monopolise the legitimate representation of the group (Brubaker, 1996). Whether it is repressive or not, the host state must be perceived as in some way posing a threat to the national minority if nationalist movements are to succeed in mobilising their potential constituencies. The perception and characterisation of the host state is itself a crucial object of struggle within the field of the national minority: it is a struggle to impose and sustain a vision of the host state as a nationalising or nationally oppressive state. A stance as a mobilised national minority, with its demands for recognition and for rights, can be sustained only if this vision of the host state can be sustained.

The contemporary Spanish state's nationalising efforts, in stark contrast to those of the Franco era, now approximate rather closely to the civic model. However, there is no strong sense of national identity; instead there are fairly widespread feelings of ambiguity about it (García Ferrando et al., 1994; Moral, 1998). This ambiguity is a crucial factor affecting relations between Spain and Catalonia and in determining the nature of the

Catalan political field. Dual identity, in fact, tends to be the norm in Spain. In 1996 half the population felt themselves to be as much from their own region as from Spain; only 27 per cent felt exclusively Spanish; and only 21 per cent identified exclusively with their region (Moral, 1998; García Ferrando and Hargreaves, 1999; García Ferrando *et al.*: 234, table 2). Although there are significant regional variations, in none of the seventeen *Autonomías* is there a majority that feels either exclusively Spanish or from their region. In 1990, as one would expect, the highest identification with Spain was found in Madrid (38 per cent). At that time Catalonia stood out as having the highest percentage of those who identified more with the region (31 per cent) and the second-highest percentage identifying exclusively with the region (14 per cent) (the Basque Country had the highest proportion of those who identified exclusively with their region at 20 per cent). Even though the proportion of those identifying more with, or exclusively with the region, was higher in Catalonia than in any other region (45 per cent in contrast to Castilla-Leon's 5 per cent), this still did not constitute the majority of the Catalan population. The latest figures show that the proportion of the Catalan population identifying more with, or exclusively with, the region has fallen to 37 per cent, that roughly the same proportion, 36 per cent, feel both Catalan and Spanish, i.e. have a dual identity, and a bigger percentage, 24 per cent, now feel they are solely Spanish. All this indicates that in Catalonia there is a strong potential basis of support not only for parties espousing exclusive nationalism, but also for those favouring an inclusive nationalism, that is, one which is more amenable to coming to terms with the central state.

Social survey evidence on such questions has its drawbacks, of course – notably its lack of depth – and over-reliance on it runs the risk of reducing the complexity of social and political affairs to what can be conveniently put into a table. Respondents may give the answers that they think are expected, or not give much thought to their answers. They usually get little opportunity to elaborate on what they mean and responses vary with the way questions are formulated, so there are always problems of interpretation. Most importantly, respondents' views are not permanently fixed: they are affected by changes in the socio-historical context and therefore always need to be related to that context to establish their significance. Such evidence always needs to be complemented with other methods and other sources of information: in particular, information on what people actually do as opposed to what they say, as we attempt to do in this study. Nevertheless, used with caution, opinion surveys can be a useful aid in helping to determine the nature of national identity. In particular, they enable information to be gathered on a large-scale nationwide basis, so that comparisons between sub-sections of a large

Table 1 *National and regional identification in Spain and Catalonia (%)*

	Identification with Spain		Dual identity		Identification with *Autonomia*/ region	
Territorial ambit	1990	1996	1990	1996	1990	1996
Spain	27	27	52	50	20	21
Catalonia	16	24	36	36	45	37

Source: García Ferrando *et al.* (1994); Moral (1998).

population may be made, as we do here in the case of the rest of Spain and Catalonia.

There is evidence of this kind to suggest that from 1976 to 1990 overall, in the new *España de las Autonomías*, strongly felt nationalist and regionalist sentiments lost ground to more moderate levels (García Ferrando *et al.*, 1994: 20–2). However, from 1979 levels of nationalist and regionalist sentiment increased in some of the *Autonomías*, notably in Catalonia where they reached their peak at the end of the 1980s (García Ferrando, 1992: 13, table 4; García Ferrando *et al.*, 1994: 182, table 8; García Ferrando and Hargreaves, 1999; Moral, 1998).[1] So, the year that Barcelona was awarded the Games, 1986, coincided with the expansive phase of Catalan nationalism and this had implications for the way that political actors and the public responded to the prospect of the Olympics and the impact the Olympics had on Catalan–Spanish relations. Between 1990 and 1996 levels of Catalan regionalist and nationalist sentiment fell (table 1; García Ferrando and Hargreaves, 1999; Moral, 1998).

Although nationalist and regionalist sentiment had grown in Catalonia

---

[1] Estimates of the level of support in Catalonia for complete independence vary considerably. See, for example, Estradé and Treserra (1990), two Catalan investigators, who found higher levels of support among their respondents. The survey was restricted to Catalonia, the number of Catalan respondents as such, at 2,100, was bigger than the CIS survey sample, and the questions put differed considerably. They found 54 per cent of their respondents considered themselves exclusively Catalan living in Catalonia and 13.2 per cent considered themselves exclusively Catalan living in Spain. Twenty per cent considered themselves Spanish living in Catalonia and 6.6 per cent considered themselves Spanish living in Spain (Estradé and Treserra, 1990: 59, table 27). Furthermore, 39.4 per cent thought independence would be desirable, against 46.1 per cent who thought it would not (104, table 50). However 44.5 per cent would vote 'yes' in a referendum on whether there should be a gradual move towards independence, against 26.4 per cent who would not (107, table 51). Political party membership and voting behaviour are also key indicators. The latter is complicated by the fact that the pattern of party support in Catalonia varies according to whether the elections are for the City Council, the Catalan government or the Spanish government (Pallarés, 1994).

prior to the Olympics, unlike in the Basque Country the pactist political culture meant that agents were well attuned to responding flexibly in a conflict. Catalans were culturally and politically self-confident and self-reliant enough to eschew violence and extremism; and the linchpin of this confidence and of their sense of identity is the Catalan language (Conversi, 1997). Sections of the Catalan political elite have successfully forged alliances with the centre in the new *España de las Autonomías* and other sections find it possible to accommodate to the centre. Political parties, movements, organisations and political entrepreneurs within the Catalan political field, with the exception of a small minority on the right of the political spectrum, are all in their way Catalanist. They compete to monopolise the legitimate representation of Catalonia to its population, to Spain and the outside world, offering significantly different versions of what constitutes Catalan identity and interests.

In the field of the national minority, the governing political party, Convergencia i Unió (CiU), i.e. the party commanding the support of the majority of nationalists, is 'inclusive': it does not demand compete independence and instead proceeds moderately and pragmatically to obtain the maximum feasible degree of autonomy for the region. The other main nationalist grouping, Esquerra Republicana (ERC) is separatist and also non-violent. These two nationalist parties attract support, in the main, from the Catalan-speaking middle and lower middle classes. The Catalan Socialist Party (PSC), though an affiliate of the Spanish Socialist Party (PSOE), is autonomous: it is as Catalanist as the nationalist parties on some questions, it is Catalanist in its general orientation, and it provides the main competition for the nationalists. In comparison to the two main parties the Catalan Communist Party, Iniciativa de Catalunya (IC, affiliated to the Spanish Communist Party, Izquierda Unida, IU), though influential in the media, universities and intellectual circles, is rather weakly represented in the Catalan parliament, as is the conservative Partido Popular (PP).[2] The parties of the left represent the Castilian-speaking voters who are predominantly working class. A crucial factor in helping to bridge the gap between these two communities and in regulating conflict between them is the fact that the parties that represent them are controlled by leaders drawn from the Catalan-speaking political elite (Llobera, 1989). The ethnic homogeneity of the Catalan political elite thus seems to be a vital ingredient in the pactist political culture that characterises Catalan politics. The structure of Catalan politics is strongly pluralist and this, combined with Catalonia's contractualist political

---

[2] Both Esquerra Republicana and Iniciativa de Catalunya have since split up into separate parties.

culture and its pactist strategy, enables it to respond remarkably flexibly and creatively in its relations with the centre. The availability of a wide variety of competing alternatives and the tradition of pactism goes a long way to explaining the absence of violence in Catalan nationalism today.

Catalan nationalism incorporates strong elements of ethnic nationalism (Hargreaves, 1998). As we have seen, its claim to the status of a historic nation and its opposition to the host state are rooted in the existence of a culturally distinct community with a very strong sense of its own national identity, which coheres, above all, around the Catalan language. Language is the primary ethnic marker distinguishing Catalans from Castilian-speaking Spain and, in particular, from that large sector of the region's population which is of immigrant origin from the rest of Spain (Barrera-González, 1995). The Catalan government is officially committed to the notion of civic nationalism, in the sense that it proclaims that Catalans are people who live and work in Catalonia, and its leader Jordi Pujol denies that his brand of Catalan nationalism is ethnic. However, in reality Catalan nationalism is more complex. The Catalan government vigorously promotes Catalan culture in every shape and form. That ethnic nationalism predominates over civic nationalism is evidenced by the many public statements that Pujol has made concerning the centrality of the language to being Catalan and, above all, by the government's policy of 'linguistic normalisation', whereby Castilian native speakers are compelled in a number of ways to become culturally Catalan. Most importantly, the school curriculum is taught in Catalan and proficiency in the language is a condition of employment in much of the public sector. The Catalan government has succeeded in some ways in Catalanising the mass media, especially the popular government-controlled Catalan-language TV channel TV3.[3]

Understandably, Pujol wishes to avoid the label 'ethnic nationalism' because of its tribal connotations and its perceived association with intolerance and violent conflict. Actually, it is a mistake to assume that the ethnic model necessarily entails such extreme forms of exclusivity: in most cases of ethnic nationalism the criteria of membership are cultural, and cultural credentials, unlike race or ancestry, can, in principle, be acquired by aspiring members of a national community, although in practice it may not be that easy to do so in given cases. In Catalonia at one level it is relatively easy to acquire the cultural credentials for membership of Catalan society. While Catalan nationalism is predominantly ethnic rather than civic, Catalans are tolerant of the large Spanish-speaking community which became established as a result of large-scale immigration from the

---

[3] Book and newspaper publishing in Catalan has grown significantly, but Catalan government attempts to enforce the use of Catalan in advertising and film have been far less successful.

rest of Spain, mainly from the much poorer south of the country, during the late 1950s to the mid-1970s. The Catalan government has prudently pursued a flexible, inclusive and consensual policy with respect to the Spanish-speaking community and has avoided pressing for complete independence for the region. Through intermarriage, bilingualism and occupational mobility the two communities overlap to a considerable extent, the boundaries between them are somewhat blurred and on the whole relations between them are remarkably harmonious. In these ways Catalan nationalism shows that ethnic nationalism need not necessarily be more 'tribal', intolerant and exclusive than civic nationalism (Brown, 1999). Nevertheless, there are ethnic boundaries between the Catalan and Castilian communities constituted by different linguistic patterns, senses of national identity, political party allegiance and, notably, by the fact that a disproportionate number of middle-level and elite positions in Catalan society are held by autochthonous Catalans (Barrera-González, 1995; Flaquer, 1996; Llobera, 1989; Llobera, forthcoming). The civic emphasis in the Catalan government's policy of cultural assimilation is a way of papering over the reality of existing ethnic divisions between the two communities, one of which, the Catalan community, in some ways tends to be dominant (Woolard, 1986). It is a successful attempt up to now, at least, to placate the working-class Castilian-speaking population which is potentially capable of being mobilised, not just by its main opponents, the socialists, who after all are Catalanists, but by latent centrist forces opposed to Catalan autonomy.

The issue here is whether learning Catalan and bilingualism entail full integration into Catalan society, in the sense of eliminating barriers to social interaction and social mobility. The evidence, such as it is, suggests it does not, if language patterns, the class structure of Catalonia, and the question of who constitutes the region's elite are taken into account (Barrera-González, 1995; Conversi, 1997; Giner, 1984; Laitin, 1989; Llobera, 1989; Shabad and Gunther, 1982; Woolard, 1989). Bilingualism does not mean that language no longer functions as an ethnic marker – rather, it means it functions more subtly as such (Woolard, 1989). Native-speaking Catalans are skilled at 'linguistic switching' as the occasion demands, speaking Catalan among themselves, notably at home in the family and among friends, and Castilian to others – a practice that clearly involves recognising who is Catalan and who is not.

'Who is a Catalan?' is a highly complex, vexatious and politicised question to which there is no definitive answer. Pujol's answer – those who live and work in Catalonia, with the caveat that to be fully Catalan one must be able to speak the language – is one answer among several possibilities. 'Autochthonous Catalans' can be distinguished for analytical purposes from 'non-autochthonous Catalans', the former being those of Catalan mother tongue and the latter consisting of first- and second-generation immigrants whose mother tongue is Castilian (Barrera-González, 1995; CIS, 1993, cited in Barrera-González). This does not settle the question, but it is a useful distinction because it is possible to establish a strong correlation between individuals' linguistic provenance and their perceptions of who is Catalan.

Between them the two groups employ a variety of objective and subjective criteria to define who is Catalan, but differ in the importance they attach to these criteria (ability to speak Catalan, being born in Catalonia, living and working in Catalonia, adapting to local customs, valuing things Catalan, wishing to be Catalan, defending things Catalan). Broadly speaking, 'autochthonous Catalans' are more demanding in their definitions and they stress, in particular, the requirement to identify positively with Catalonia more than objective factors like ability to speak Catalan. The 'non-autochthonous Catalans' are less demanding and not so certain: they tend to stress objective factors that give putative claimants to being Catalan easier access to that status, such as living and working in Catalonia. Views on the question also correlate with individuals' level of education, voting choice, political party affiliation and age. The young, the old (those beyond middle age), the better educated and those leaning towards the two nationalist parties, CiU and ERC, are again more demanding and put more stress on positive identification with Catalonia as the most important criterion.

It must be emphasised that the divergence is not simply between Catalan native speakers and Castilian speakers. The majority of the latter understand Catalan and many speak the language. To this rather complicated picture must be added another factor. Explicit views on what constitutes being Catalan co-exist with implicit views which are not readily amenable to investigation by opinion survey. The fact that 'autochthonous Catalans' relegate speaking Catalan to a relatively low position when explicitly asked to rank a list of criteria for being Catalan in order of importance, is surprising at first glance, given the salience of the language otherwise as an ethnic boundary marker. One explanation that has been advanced for this is that 'autochthonous Catalans', i.e. those often labelled by people in both linguistic communities as the 'real Catalans', do not wish to discriminate against Castilian speakers. Their attitude is one of tolerance of linguistic difference, indicating the existence of a consensus whereby potentially damaging divisions between the two linguistic communities are obviated (Barrera-González, 1995). While, no doubt, consensus does exist at some level, this deference to Castilian speakers' sensibilities does not prevent 'autochthonous Catalans' from being much more strongly in favour of the use of Catalan as the vehicular language in schools than their 'non-autochthonous' compatriots (Barrera-González, 1995: 35). This reveals an implicit acknowledgement of the high salience of the language boundary on the part of the former.

The implicit centrality of language for 'autochthonous Catalans' is brought out in the differences between them and 'non-autochthonous' Catalans in the strength of their national identity (CIS, 1993, cited in Barrera-González, 1995: 58). In the 'autochthonous Catalan' group – defined in this study, it should be emphasised, as those whose mother tongue is Catalan – the large majority (70.5 per cent) say they are 'only Catalan' or 'more Catalan than Spanish'. On the other hand, the only group with anything approaching this strength of conviction as to their national identity is the 'non-autochthonous Catalan' group who have little or no competence in Catalan, 61 per cent of whom say they are 'more Spanish than Catalan', or 'only Spanish'. The non-autochthonous Catalans claiming to be competent Catalan speakers are much less certain: only 21 per cent say they are 'only Catalan' or 'more Catalan than Spanish', while 27.5 per cent say they are 'only Spanish', or 'more Spanish than Catalan'. Of the small minority of genuine bilinguals (those whose mother tongue was equally Catalan and Spanish), 58.5 per cent feel 'only Catalan' or 'more Catalan than Spanish' and 39 per cent feel 'only Spanish' or 'more Spanish than Catalan'.

'Autochthonous Catalans' are much more likely to be middle class than first- and second-generation immigrants. They dominate medium and small-scale business, the professions, culture and politics, whether they are nationalists or not, and even where the language of these spheres, notably commerce and politics, is Castilian. This is why Catalan is the prestige language of the region and why Castilian-speaking immigrants are eager to learn it.[3] So there are clearly major ethnic differences in Catalonia between native Catalans and others, despite official disclaimers (Hargreaves, 1998). The ethnic element, i.e. the tendency to exclusiveness and a certain degree of obsession about the vernacular culture, is most evident among the separatists.

---

[4] According to a survey carried out by the Institute of Political and Social Sciences at the Autonomous University of Barcelona, the proportion of people in Catalonia whose usual language is Catalan has decreased quite sharply in recent years and the proportion of people whose usual language is Castilian has risen (Flaquer, 1996). The trend seems to be stronger among the younger generation who have a good understanding of Catalan, having gone through a school system where the curriculum was taught in it. What this means is not entirely clear, but taken together with the trend in the 1990s to identify somewhat less with Catalonia and more with Spain, it might mean that language is becoming less central to Catalan identity and that nationalist politicans may find it increasingly difficult to gain support by making defence of the Catalan language the central plank of their campaigns.

Catalan nationalism, having captured political power in the region, also exerts considerable leverage on central government, to the extent that the last two governments have relied on CiU support to stay in power. Catalan nationalists are therefore in a position to use state power both directly and indirectly to further their interests. Catalonia is one of the richest regions in Spain and its government commands considerable revenue resources and powers of expenditure. It possesses certain powers with respect to law and order, the administration of justice, and economic development, and full powers over language and culture, health, education and social policy. It was this power position which was to prove so crucial in the conflict over the Olympic Games.

3 The relationship between Olympism, globalisation and nationalism

Globalisation

Olympism is a world-wide sports movement with its own structure and culture whose activities have important political, economic and cultural ramifications. An important part of the explanation of how it may be linked with nationalism therefore needs to be understood in terms of recent developments at the international level. The most important of these are: the ending of the superpower conflict and the reconfiguration of the interstate system into the 'new world order'; the accelerated internationalisation of financial markets, technology and certain sectors of manufacturing and services since the 1970s; the salience of the activities of multinational capitalist enterprises; the expansion of new communications and information technology; vast population movements; growing environmental problems that transcend frontiers; and the apparent emergence of a hybrid, cosmopolitan 'global culture'.

The notion of globalisation is commonly invoked to make sense of such changes. If Olympism is to be conceived as an aspect of globalisation, care needs to be exercised, because it is relatively easy to misconceive the significance of recent changes in such terms. The 'strong version' of the globalisation thesis argues that distinct national economies, polities and cultures are subsumed and re-articulated into a new system by international processes and transactions (Robertson, 1990). The emergent global system becomes autonomised, i.e. it is socially and nationally disembedded, so that economic, political and cultural processes are no longer capable of being understood, regulated and controlled as in the previous age. Notably, the capacity of the 'nation-state' to exert control over economic, political and cultural life is being challenged and the 'nation-state', national identity and nationalism are being eroded and superseded by a globally generated system of governance, a global identity and a global culture.

However, this strong version of the globalisation thesis does not stand up to rigorous examination. Essentially it rests on half truths, vaguely formulated and untested propositions, and exaggerated projections of developments at the international level, and it suffers from an almost complete lack of historical awareness (Hirst and Thompson, 1996). One wonders why it has caught the intelligentsia's imagination and swept across the social sciences and cultural studies so successfully.

The present highly internationalised economy is by no means unprecedented: rather, it is one of a number of distinct conjunctures that have existed since an economy based on modern industrial technology began to be generalised from the 1860s (Hirst and Thompson 1996). The world economy is far from 'global'. Rather, trade, investment and financial flows are concentrated in the triad of Europe, North America and Japan and the third world remains marginal to both investment and trade – a small minority of newly industrialising countries apart – and this dominance seems set to continue. America, the leading nation-state, although economically weakened, remains the world's biggest economy and the powerhouse of world demand. The major economic powers, the G8, have the capacity to coordinate policy and to exert powerful pressures over financial markets and other economic tendencies. Thus global markets are by no means beyond national regulation and control and the 'nation-state' remains a key player in suturing the local, regional and international (Hirst and Thompson, 1996; Mann, 1993).

Genuinely transnational companies are relatively rare. Most companies are nationally based and trade multinationally on the strength of a major national location of production and sales, and there seems to be no major tendency towards the growth of truly international companies. Their activities often provoke nationalist opposition in the foreign countries in which they operate and quite frequently national governments (including third world governments) impose their own terms on them.

Neither is there much sign of the development of a global system of governance superseding the 'nation-state'. Since the collapse of the Soviet bloc, the bi-polar configuration of capitalist versus communist blocs has been superseded by a polycentric shifting one in which 'nation-states' are, if anything, more prominent. Global agencies like the United Nations, the International Monetary Fund (IMF) and the World Bank are heavily dependent for their effectiveness upon the cooperation of a few leading 'nation-states', and here again America is the key player. As the leader of NATO, a regionally based organisation – not a truly international one – it is the hegemonic military power. Some indication of the problems that creating a global identity would present is provided by the example of another regionally based putative transnational organisation, the European Union, whose difficulties in reconciling, let alone overriding, the national interests of its member states have multiplied, despite increasing economic integration. The formation of a European identity as an alternative to national identity remains a chimera and the EU has been virtually powerless to combat the resurgence of nationalism in Europe.

Economic, political and demographic developments have accentuated national divisions and aspirations and we have witnessed the resurgence of ethnic minority or 'peripheral nationalisms', and a renewal of ethnic majority and state nationalisms across the world. Economic competition between third world countries and between them and Western countries, the economic difficulties encountered by the former, the explosion in their populations, the political tension, breakdown and war that characterises the 'new world order' in many parts of the non-Western world, the attempts of their inhabitants to migrate to the West on a mass scale, and the resultant immigration policies and nationality laws, have raised national barriers, increased the salience of national identity and fuelled nationalism.

To some observers the increasing contact between, the mixing up and the juxtaposition of different cultures is the most convincing evidence of the existence of a new global age. Doubtful as that proposition is, it comes closest to vindication in the cosmopolitan culture that has developed unevenly and most fully in the West, and which perhaps constitutes in outline a culture of truly global dimensions. This culture is a pastiche of motifs and styles underpinned by a universal scientific and technical discourse. The circulation of mass commodities at its centre is dependent for its success to a great degree on the fact that consumer culture draws its content from a global repertoire – from traditional, folk or national motifs and styles stripped of their context. The ideology it espouses is a vague internationalism and an equally vague concern with human rights and values. Above all, perhaps, its growth is facilitated by the new computerised information and communication system encircling the globe which is beyond the control of any individual state. Global culture in this sense is different from other cultures in that, since it is diffused world-wide, if unevenly, it seems to escape connection with any particular time or place. It is unique in its degree of self-consciousness, self-parody and sense of irony. It is calculating, capricious and affectively neutral with respect to whatever it signifies. Above all, it is relativist, permeated by the idea that our selves, knowledge and morality – indeed, cultures – are nothing but imagined constructions within particular discourses and language conventions, and that the process of construction is unlimited.

If the outlines of a global culture are discernible, there are nevertheless strict limits to the construction of a global culture *sui generis*, and these lie in the existing plurality of cultures, each embedded in a specific history and attached to a specific location. This applies especially to the existence of national cultures with their own memories, traditions, identities, values, myths, customs and sense of destiny, each of them tied to a specific time and place (Smith, 1990). Cultures are by their nature discriminatory devices: they mediate the transnational stream of information, ideas and images transmitted via the mass communications apparatus. To one or other extent they insulate their members from direct exposure to global influences and enable them to interpret 'global culture' according to their own values, and to reformulate and use it according to their own interests. In other words, communication always takes place within a given cultural context. Unless the content of global culture can be harmonised with a given national culture, establish a continuity with it, and be compatible with the prevailing sense of collective identity and destiny, it has little or no chance of surviving and flourishing, for global culture draws its content from, among other sources, such already constructed national cultures. The more there is a tendency towards the emergence of a global culture, the more the plurality of national cultures is accentuated (Smith, 1990).

In so far as it does exist, we would expect to find specific cultural, ethnic and national components of global, cosmopolitan culture, and it is no accident therefore, that it displays a high degree of Westernisation and, in particular, of Americanisation. Such a recognition does not entail reverting to notions of Western or American cultural imperialism as an alternative to any notion of global culture. It is to recognise its specific character and limits, and its relation to contemporary 'nation-states', national identity and nationalism. Of course the West compared with the rest is, on the whole, more powerful in political, military, economic and, in some respects, cultural terms. However, the fact of the matter is that power resources are not exclusively controlled by Western capitalist states, and they are not able to impose themselves willy nilly on the rest. The economic power of some Asian economies, the political and military power of China, and the cultural power of Islam are sufficient demonstrations of this point. To deny this is to take a determinist view of power relations and to discount the wealth of empirical evidence on the diversity of cultures, their power to resist Western influence, and in many cases the willingness, indeed eagerness, of the non-West to enter into relations with the West in order to exploit the perceived ensuing advantages. Fashionable thirdworldist talk of Western hegemony, domination and exploitation also conveniently neglects the fact that the parlous, dependent condition of many third world countries, particularly the ex-colonies, is often due to their corrupt, inefficient, dictatorial regimes and inappropriate cultural practices.

Americanisation refers to a perceived tendency towards a universal homogenisation of lifestyles and social institutions on the lines of the American model. The idea is most easily evidenced in the character of consumer culture in the advanced societies and the strivings of an envious rest of the world to emulate them. Plainly, American mass culture is a very powerful, pervasive influence in the modern world, a dimension of American power closely associated with its economic, political and military power. However pervasive, meretricious, vulgar, morally offensive and aesthetically deficient it may seem to its detractors, there is no reason to conclude that it is dominant to the extent of having the capacity to override other national cultures, although plainly it more successfully penetrates the Anglophone world and exerts more influence there than elsewhere. American culture can be imported, selectively absorbed, and reinterpreted so that it is consonant with, and can be made to represent, quite different cultures. Take the American game of baseball. Exported to Japan and Cuba, two sharply contrasting cultures, as part of a growing American influence, it was enthusiastically taken up and became the national game in each of them. In both cases this game is now popularly understood as theirs, and it has come to express, not American culture, but specific aspects of Japanese and Cuban culture. Just as it cannot be concluded that America rules the world or controls the world economy, even though its military power is awesome, so it cannot be concluded that America is able to impose its culture world-wide. The importation of American culture whether imposed or otherwise is just as likely, if not perhaps more likely, to stimulate feelings of national resentment, and in consequence to fuel nationalist movements, as it is to lead to cultural homogenisation in the American mould. Indeed, resentment against the world's leading power which is often perceived as interfering in other countries' affairs, has played a major part in stimulating nationalism across the globe since the Second World War.

We can accept then, that there have been some extremely important developments at international level in the last quarter of the twentieth century, which can be understood as globalisation, if by that we mean an expanded internationalisation process that is an integral part of modernisation, i.e. it is an extension of modernisation, in which the 'nation-state' remains and is likely to remain a key player, and in which national identity and nationalism are key features. These developments compress time and space, so that the effects of events and processes occurring at local, national and global levels are increasingly communicated and felt at all three levels virtually simultaneously, making for a much higher degree of interdependency between them (Giddens, 1990). This is a more opaque, less knowable, less predictable and controllable world, where states' control of what happens within their territory is loosened, their capacities to control are challenged and the national culture is threatened. But it is still a world in which 'nation-states', national identity and nationalism flourish and in which the impact of globalisation processes, though an important feature, is limited.

Olympism and politics

There are few genuinely transnational entities and it turns out that Olympism is one of them. In analytical terms Olympism is primarily an aspect of global culture in the sense we have defined it here. It is frequently pulled into politics, notably nationalist politics, and it is implicated in the global economy.

At the apex of the Olympic movement and situated at the centre of a global network of international non-governmental sports organisations, the main function of the International Olympic Committee (IOC) is to control and regulate Olympic sport. It is almost impossible to exaggerate the IOC's global reach and the scale of the activities generated by the development of the Olympic movement.

A self-perpetuating body headed by the president, currently Juan Antonio Samaranch, the IOC consists of approximately 106 notables, drawn from a relatively wide variety of countries. Members are appointed by the IOC itself, so officially they do not represent their own countries, but there is, in fact, an element of state representation since a proportion of members are nominated by governments. The members meet infrequently as a whole body and so power is heavily concentrated in the hands of the president and an inner circle of associates, staffed by a bureaucracy located at the IOC headquarters in Lausanne. Affairs are administered by a nine-man Executive Board supported by twenty-three Commissions dealing with areas of particular importance, such as the sale of broadcasting rights. Membership tends to interlock with membership of other powerful international non-governmental international sports organisations, some of which constitute potential rivals to the IOC. Of particular importance are the international sports federations like the International Amateur Athletic Federation (IAAF) and the International Federation of Football Associations (FIFA), the Association of National Olympic Committees, the General Assembly of International Sports Federations, and the Association of Summer Olympic International Federations. The IOC alone determines which countries may enter the Games and in order to participate a country must have a National Olympic Committee (NOC) recognised by the IOC. Thus, through the international sports federations and NOCs the main sectors of organised sport throughout the world are integrated into the Olympic movement and the IOC thereby exerts influence over the development of sport at the national as well as international level. In fact, in this way the vast majority of the world's states, currently numbering approximately 200, are linked up and integrated into the Olympic movement.

The fact that states are the representative units in Olympic sport, i.e. individuals cannot compete unless they are selected for a 'national' team, means that the IOC has acquired *de facto* if not *de jure* diplomatic functions, and the Olympic movement has become a forum for the airing of political issues and a means for states and nations to exert political pressure in pursuit of their interests. Reference has already been made to some pertinent examples of regimes taking advantage of their position as host to the Games, but there are many other ways in which Olympism and politics are entwined. Indeed since the inception of the modern Olympic Games it has rarely been otherwise (Hargreaves, 1992). In the 1930s it became more systemic and since the 1950s, against the background of the cold war between the US and former USSR and the 'new world order' following the latter's collapse, it has become a standard feature. Some notable instances are the dispute between the 'two Chinas' and the 'two Germanies' when the People's Republic of China, Chinese nationalist Taiwan, the Federal Republic of Germany and the former German Democratic Republic used the Olympic movement to resolve the question of international recognition of their regimes. The anti-apartheid lobby had South Africa excluded from the Games. The Arab–Israeli conflict has spilled over into the Games with Palestinian terrorist attacks on Israeli athletes at the Munich Games and Arab pressure to have Israel excluded from Olympic-sponsored competitions. Such examples raise the questions of whether the Olympic movement and its leadership are pliant instruments of political forces, simply providing points of access for them to the international system, and whether the Olympic movement is powerless to prevent itself being used in this way, or whether it mediates and modifies their influence, or even counteracts and successfully resists political pressures, so that it could be said to be genuinely autonomous.

Some commentators have characterised the IOC in conspiracy theory terms as a right-wing, undemocratic and venal international organisation, willing to come to terms with any commercial interest or political regime as long as it furthers its own interests (Jennings and Simpson, 1991; Jennings 1996; Hoberman, 1995). It is certainly true that there is a conflict between the ideology of Olympism espoused by the founder, de Coubertin, and laid down in the Olympic charter, which has been articulated and elaborated *ad infinitum* subsequently by the IOC, and how in reality it functions. The ideology stems from de Coubertin's belief in the efficacy of physical culture as supposedly practised by the ancient Greeks at the ancient Olympic Games, and as it was practised in the late nine-teenth-century English public schools under the auspices of the cult of athleticism. He was convinced that such practices developed dynamic 'moralised' individuals; that they would help to regenerate his own country, France; and that organised on an international scale in a revived Olympic movement they could promote peace and international under-standing (Guttman, 1992; MacAloon, 1981). The movement he inaugu-rated and inspired was in keeping with a trend in the later nineteenth and early twentieth centuries for voluntary organisations embracing a type of internationalism to emerge, of which the Red Cross, Esperanto and the Boy Scouts are examples (Hoberman, 1995).

De Coubertin saw no incompatibility between patriotism and interna-tionalism: love of one's country for him did not entail antagonism towards other countries. What he was against, apparently, was chauvinism. But the history of the Olympic movement clearly manifests political influences going well beyond mere patriotism and which certainly conflict with liberal-left notions of internationalism, and it is a moot point as to what internationalism means for the IOC. To argue that the IOC's internationalism has a right-wing authoritarian slant and that the IOC has fascist affinities exaggerates the influence of certain features of the IOC. For a long time IOC members were recruited overwhelmingly from the upper echelons of society, with a good proportion from the aristo-cracy, giving it a pronounced hierarchical, anti-democratic, right-wing character. To a great extent the undemocratic, secretive club ethos still exists, but nowadays there are fewer aristocrats and under the so-called 'Olympic revolution' carried out by the current president the modernised IOC is technocratic, professional, business-oriented and politically prag-matic. Members are more likely to possess a sphere of expertise and be wealthy businessmen, executives, lawyers or other types of professional, or to be ex-politicians, ex-military, or top sports officials. Some members are even retired communist bureaucrats. The current president was Franco's sports minister and later one of his provincial officials (Boix and Espada, 1991), a prominent German member of the recent past was in the Nazi Party, a current member was chief of the Korean CIA when that country was under the military regime, and there are some other members who justifiably have unsavoury reputations (Jennings, 1996; Hoberman, 1995). A majority of members come from countries where democracy is extremely fragile or non-existent, i.e. communist and ex-communist countries, the Arab world, Africa and Asia. However, conspir-acy theory, while it reveals the yawning gap between the IOC's professed beliefs and its character in reality, does not take us very far in analytical terms. After all, the IOC is no different from many other international organisations, both governmental and non-governmental, in having skeletons in its cupboard, in departing from its ostensible aims and behaving in a self-interested manner. If all organisations involving individuals associated in some way with repressive political regimes are to be held up for castigation, many international agencies, governmental and non-governmental, many multinationals and not a few democratic governments would not survive much scrutiny.

Like the Catholic church, the IOC is one of the few genuinely 'offshore operations' that transcend frontiers and are not controlled by any single state or international body (Hoberman, 1995). Although the IOC's headquarters are located in Lausanne, for the convenience Switzerland provides as a traditionally neutral state, the IOC, like the Red Cross, is by no means a Swiss body under Swiss control.

The extent to which the IOC is autonomous can be tested by examining some key instances where political pressure was applied to it. As is the case with any powerholder, the IOC's power rests upon its legitimacy, prestige and authority, the material resources at its disposal and its organisational capacity. As well as political pressure the Olympic movement has to withstand pressure exerted by economic and cultural interests.

The Berlin Olympics of 1936 is a clear instance of the Olympic Games being used for state nationalist and, in this case, fascist purposes. Most accounts reveal the complicity of the IOC (Mandel, 1971; Guttman 1984; Hoberman, 1995; Eisen, 1984) and agree that the Nazis achieved a propaganda victory out of the Games, but it should be noted that the Nazi regime, nevertheless, had to compromise somewhat. It was obliged to remove the more obvious anti-semitic propaganda at the behest of the IOC and Hitler was denied the more central role he wished to play in the Games' proceedings (Mandell, 1971). Whether this constituted a significant restraint and made any difference to the Nazis' achieving their objective is a moot point. Indeed, it could be said to have cloaked the real nature of the regime and contributed, therefore, to the propaganda victory. The key point is that from this time onwards the Games were politicised, in the sense that all host countries, no matter what the nature of the regime, used the Games to project a favourable image abroad and to boost the morale of their populations.

In this particular case Olympism favoured fascism; later it was to favour other hosts to the Olympics with a political axe to grind: Mexico's authoritarian one-party state (1968), Soviet totalitarianism (Moscow, 1980), American crusading liberal-democracy (Los Angeles, 1984), and the

Korean military regime (Seoul, 1988). They all took advantage of the occasion to project a favourable political image of themselves. Olympism shows no particular political bias in this respect, providing regimes of whatever political hue with the opportunity to promote their national identities, although it should be noted that in only one of the above cases, the Berlin Olympics, did Olympism become entangled with nationalist politics, strictly speaking.

It would seem from these examples that Olympism is simply at the disposal of regimes determined to use it for their own purposes. However, closer inspection of the IOC's dealings with governments subsequently, reveals that this is by no means the case. At the time of the Berlin Olympics (1936) the IOC lacked experience of dealing with totalitarian regimes and 'was perhaps flattered and overawed by the unprecedented degree of importance Nazi Germany gave to the Games. It must be remembered that the IOC was not alone in its apparent naivety about the Nazis at this time. The Nazi regime was still a relatively unknown quantity: like fascist Italy it had been internationally accepted, and it had not yet acted out its expansionist and genocidal impulses. The IOC was no exception in its supine behaviour. For example, the England football team was instructed on Foreign Office advice to give the Nazi salute in the ceremony prior to a match with Germany, on German soil, in 1938. Until the outbreak of war between Britain and Germany no government opposed the latter and some, like Britain in the Munich Agreement, and the USSR in the Nazi–Soviet Pact, actively sought accommodation with it.

In fact, the IOC was never so compliant again, showing its independence and a capacity to resist political pressure in several notable instances involving, directly or indirectly, great pressure from the superpowers. East Germany (DDR), supported by the USSR, pressurised the IOC from the 1950s to the 1970s to recognise it as a way of ending its diplomatic isolation. The IOC responded by insisting that it join West Germany in forming an all-German team, a solution that neither of the two Germanies wanted, and which went further than, and was in advance of, what was demanded by the UN and other international political bodies. This was when any hint of a united Germany was anathema to the superpowers, and also when several powerful international sports federations had already conceded recognition to East Germany. It was only when East Germany had made progress in gaining full diplomatic recognition within the broader international community that the IOC conceded recognition to it (Houlihan, 1994).

From 1950 for thirty years the People's Republic of China (PRC) and the Chinese nationalists in Taiwan used the IOC as a forum to promote their claims alone to represent China. In this case the IOC responded by adopting the 'two Chinas' formula and resisted pressure from the US and USSR to favour their allies. Because China withdrew from mainstream sport during the cultural revolution in the 1960s, Taiwan was the unchallenged representative of China in the Olympic movement. In 1975 the PRC applied for membership on condition that Taiwan be expelled. Despite the fact that the most powerful international federations (FIFA and the IAAF) complied with this demand, that the host country of the 1976 Olympics, Canada, refused to allow the Taiwanese team visas, and that the UN had expelled Taiwan, the IOC forced the two Chinas to compromise by agreeing to separate membership under the names of the 'China Olympic Committee' (PRC) and the 'Chinese Taipeh Olympic Committee (Taiwan)' (Houlihan, 1994).

In 1980, in the course of an attempt to enforce an international boycott of the Moscow Olympic Games, the US brought great pressure to bear on the IOC to have the Games relocated. The IOC refused, gave these Games its full support, and the majority of countries followed this lead and participated (Killanin, 1983).

The way the IOC has handled the Arab–Israeli conflict, on the occasions it has impinged on Olympic sport, is an example where it has adopted a less independent stance, at times capitulating to Arab nationalism. When, in 1980, the USSR sided with the Arabs and demanded that Israel be excluded from the Moscow Games, the IOC refused and made it a condition of awarding the Games to Moscow that all countries invited by the IOC be permitted to attend (Killanin, 1983:8). On the other hand, the IOC has done very little about the recurring problem of Israel's exclusion from other competitions with which the IOC is associated, due to Arab pressure. In the early 1970s Israel's request to join the European Regional Games was turned down at around the same time as the IAAF granted Palestine membership. When the host country, Indonesia, excluded Israel from participating in the Asian Games in Jakarta in 1962, the IOC suspended the Indonesian Olympic Committee. In response the Indonesian government, with China's support, successfully organised an alternative Games, the 'Games of the Emerging Forces'. Alarmed at the prospect of international sport being successfully organised by governments, the IOC reinstated Indonesia in 1964 and Israel continued to be excluded from the Asian Games, apparently with the connivance of the IOC. In 1982 the host country, India, did not invite Israel to participate, a decision questioned by the IOC, but when the organisers withdrew their request for Olympic patronage of the Games as a tactical manoeuvre, the IOC accepted this and the president and several IOC members attended the Games in person. The new body set up subsequently to replace the

Asian Games Federation, the Olympic Council for Asia (OCA) is funded substantially by Arab oil money and it did not invite Israel to join. In contrast to the IOC, several international sports federations, like FIFA and the IAAF, took a stronger stand against the anti-Israeli lobby. It is difficult to escape the conclusion that the IOC's capitulation was at least in part due to its reliance on Arab money to sustain its support for Asian sport (Houlihan, 1994).

The Olympic movement then, does provide access to the international system for states to pursue their interests and an access point for nationalist politics to come into play, but the Olympic context also limits and constrains these forces by mediating, modifying and at times successfully resisting them when they threaten the viability of the enterprise. The IOC has compromised with, and responded to, the influence of quite different and opposed political forces, because its prime objective, like that of most long-lasting organisations, is self-preservation and self-interest. It is little wonder then, that it is prepared to compromise with states pursuing their 'national interests' and with nationalism, whether for or against the state. The key point to bear in mind is that this does not mean it simply reflects such forces.

The IOC's legitimacy and authority has grown with the increasing size and importance of the Games, its demonstrated organisational capacity and its experience in dealing with major powers and difficult political issues. Just as the third world countries were able to play off the superpowers against each other, the IOC can do the same with the major powers today. One of the ways it has done this has been by expanding the membership to include not only more countries from the communist bloc but also from the third world.

The economic dimension of Olympism

The IOC can also withstand pressure because it enjoys a fortunate economic position. Supported by their respective states, the world's major cities vie with each other, not only for the political and cultural prestige, but also for the potentially immense economic benefits that now accrue to those fortunate enough to be awarded the Games by the IOC. The IOC alone has the power to confer this privilege.

The main way in which the political, economic and cultural significance of Olympism has been enhanced, and the power and influence of the IOC concomitantly increased, has been through the transformation of the Games into a mass media spectacle, with a global audience of possibly 3.5 billion and at the very least 1 billion (Moragas, 1992). Fifteen thousand athletes, at least the same number of officials, even more journalists, and vast numbers of spectators, migrate to the summer Games from all points of the compass, making them a major stimulus to the international travel, tourism and leisure industries. Through the intervention of television and steadily advancing commercialisation since the 1980s, Olympism has become a very lucrative branch of the world-wide entertainment industry. The huge TV audiences for the Games attract advertisers willing to pay premium rates to the TV channels and the sale of TV rights to broadcast the Games has become the Olympic movement's largest source of revenue over the last twenty years. The American networks have played the pivotal part. For the last three Olympics NBC has acquired the US rights by bidding up against its main rival, ABC Television, a process culminating in a payment of $715 million for the rights to broadcast the Atlanta Games in 1996. Revenue from NBC amounts to nearly twice what the rest of the world's TV channels pay for the Olympics. It is no accident that one of NBC's top executives has a seat on the IOC. Consequently, the scheduling of Olympic events has to take account of the demands of prime-time American television. The Olympics are now marketed by the IOC in conjunction with the Games organising committees, like any other commodity. ISL, the international marketing company founded by Horst Dassler, the head of Adidas, handles the IOC's TOP sponsorship programme, giving world-wide rights to a dozen multinationals to exclusive use of IOC symbols. Coca-Cola alone provided $179 million for this privilege on the occasion of the Atlanta Games in 1996 (Real, 1996). Apart from this, the IOC and the Games organising committees have other kinds of sponsorship and advertising arrangements whereby hundreds of companies world-wide have purchased the Olympic symbols, the Games logo and mascots to advertise their products and enhance their corporate images. The top athletes make fortunes from endorsing well-known brand names and products. Revenue from the sale of TV rights, sponsorship deals and advertising is the life-blood of Olympism. It is not only the host cities and countries that are drenched in advertising and corporate imagery linked to the Olympics but virtually the whole globe, as advertisers and sponsors take advantage of the media coverage of the Games. A variety of American multinationals like Coca-Cola, Kodak, IBM, Rank Xerox, Nike, Mars, 3M and USPS have been particularly prominent in these kinds of developments. The IOC's own marketing department estimated that Olympic revenue programmes generated $1.8 billion over the three-year period 1989–92 (Miller, 1992: 46).

With an annual budget of $15 million, reserves in the region of $100 million, derived largely from income from ownership and control of broadcasting rights to the Games from which the IOC takes a percentage, sponsorship from eager multinationals, and advertising and franchising deals, clearly the IOC plays in the multinationals' league. And it must be emphasised that the privilege of staging the Games, which involves sums that dwarf these expenditures, is paid for by the host city and country, not the IOC. The sums involved here are truly staggering. The budget of the Barcelona Games Organising Committee alone was $1,700 million and the total direct investment in the city and region generated by the Games, from the public and private sectors combined, is estimated at £5–6.5 billion (Brunet, 1992). Indeed, economic activity generated by the Games may be of such a magnitude, as in the case of the Barcelona and Seoul Games, that it has a significant impact on a country's GDP and economic growth (Brunet, 1992; Kim, 1989).

Clearly, Olympism is thus enmeshed in a global capitalist economy, but it is a mistake to conclude from this that Olympism is primarily driven by the imperatives of advanced global capitalism (Gruneau and Cantelon, 1988), or controlled by any single economic interest, such as the sports goods manufacturer Horst Dassler, head of Adidas (Jennings, 1996). It is more than likely that from time to time individuals and particular enterprises exert influence over the IOC, as is normal with any organisation, but it is fanciful to depict any one of them as the power behind the IOC. More to the point, the IOC is not a publicly quoted, profit-maximising, business enterprise owned by shareholders and subjected to market forces and to takeovers, as such organisations are. Like any international non-governmental organisation operating in a capitalist environment it has to balance its books, but that imperative is of a different order from the imperative to maximise profits, a discipline which is exerted by the market on capitalist enterprises. The relationship of the IOC to capitalist enterprise is that, like all sporting and cultural organisations run on non-profit-making lines, its activities create economic opportunities which capitalist enterprises take advantage of and with whom the IOC then enters into relationships. Thus, the IOC is financially reliant upon the revenue it obtains from NBC and from its multinational sponsors. But TV companies and major sponsors have to compete in the market to obtain the rights to televise the Games and to be associated with this prestigious event. The IOC can diversify its sources of revenue when it finds itself becoming over-reliant on any one source or group of sources, because there is a strong demand for its unique product which it alone owns and controls, i.e. it is in a quasi-monopoly position. It can therefore limit the impact of market forces on the Olympic Games. For example, while it is true that amateurism has collapsed, that the top competitors are now highly paid professionals and that the Games are marketed like any other product, host cities and countries are not selected on economic grounds alone, and sponsors' logos and advertising displays are still not allowed in the Olympic stadium.

Olympic culture

Given the global magnitude of the media audience for the Games and the massive migration across the globe on the part of participants, spectators, officials and professionals as well as technical experts of all kinds to attend and service them, arguably the Games have become the focal point of interest for more people than any other single event at any one time in history, constituting a forum for intercultural communication and exchange on an unprecedented scale. What in all probability constitutes the largest festival the world has ever witnessed has been characterised as an eclectic mix of classical allusions, militaristic triumphalism, fashion show glamour and national sentimentality, and as representative of a global, rootless ahistorical 'third culture' (Houlihan, 1994). Eclectic it certainly is, and apart perhaps from the militaristic element which has significantly declined, this depiction is not too far from the truth, but it needs to be amplified and characterised in more specific terms than as a 'third culture'.

Olympism is multilayered: it is made up of very different components which interact with each other and which may not always be compatible or easily accommodated. There are tensions in the Games between the more festive, celebratory aspects, the formal ritual and ceremonial aspects, originally designed to express the official Olympic beliefs and values, the show business spectacle that the Games in key respects have become, the internationalist theme, and the manner in which nations may be projected.

The ritual and ceremonial aspect articulates a certain traditional 'universalistic humanist' morality and an associated set of ideals about sport and internationalism which are held to be sacred. To participate in Olympic sport with sportsmanship and according to the rules, and to conduct it impartially, is to put into practice these ideals. Honour and glory accrue to the winners: they are heroes who serve, not themselves primarily, but the higher collective ends of Olympism – the formation of disciplined, responsible, spiritualised individuals and the achievement of peaceful relations between nations and peoples. The intended function of the plethora of Olympic ritual practices and ceremonies during the Games, from the reception of the sacred flame to the taking of the Olympic oath, the victory ceremonies and the handover ceremony to the representatives of the next Olympic city, is to convey the message of what is, essentially, a form of pagan religion.

In contrast, Olympism as show business spectacle is modern, as opposed to traditional, cosmopolitan rather than internationalist, amoral as opposed to moral, materialistic as opposed to idealistic, and profane as opposed to sacred. Winning and individual success is everything; defeat is disaster. Rampant triumphalism is the norm. Performance is thoroughly personalised. The concept of glamour replaces that of honour and hero worship is replaced by the image of the star as the object of worship. Success is measured almost exclusively in terms of record performance and material reward. Rules are not sacrosanct: they are obstacles to be circumvented. Drug-enhanced performance is tacitly allowed and increasingly condoned. Show business means that the show, as such, must take priority over everything else: it entails projecting and selling an image of the Games that is dramatic, exciting and, above all, sensational. Occasions demanding solemnity and dignity are antithetical to show business and when such occasions occur in the context of show business they tend to take on a comic-opera aspect, appear faintly ridiculous and inauthentic and are never very far from farce. Thus their objectives run the ever-present risk of being undermined. Olympism as show business is, of course, an integral part of a hedonistic consumer culture on a global scale.

The entertainment world, of which Olympism is now a part, was primarily generated in America: its techniques were pioneered in Hollywood and in American television. In this connection it is interesting to note that of the last four Olympics two have been held in America (Los Angeles, 1984 and Atlanta, 1996). Continuity in the style and ethos of the Games is ensured, for example, by the fact that some of the personnel that choreographed, directed and produced the shows have worked on successive Olympic Games. It is also ensured by the fact that Olympic city organising committees study intensively the management, planning, design and techniques of previous Games. If American expertise and know-how have been influential and reach their apogee when the Games are held in an American city, nevertheless there are few more striking examples of an emergent, if unstable and unevenly spread, global culture than the fact that the professional, managerial, commercial, artistic, scientific and technical expertise necessary to produce a modern Olympic Games is drawn from across the globe.

The Games are also a multifaceted festival, an in part serious, civil–religious celebration, but in large part also a celebration with an exuberant, non-serious, carnivalesque, spontaneous impulse, which sometimes seems to border on anarchy. These latter qualities can be seen particularly in the behaviour of the crowds in and around the stadia. Despite superficial similarities between the festive and show business elements, analytically they are not the same at all. Festival is organic, embedded in tradition, in place and time. Show business is rootless and parasitic on tradition. A standard feature of the Games is that host cities, communities and nations take the opportunity afforded by the Olympics to put on a festival celebrating their own local community and nation.

The nation – or, to be more accurate, the state-nation – enters the Olympic arena because, in the first instance, it is the constituent unit of Olympic sport. We have already commented on how crucial the deployment of symbols of the nation is in the formation of national identity. The unique feature of the Olympics compared with other international phenomena, including other sporting events, is the extraordinarily rich opportunity it affords for deploying symbols of the nation. Each in their own way, the three aspects discussed above – the ritual and ceremonial, the show business, and the festival aspects – enable a panoply of national symbols to be deployed in the course of the Games. National flags and anthems of course are omnipresent, but there are a multitude of other ways the nation may be symbolised, given the ritual and ceremonial, the show business treatment and the festival impulse – the theatricalised presence of persons symbolising the nation like heads of state and politicians, and the use of languages, parades, music, folklore, uniform, costume, song, dance, literature, poetry, the visual arts, historical allusions, and so on.

Simultaneously, however, Olympism strongly signifies internationalism. It needs emphasising that there is no necessary incompatibility between the mobilisation of national sentiment in these ways and the strongly internationalist sentiment that is symbolised, for example, by de Coubertin's five-ring Olympic flag. The meaning of internationalism here is not the supersession of the 'nation-state' and national sentiment and their replacement by some supra-national body with which the people of the world identify, but rather, given the will and institutions to bring them together, such as the Games, nations can exist together peacefully. Neither is Olympic internationalism incompatible with one kind of nationalism, namely, minority nationalism. Minority nationalism represents a form of conflict within the 'nation-state' not between states, unless another state or states intervene in the conflict. Furthermore, minority nationalist strategy usually attempts to mobilise external support for its cause and thereby legitimate its struggle internationally, and a supra-national body like the Olympic movement provides a convenient vehicle for achieving these objectives. This is quite different from the behaviour of 'nation-states' in conflict with each other, who like the superpowers in the cold war era, or like the fascist powers in the inter-war period, treated the Games as a war without weapons, a form of participation which plainly is antithetical to internationalism.

Olympism, as an aspect of a cosmopolitan, global culture, co-exists and interacts with local, national cultures. Rather than helping to reduce their significance it is perfectly compatible with the existence of strong senses of national identity in participant countries and with the presence of nationalism as a major political force. Indeed, far from being eroded, nationalism can be stimulated by global developments such as Olympism, as we will presently demonstrate with reference to one particular case, the Barcelona Games in 1992.

To those of a fashionable 'thirdworldist' persuasion, Olympism is a form of Western cultural imperialism. There is little reason to believe that 'Olympic universalist humanism' and Olympic scholarship function as instruments of Western domination (MacAloon, 1996), or that once non-Western states are successfully involved in Olympic sport they inevitably sacrifice their autonomy and that they legitimate Western values and rationality (Houlihan, 1994). Cultural determinism of this kind tends not to be too enlightening when it comes to analysing the relationship between Olympism and nationalism. What is being overlooked by such commentators is also the willing and active involvement of most third world and other non-Western countries in the Olympic movement and their capacity to use it adeptly to their own advantage. We have already cited some examples – China, Cuba, Kenya, South Korea, South Africa, the Arab states – and there are many more. The IOC, mostly at their behest, is extending its global coverage and strengthening its global links, by promoting sports development in third world countries, which it finances through its 'Olympic Solidarity' programme. Approximately one half of the IOC's membership comes from non-Western countries and we may be sure that they are not there simply to pursue Olympic ideals.

Olympism, then, is an aspect of global culture in the restricted sense of the concept of globalisation used here, i.e. not in terms of globalisation as a new stage in development. It is an integral part of a process of modernisation on a global scale, which has accelerated since the 1970s. Olympism brings the world to chosen localities in a uniquely concentrated form, subjecting them to the most advanced aspects of modernisation – capital flows and financial techniques, industrial technology and services, new communications and information technology, the mass media, managerial and political techniques, diplomacy, security management, the art of presentation – and to cultural flows, notably mass consumer culture. Simultaneously, the Games project these localities on to the world stage, providing them with opportunities to exert influence and to further their interests. The resultant increased interpenetration of the local and the global presents new challenges and opportunities and its impact may be threatening in some ways to those involved. Whether or not Olympism stimulates nationalism depends on particular conditions that pertain in given instances. In the case of the Barcelona Games circumstances were such that Catalan nationalism was stimulated. How this occurred is analysed in the chapters that follow.

4   The war of the flags and the *paz olímpica*

When Juan Antonio Samaranch, president of the International Olympic Committee, announced on 17 October 1986 that Barcelona, the capital of Catalonia, had been awarded the 1992 summer Olympic Games, there were scenes of jubilation in the city.[1] But in the six-year period between that moment and the opening ceremony, Catalan and Spanish national interests were to impinge increasingly on the preparation for, and organisation of, the Games. In this chapter the development of the ensuing conflict is analysed, concentrating on the four-and-a-half-month period preceding the opening of the Games, and showing how disruption of the Games and a confrontation between Catalan nationalists and Spain were very narrowly avoided. The analysis focuses, in particular, on the way Catalan ethnonational symbols were deployed in this power struggle, and how they coexisted and interacted in tension with symbols of the Spanish state-nation.

The political protagonists' interests, objectives and strategies

Barcelona's bid for the 1992 Olympic Games was instigated in 1981 by the then socialist mayor of Barcelona, Narcis Serra (later Spain's vice-president), in the immediate aftermath of an aborted military coup and with the threat of a further coup in the offing (Preston, 1986: ch. 7). Serra, apparently, reasoned that Catalonia needed a morale-booster at such a tense and dangerous phase in Spain's transition to democracy. One of the main reasons for the attempted coup was indeed the *franquista* die-hards' fury at the legislation granting regional autonomy to Catalonia, which to the 'bunker', as they were known, threatened once more the integrity of the Spanish state, for which they had fought so determinedly under Franco. In October 1980 Juan Antonio Samaranch – a Catalan and reconstructed *franquista* politician, who became Spanish *ambassador* to

[1] Hill (1992: ch. 9) describes the immediate background to the success of the bid.

Moscow after Franco's death – had succeeded to the presidency of the IOC, and Serra had intimated to him Barcelona's desire for the Games, to which Samaranch is said to have replied: 'I accept your challenge' (*La Vanguardia*, 14 June 1992). Serra approached the king for his authorisation to bid on 30 May 1981, and it was thus that the city's candidature came to receive the full support of the state at local, regional and national levels.

All the main political interests in Spain and in Catalonia rallied behind the bid when it proved to be successful and the Barcelona Games Organising Committee (COOB) was constituted in March 1987. The agreement to form this consortium was made by the Spanish government, the Generalitat, the Barcelona City Council and the Spanish Olympic Committee (COE). The agreement was signed by Pasqual Maragall, as mayor of Barcelona, Jordi Pujol as president of the Catalan government, Javier Solana, then Spanish minister of education, and Carles Ferrer Salat, the president of COE. Financial responsibility was shared between the three levels of government. The different political parties in power at the three levels of government reflected the divergent interests of centre and region, and also divergent interests within the national minority region, notably between the city and regional governments. Although they all rallied around the Games, together with the political parties not in power and the influential interest groups in the offing, they did so for very different reasons, and they pursued different objectives in relation to the Games. Power at the centre was held by the Spanish Socialist Party (PSOE) under the leadership of Felipe González. The autonomous Catalan government was formed by Convergencia i Unió (CiU), an alliance of two moderate nationalist parties lead by Jordi Pujol.[2] In the host city power was held by the Catalan Socialist Party (PSC), an affiliate of PSOE, led by the mayor, Pasqual Maragall.

The importance that was attached to COOB can be seen by the fact that government at all three levels was represented by the relevant ministers and high-ranking officials. As mayor of the host city, Maragall was appointed to the most important office in relation to the organisation of the Games, the presidency of COOB. The Spanish minister of sport, and the Catalan secretary general of sport, together with the president of COE, were appointed as vice-presidents. It seems that an understanding was reached early on within COOB that the Games would reflect Catalan culture, but the details were left rather vague.

Broadly speaking, the centre and the region were divided in the way the

---

[2] Convergència Democràtica de Catalunya (CDC), which is Pujol's own party, and Unió Democràtico Cristiano (UDC).

Games were perceived and, thus, over the objectives to be pursued in relation to them. The Spanish government saw the Games primarily as a matter of national prestige: it was determined to show that Spain is a fully modernised, mature democracy and member of the European Community. The poor performance of the Spanish football team in the 1982 World Cup, which was held in Spain, was widely interpreted as a national humiliation and the relevant authorities were determined this would not happen again.[3] Catalan nationalists, on the other hand, feared that the Games would be used by central government to interfere in their affairs and they were determined to oppose this and to Catalanise the Games for their own benefit. In the new *España de las Autonomías*, the Spanish government is much concerned with the problem of managing strong regional interests, and, in the case of the Basque Country and Catalonia, containing the tendency for them to spill over into ethnonationalism and support for separatism. Understandably, it was sensitive to the possible effects of the Games on relations with Catalonia and on Spain's image abroad, should the Games become the focus of any conflict. Furthermore, the Games provided the perfect opportunity to stimulate the national as well as the regional economy, through the massive public and private investments in the infrastructure the Games required. Government strategy, therefore, was to be accommodating to demands for Catalanising the Games and for financial support, but to limit these demands through its power position within COOB and, in particular, through its control over the purse strings as the single biggest investor in the total costs of the Games.

In contrast, in Catalonia there was a strong tendency across the political spectrum to see the Olympics as an opportunity to remedy the relationship with the centre. Catalonia is the most economically advanced and prosperous region in Spain and the resultant fiscal imbalance between it and the rest of Spain induces resentment in the region at what is perceived as the exploitation of Catalonia (Cabana *et al.*, 1998). It was in both the Catalan government's and the City Council's interest to use the Games as a lever on central government to extract the resources that they felt were long overdue to them.

The Catalan government had its own specific objectives. As a nationalist, Pujol saw the Olympics in terms of a long-term project of enhancing the prestige, economic development and political autonomy of Catalonia, so it was in his interest also that the necessary resources were

---

[3] Interview with Manuel Fonseca, director general, Consejo Superior de Deportes (Spanish Sports Council). Fonseca was COOB's director general sports and a member of its standing committee.

extracted from the centre and that the Games went well. He was, however, concerned that his main political rivals in Catalonia, the PSC and Maragall, should not benefit at his expense. Although suspicious that Maragall would accumulate political capital from the Games, Pujol could not afford to remain completely aloof, so the Catalan government's strategy was to avoid close involvement, and to monitor and control developments through its membership of COOB. It could exert leverage as a major financial partner in the enterprise and through the legal powers it possessed over planning and development in the region. Direct responsibility for the management and organisation of the Games (and, with it, for anything that might go wrong) was thus in the hands of the municipality.

The latter had a precise objective – the renewal and modernisation of Barcelona's urban infrastructure, which was sorely overdue and for which it had been unable to obtain sufficient resources from the centre prior to the mid-1980s. It would have been counterproductive for the central government, given its objectives, to withhold the necessary resources, so there was a happy coincidence of interests. In achieving this objective and in thus placing Barcelona in the vanguard of economic development in that dynamic European region encompassing the Barcelona–Toulouse–Montpellier triangle, Maragall and the PSC hoped to strengthen themselves politically against their main political rivals, Pujol and the CiU, both in Barcelona where the socialists held power, and in the regional government where the socialists were in opposition. This was in the interest of central government too, since it potentially weakened the representation of CiU in the national assembly. It is necessary to understand that the socialist central government did not comply with Maragall's demands merely because Barcelona was socialist. Other regions where the socialists were in power, such as Andalucía and Extremadura, were resentful, if not opposed to the diversion of funds to Catalonia, which they coveted for the development of their regions. Maragall and the PSC, then, in common with the nationalists, represented a particular local–regional interest in this respect.

Pressure to Catalanise the Games came from a variety of sources within the nationalist camp. Pujol, the leader of the main nationalist party, CiU, pursued a more moderate pragmatic course of action, but other elements in the party were more radical, especially the youth section.[4] Acció Olímpica, an activist campaign group, was founded to agitate for the Catalanisation of the Games by the influential pressure group on Catalan cultural affairs, Omnium Cultural, which counted many CiU members

---

[4] The Joventut Nacionalista de Catalunya (JNC).

and supporters among its membership. Acció Olímpica may have been financed, in part at least, by Pujol's party and the Generalitat. According to one source sceptical of Pujol's motives, Pujol and the Generalitat initiated the formation of Acció Olímpica, ensuring that it was generously financed by the Generalitat, CDC and town halls controlled by the nationalists (Antich, 1994: 276). Esquerra Republicana (ERC), the main separatist party, with the third largest number of seats in the Catalan parliament, was one of the most powerful forces behind the drive to Catalanise the Games. La Crida de la Solidaritat, a militant *independista* pressure group, influential among university students and radicalised middle-class youth, also played a substantial part.

The Catalan Olympic Committee (COC), lead by Miró Ardèval, a former minister in the Catalan government, was formed in opposition to the official Spanish Olympic Committee for the express purpose of obtaining recognition from the IOC for a separate team representing Catalonia to participate in the Games. Ostensibly, a 'non-political' body designed to mobilise support among the Catalan sports federations for this objective, it was, in fact, an umbrella organisation for the main elements of the nationalist movement to Catalanise the Games until the later stages of the campaign. The strategy served to focus sustained attention on the Games as a Catalan national issue by articulating certain core demands concerning the place of the main Catalan symbols – their flag, national hymn and language – in the Games. In May 1989 the Generalitat adopted a resolution to support the COC in its quest to be recognised by the IOC. With respect to language, television coverage in Catalan was a further bone of contention for the nationalists, since Spanish national television (TVE), based in Madrid, controlled the Spanish rights to cover the Games, and was refusing to allow coverage in Catalan.

Urban redevelopment schemes necessitated by the Olympics had generated some controversy, particularly those which displaced the inhabitants of older areas of the city, like the Barceloneta, with its many tiny restaurants and bars, and the old industrial part of Poblenou, where the Olympic village was to be located and the sea front redeveloped (Tejero 1992; Vazquez Montalbán, 1992). Such schemes did not disturb nationalist sensibilities to any great extent, for they greatly improved the city, and whatever disquiet local inhabitants felt was very well managed by the City Council.[5] The alleged threat to the environment caused more upset in certain instances. COOB had selected Banyoles, a beauty spot with a suitably large lake, and which also happened to be a nationalist strong-

---

[5] Interview with Manuel de Forn I Foxà, Commission for the Strategic, Economic and Social Plan of Barcelona.

hold, as the site for the rowing events. Local nationalists' objections took some time to allay.

The design for the Games mascot, 'Cobi', also caused problems. Cobi's creator, Javier Mariscal, one of Spain's most successful designer-artists with an international standing, had submitted a design devoid of any familiar reference points, to the extent that even to describe it presented some difficulty. It was neither a Disneyesque character nor an abstract, naïve Picasso-style figure; nor was it a conventional sports mascot, like the Russian bear of the Moscow Olympics. The jury had gambled on something strange and 'avante-garde' being acceptable to the public – a creature that resembled a small two-legged brown dog, with no hair or tail, that first had been drawn on paper, was then cut up, and finally, pasted together.

In fact, Cobi had his origins in the drawings and figures of fiction created in the 'countercultural', anti-classicist tradition of the underground comic, a genre in which Mariscal had worked in his early career. The image was inspired by the Garriris and Perro Julian figures he created when working with the comic magazine *El Víbora* (Busquet, 1992). As soon as the COOB jury revealed its decision in February 1988 to adopt Mariscal's design as the Games mascot, it provoked a hostile reaction among nationalists, particularly the *independistas*, as well as among groups on the left, such as the anarchists. They disliked it because what was intended by COOB to function as a well-recognised, popular representation of Barcelona and a profitable commercial product, represented for them an ugly monstrosity, not remotely Catalan. They would have preferred a symbol fixed in the Catalan tradition, like the dragon, a creature that figures prominently in Catalan mythology and was reputedly slain by their patron saint Sant Jordi (St George).

The critics were by no means alone in their dislike. In an opinion poll conducted in Barcelona by *El País* a month or so after the mascot was first revealed to the public, over half the city's population came out against it (*El País*, 21 March 1988, cited in Busquet, 1992: 100). Meanwhile, its designer, Mariscal, a Valencian resident of Barcelona for twenty years, exacerbated the polemic in an interview he gave to the Valencian newspaper, *Las Provincias*, in which he, naïvely, flippantly characterised Catalan nationalism. Barcelona, according to him, was marvellous but also horrifying: there were so many Catalans in Barcelona and that horrible little man, Pujol, cultivated a small-town, closed mentality, so that if he had his way there would be Catalanism, fatherland and nothing else. Predictably, the nationalists were outraged, putting the worst possible construction on his remarks, even though he later claimed, with some justification, that they were taken out of context and were meant as a joke.

Pujol took the remarks as an insult to Catalonia and declared the country had the right to defend itself against such attacks. Representatives of the Generalitat blamed the City Council and the government for choosing Mariscal as the designer of the Games mascot, and for the consequent 'crisis' that had developed in the relations between Catalonia, the City Council and central government. The reaction of the central government's delegate to Catalonia was to suggest that Pujol and his party were politicising the issue of the mascot design as a pre-election manoeuvre. *El País* commented that Pujol had a hidden agenda, namely, his objection to the appointment of Josep Miquel Abad as director general of COOB (*El País*, 2 February 1988). The latter, a former communist deputy mayor of Barcelona, was appointed by Maragall, the socialist president of COOB.

An indignant La Crida mounted a campaign against Mariscal's design, called on the public to boycott it, and declared that if COOB did not replace it with another it would be endorsing Mariscal's insults. Some dealers and traders did boycott the symbol, but to what extent such actions were motivated by nationalism is not clear.

COOB stood firmly behind Mariscal's design, and resistance to Cobi faded as the mascot steadily achieved widespread public recognition (not least because of its prominence in marketing a wide range of products and services) and growing approval among the majority of Catalans, although only a year before the Games an *Avui* newspaper survey found approximately a third of Catalans still disliked the symbol (*Avui*, 27 July 1991, cited in Busquet, 1992). Paradoxically, its growing familiarity with, and acceptance by, the public afforded the nationalists with opportunities to appropriate and exploit the symbol politically. Suitably altered in innovative ways, the image was deployed in their own campaigns. Politicised versions of the image and 'anti-Cobi Cobis', proliferated – the 'police Cobi', unmasking the Games as an instrument of repression; a mad Cobi making obscene gestures ridiculing the whole enterprise; a smart Cobi, illustrating the Olympics as a get-rich-quick event; a hanged Cobi, hanged by independence groups; a beaten-up Cobi, victim of anarchist groups; a burned Cobi, signifying destruction of the Spanish enemy in the imagination of certain nationalist groups; a 'Freedom for Catalonia' Cobi; a Catalan Olympic Committee Cobi; and an *independista* Cobi. In this way the symbol was returned to its subversive origins in the underground counterculture.

The threat to the Games against this kind of background was either excessive Españolisation or excessive Catalanisation and the possibility of the Games collapsing in a fiasco. After all, the Games were to take place in the very stadium that in 1936 has been designated as the venue for the alternative anti-fascist 'Workers Olympics', an event which had been supported by the Catalan government and aborted at the last moment by Franco's coup (Pujadas and Santacana, 1992).

A foretaste of possible trouble on the Olympic horizon, and of how easily the Olympics might damage the delicate relationship between the centre and Catalonia, had occurred on 8 September 1989 at the inauguration of the refurbished Olympic stadium, when the king, attending the occasion as head of state, together with the Spanish team, was whistled and jeered at by the crowd (Antich, 1994; Crexell, 1994). Nationalist propaganda, the rather heavy-handed security measures, the bad weather and the delayed arrival of the king all contributed to the crowd's ill-tempered demonstration against the centre on this acutely embarrassing occasion for the authorities. If this kind of demonstration were to have happened again during the Olympics, when the eyes of the world were on Barcelona and Spain, the effect would have been catastrophic. There was also the serious possibility that the Games would become the target of terrorism, from either ETA, the Basque terrorist organisation that had posed the most serious threat to the integrity of the Spanish state up to that time, or from some other group. Counter terrorist operations and the heavy deployment of security forces, in a historic context of tensions between this region and the centre, would thus test public confidence in the capacity of the state to maintain social and political order efficiently and democratically.

Maragall and the executive arm of COOB, caught in the middle between the centre and the nationalists, and faced with the hazards of either excessive Españolisation or Catalanisation of the Games, had to face both ways and take pressure from both directions. At one point, indeed, fearing that Maragall would not be able to resist pressure from the nationalists, central government was rumoured to have attempted to replace him as president of COOB with their own man – a move that was successfully resisted by Maragall. The strategy adopted to cope with this situation was to neutralise these pressures and accommodate the competing demands as far as was possible. It was also in the interest of the IOC to see that disputes between centre and region were minimised. Perhaps no one was in a better position to help accomplish this task than Juan Antonio Samaranch, its president – a Catalan and also a long-standing member of Spain's political class, who could present himself as a friend equally to both (Boix and Espada, 1991; Jennings and Simson, 1991; Jennings, 1996; Miller, 1992).[6]

[6] Boix and Espada (1991), Jennings and Simson (1992), and Jennings (1996) are controversial exposés of Samaranch's career. Samaranch successfully sued Jennings and Simson in a Swiss court rather than a British one where potentially the publicity would have been highly damaging. Miller (1992), a sports journalist very much in Samaranch's confidence, stresses his positive achievements.

At all levels there were particular interests at stake and potential, if not actual conflict between them, but there was also a powerful inducement to accommodate those interests, if potential gains to all concerned were not to be jeopardised. Broadly speaking, the strategies that were adopted by all the interested parties aimed at balancing the gains they could make at their opponents' expense against the potential losses, if the conflict was not contained and if the Games, in consequence, went badly.

The campaign to Catalanise the games: achieving the paz olímpica

The different nationalist groups and organisations, acting individually or sometimes in concert, noticeably stepped up the pressure from February 1992 onwards (the Games opened on 25 July). All the different authorities concerned felt this pressure to a greater or lesser degree – central government, the Generalitat, the municipality, COOB management, COE and the IOC. But it was the central government that was most shielded, while Maragall's socialist administration took the brunt and stood to lose most politically if anything were to go wrong.

Acció Olímpica's campaign opened on 3 February 1992 with a public meeting at the Barcelona College of Lawyers. Pujol's wife Marta Ferrusola, the president of COC, Miró Ardèval, and another figure prominent in the leadership of CDC, the historian Ainaud de Lasarte, were present. The presence of Pujol's wife in particular signified that the campaign had Pujol's endorsement (Antich, 1994: 278).

The gains made by ERC and the return of the nationalist government in the election to the Generalitat of 15 March seem to have given an impetus to the campaign that was building up for Catalanisation of the Games (El País, 21 March and 3 April 1992).[7] Angel Colom, the ERC leader, almost immediately threatened protest actions during the Olympics if his minimum demands were not met. He called on the IOC to allow the same treatment for Catalans as it allowed for countries in the former USSR, who now formed a unified team, i.e. to march under the Olympic flag and display armbands with their countries' flags. He also called for the Catalan flag to be hoisted and the Catalan hymn played when a Catalan athlete mounted the podium. If a Spanish team were to win, he wanted the medals to be presented to the sound of the Olympic hymn and under the Olympic flag (El País, 27 March 1992). He also

---

[7] ERC made the biggest gain in seats, nearly doubling their total to eleven. CiU won seventy to gain an absolute majority; PSC won forty; seven went to Iniciativa de Catalunya (IC), the former Communist Party of Catalonia.

proposed that the Catalan athletes march together, somewhat behind the Spanish team, to close the march past, so fulfilling the role of the host country (*El País*, 3 April 1992). Not to be outdone, Pujol called for a greater presence of Catalan symbols, and came out in support of the IOC recognising COC. He was also reported to be behind efforts to have the Catalan sports federations internationally recognised and separated from the Spanish federations, and to be manoeuvring for a role for himself in the opening ceremony – accusations he vigorously denied (*El País*, 27 March, 1 April, 2 April, 3 April, 4 April, 1992). Simultaneously, Miró Ardèval, president of COC, adopted a softer, more flexible approach than ERC in suggesting that the IOC could allow Catalan athletes to be present with their own flags; that under the Olympic Charter COC could be recognised or accredited as an aspiring member of the IOC; and that Catalan athletes could carry both Spanish and Catalan flags on the podium (*El País*, 1 April 1992).

On 26 March, Samaranch himself appeared to be joining the Catalan nationalist chorus when he agreed there should be more Catalanisation, in response to La Crida demonstrators, who had disrupted a public meeting he was addressing with their demands. They warned him that the success of the Games depended upon him (*El País*, 27 March 1992).[8] He cleverly passed the buck to COE and COOB when asked to give the specific ways in which it would be done, saying that it was their responsibility to agree this. Three days before the election he was reported to have positioned himself favourably with the Catalans by making pro-Catalan remarks and allowing his wife to appear in public in a 'triumphalist' meeting of a local branch of CiU (*El País*, 5 April 1992).

This agitation seems to have caught the IOC, the Spanish Olympic Committee (COE) and COOB unawares. The IOC vice-president, Keba M'baye, in response to Colom, arranged a meeting between COC and COE, to be attended by Samaranch in Lausanne in early April, a response which was interpreted by the nationalists as giving COC equal treatment with COE. COOB and COE took a firm stand at first, arguing there was already sufficient recognition of Catalonia in the agreement approved by the four constituents of COOB – the government, the Generalitat, COE and the Town Hall – and that any changes must be put to, and approved by, COOB (*El País*, 5 April 1992). The agreement apparently reached on 15 October 1991 (*El País*, 1 April 1992)

[8] Views differ on why Samaranch conceded to the nationalists. La Crida spokesman, Jordi Sánchez, suggested in an interview that the concession was reluctantly wrung out of him by La Crida's intervention. Others, like the *El País* team which included Antonio Espada, one of Samaranch's biographers, argue that it was a ploy to whitewash over his *franquista* past – see *El País*, 3 April 1992.

constituted an 'almost secret pact' as *El País* called it (*El País*, 4 April 1992).) Some aspects had leaked out during the previous few months: a fair/reasonable use of the four languages (French, English, Spanish and Catalan); Catalan as the primary language for the public address system; Maragall's and Samaranch's addresses to be partially in Catalan; Maragall's address to evoke the memory of the Republican president of the Generalitat during the civil war, Lluis Companys, who had also been president of the organising committee of the *Olimpiada Popular* (the 'Workers' Olympics') and who was executed by Franco in 1940; the march-past to be in alphabetical order according to the French–English denominations; each delegation to be proceeded by a banner with the name of each country in the four official languages, in such a way that none had precedence; Catalan flags to be present in all the installations and buildings employed by the Games; the Catalan flag to fly with the Olympic, Barcelona and Spanish flags; all public buildings in which the Spanish flag was installed to fly the Catalan flag; and the musical programme of the inauguration to include an interpretation of the Catalan patriotic song 'El Cant de la Senyera'. At that point the pact certainly did not envisage conceding everything the *independistas* wanted, nor did it foresee even the possibility of the Catalan flag marching past in the Olympic stadium during the opening and closing ceremonies. COOB sources let it be known that Pujol's attempted revision had caused deep annoyance among his associates in COOB, 'so much so that they consider he has broken the Olympic pact', and that he would not have done so had he not been encouraged by Samaranch (*El País*, 1 April 1992). Pujol denied he had broken the pact and said that he had been very positive about the language aspect; that COC was a popular idea; and that the Generalitat could not obtain recognition for it on its own. He reiterated that he was in favour of a bigger presence of the Catalan flag, but would accept the final details when they were decided (*El País*, 2 April 1992). COC spokesman Miró Ardèval denied that the Generalitat had been helpful to them and doubted whether Samaranch's call for Catalanisation was anything other than mere rhetoric. He now put forward specific demands, while conceding that COC would not be recognised by the IOC in time for the Barcelona Games and that the Catalan and Spanish athletes should march together. Instead, Catalan Olympism should be represented by a group of presidents of Catalan sports federations, or retired Catalan Olympic sports participants, in the march past; when a Catalan athlete member of a Catalan federation mounted the podium, the Catalan as well as the Spanish flag should fly and a verse of the Catalan national hymn should be played; and members of COC should be accredited in the Barcelona Games. If these demands were not met COC would denounce the fact that in a Games hosted by the Catalan nation that nation's symbols were excluded.

ERC next pressed home their attack by putting a motion to the Catalan parliament that the minimal level of Catalan symbols be stipulated in law to guarantee their presence. Colom demanded that the constituents of COOB and the political parties clearly pronounce on this. He threatened to mobilise the population of Catalonia in the summer to receive the Olympics with flags, and applauded Pujol's and Samaranch's calls for more Catalanisation as a rectification of their previous positions (*El País*, 4 April 1992).

By 7 April COOB was making conciliatory moves, letting it be known via the press that the 'basic pact' in principle incorporated the *senyera* in the opening ceremony, and that the exact way it would be included was being negotiated. The COC proposal, that it be carried by presidents of the Catalan sports federations in the opening and closing ceremonies, was the greatest possibility. The Spanish team would include Catalans marching under the Spanish flag with Prince Felipe, the heir to the throne, as standard bearer. The four constituents of COOB were also negotiating the possibility of 'Els Segador' being played at a suitable moment in the opening ceremony, but explained that this was delicate, since if it were on the same level as the Spanish national anthem the government would object, and if it was treated merely folklorically the Generalitat would object. Socialist sources intimated that Maragall had already initiated the inclusion of 'Els Segadors' with the executive director of COOB before the polemic had started a month previously. Maragall, while showing his disapproval of Pujol's and Samaranch's interventions, stated that COOB was always open to initiatives to improve the ceremonies, as long as they were put to the 'heart of COOB'. For his part Pujol declared that his generic demand for greater Catalanisation would be concretised by the presence of the *senyera* in the march past (*El País*, 7 April 1992).

Maragall was in a difficult position. It must have seemed to him that Pujol and Samaranch were ganging up on the socialists. If the charge of not sufficiently supporting Catalanisation were to stick, he could be wrongfooted by his nationalist opponents; but if he conceded to nationalist demands at this stage he would, perhaps, fall foul of Madrid, undermine his own support and encourage further nationalist demands. Pujol and the nationalists, on the other hand, had their suspicions increased that Maragall was accumulating political capital out of the Games at their expense, and intending to minimise Catalanisation. Pujol could not afford to be upstaged by ERC, which was using the issue to put pressure on CiU to form a nationalist block against the 'Españolistas', which might split the more radical nationalists away from the leadership – hence his propensity to join the nationalist chorus to strengthen the Catalan presence in the Games (*El País*, 8 April 1992).

The conciliatory moves seemed to work momentarily. On 9 April The Generalitat, COC, Omnium Cultural, La Crida and the Catalan parties with representation in parliament were reported as expressing their satisfaction at the inclusion of the *senyera* in the march past and the 'agreement' to give a greater presence to Catalan symbols. The Generalitat was careful to add that it was not to be supposed that all its aspirations were fulfilled, which presumably referred to the fact that negotiations about the possibility of including the delicate matter of 'Els Segadors' were continuing among the associates of COOB (*El País*, 8 April 1992).

Three days later the polemic broke out again, however. The occasion was the *rapprochement* between Samaranch and Maragall, signified by their joint appearance and statement to a press conference convened by the IOC Supervising Commission for the Games (*El País*, 9 April 1992). Town Hall sources were reported as saying they had demanded a public statement from Samaranch over the controversy. He declared his support for the 'agreement', reached a couple of days before within COOB, reaffirming the Catalanity of the Games and welcoming modifications, as long as they were put to 'the bosom of the Committee'. He made a call for unity and denied that his declaration of 26 March could be interpreted as stoking up the polemic. Crucially, he went on to withdraw authorisation for the COE–COC meeting previously proposed by Keba M'baye, the IOC vice-president, saying that the only interlocutors of the IOC were COOB and COE.

Maragall, somewhat unwisely, asserted that Samaranch's declaration definitively closed a debate that should never have been opened. The Catalanity of the Games was guaranteed and had always been so, and COOB was always open to perfect them. This matter should not be politicised. He confirmed that the *senyera* and 'Els Segadors' would be present in the ceremonies, but warned that it would not be 'in the hands of those who have demanded them at the last minute' (he declined to specify to whom this referred). According to an *El País* informant, he said privately that it was Angel Colom, but 'municipal sources' said it referred to the Catalan government, CiU and its affines (*El País*, 11 April 1992).

COC and the *independistas* reacted furiously to the joint statement. While declining to comment on Samaranch's words until confirmation that the COE–COC meeting arranged by the IOC was cancelled, COC warned it would be present inside or outside the stadium. Colom announced he would not tolerate 'an undervaluing contempt' for the Catalan symbols, and deplored Samaranch's action in de-authorising the COE–COC meeting, pointing out that the debate had only just began, and that on St George's Day the ERC youth organisation would demonstrate by surrounding the Olympic ring (the road running around the Olympic complex on Montjuic where the main stadium was located) with a *senyera* three kilometres long. La Crida characterised Samaranch's attitude as violent and insulting and as making it difficult to celebrate the Games in full normality, a clear warning that if this went on the Games would be disrupted (*El País*, 11 April 1992).

The nationalists now seized the initiative, forcing the authorities back on to the defence, the momentum of their campaign increasing with threats and actions virtually on a daily basis. Colom warned that if the maximum level of Catalanisation was as Maragall proclaimed, 'there would not be a tranquil Games . . . there will be a mobilisation of the population of Catalonia' (*El País*, 12 April 1992). La Crida announced it would mount a 50 million peseta campaign that would include: disposing of 100 entry tickets to attend the opening ceremony; deploying 2,000 *independista* volunteers, dressed in uniform, to inform Olympic visitors of the discrimination that Catalonia suffered; and buying publicity space on foreign TV channels to diffuse a video on this theme. Pujol, while supporting the Maragall–Samaranch accord and expressing satisfaction with the presence of the hymn and flag as a means of showing Catalonia to the world as an authentic nation, stirred the pot somewhat by adding, 'I will be even happier if the Games go well and demonstrate that Barcelona, capital of Catalonia, is capable of organising them' (*El País*, 12 April 1992).

Colom and Miró announced they would be inviting La Crida, Omnium Cultural and other Catalan entities to prepare a demonstration finishing in the immediate vicinity of the Olympic stadium, at the same time carefully emphasising that it would not interfere with or in any way spoil the Games. They warned again that they would not tolerate the relegation of Catalan symbols to a folkloric role, e.g. the inclusion of 'Els Segadors' in a medley of forty tunes. Colom reiterated his minimum demands on the constant presence of Catalan symbols in the inauguration, unfolding and closure of the Games, and that there should be a dignified presence of the *senyera* and 'Els Segadors': 'We do not want the flag to spring up like a toadstool' (*El País*, 14 April 1992). He asked for 'generosity' from Spain so that the Catalan flag could fly and the Catalan hymn sound when a Catalan obtained a medal. Miró did not go as far, saying COC would concur with the use of both national anthems in such an eventuality, and he sounded an optimistic note in expressing confidence that the mobilisation would not be necessary and that 'the door to dialogue so brutally closed . . . by the IOC will open again' (*El País*, 14 April 1992).

Maragall responded indignantly to what he characterised as 'useless and unnecessary polemics' and called on the Generalitat to redirect certain groups' proposals through its representatives on COOB, and for 'respect and patriotism from these minority groups.' In the name of Barcelona and Catalonia he called on everybody to give, not an image of confrontation to the world, but one of rigour, good organisation and happiness. The PSC secretary general also approached Pujol to restrain Miró, as a member of his own party (*El País*, 15 April 1992).

ERC pressure continued with a threat from one of its deputies that there would be a boycott of the torch relay in localities where there were Republican councillors, if the level of Catalanisation was not raised (*El País*, 17 April 1992). Representatives of the conservative Partido Popular (PP) at the central state level now joined the polemic, calling for resistance to Catalanisation of the Games, and claiming that central government investment in the Games had detracted from that in other regions and that the majority of provinces were alienated by this. Catalanisation was causing regional tensions and damage at all levels, and aspects of this process were thought to be contrary to the Spanish constitution. The PP representatives were also worried about the authorities' apparent solicitude for recognising COC (*El País*, 21 April 1992).

Maragall, addressing the general assembly of COOB, warned of possible nationalist intentions to repeat their boycott of the Olympic stadium inauguration in September 1989, and a Partido Popular representative expressed anxiety about nationalist mobilisation during the Games, and the rejection of Catalonia it was causing in the rest of Spain. Maragall, somewhat contradictorily, insisted the controversy was closed and, adding a few more details, reiterated his assurances about the presence of Catalan elements (*El País*, 22 April 1992). At the same time, Pujol, who was opening the Catalan Pavilion at Expo in Seville, declared that he would increase the pressure (*El País*, 22 April 1992).

As promised, on 23 April, St George's' Day, 3,000 members of the ERC youth wing (JERC), joined by Colom, La Crida spokesman Jordi Sánchez and the Lithuanian minister of culture among others, duly encircled the Olympic ring with their three-kilometre *senyera*.[9] The JERC secretary stated that the act 'initiated the first phase of the warning of a campaign that will extend to all the Olympic sites and whose objective is to secure the Catalan symbols as the only ones of the Olympics'. In a reference to police action against demonstrators at Expo in Seville, he said

---

[9] Nationalist propaganda draws a parallel between the position of small oppressed nations in the former USSR and that of Catalonia, and relations were cultivated at various levels with the Baltic states. The director general of COC, Xavier Vinyals, became the official representative of Lithuania in Barcelona, hence the appearance of the Lithuanian ambassador at the demonstration.

the action was 'a show of strength and the counter-attack to the show of fascist strength at the inauguration of Expo' (*El País*, 24 April 1992). La Crida stated its minimum demands: the Catalan language to have equal status with other Olympic languages; use of the Catalan flag and hymn like other countries; and a Catalan delegation at the opening and closing ceremonies. It also revealed details of its 'Freedom for Catalonia' campaign: production of a sixteen-page publicity booklet containing the nationalist demands; direct, non-violent action at the Olympic sites; distribution of stickers showing the image of Cobi the Olympic mascot with an *independista* flag, the inscription 'Freedom for Catalonia' and the COC banner.[10] The slogan was couched in English to achieve maximum international impact, and at the same time was easily understood at home. That night 500 people, mostly young *independistas*, demonstrated in the Rambla de Catalunya, chanting *independista* slogans, demanding amnesty for Catalan nationalist prisoners in Spanish jails (some of whom were convicted terrorists), and demanding Catalanisation of the Games (*El País*, 24 April 1992).

On 5 May a large meeting in support of COC was held in the Central University attended by, among others, Miró (president of COC), Jordi Sánchez (La Crida spokesman), figures from Catalan sport, Colom, JERC representatives, Joan Rigol (the president of UDC, Pujol's partner in the CiU alliance), Jaume Camps and Carles Campuzano (CiU deputies), Marta Ferrusola (Pujol's wife), and his son. Thus, figures belonging to the Catalan political establishment aligned themselves with *independistas*. Sánchez criticised Samaranch, Maragall and Corcuera, the minister of the interior, and warned the latter that he would be responsible for a tarnished image of the Games if he acted against demonstrators as he had done at Seville. Miró argued that a boycott would be counterproductive. Sánchez said that La Crida would not stage a boycott as such, but that the people would take to the streets to protest and demand Catalanisation. About this time CDC (Pujol's side of CiU) issued a communiqué that a big demonstration of Catalanity would be precisely what would make the Games successful and its executive promised to support initiatives to this effect. Ten days previously, however, Pujol had given instructions to the National Council of CDC that no CDC militant should torpedo the Olympic celebration (*Avui* 6 May 1992; *El País*, 6 May 1992). It was no wonder that there were suspicions about Pujol's adherence to the pact.

---

[10] The 'Freedom for Catalonia' slogan had been used previously in nationalist demonstrations on sporting occasions: at the inauguration of the Olympic stadium on the occasion of the World Athletic Championships, 8 September 1989; the debut of the Barcelona American football team, the Dragones, in 1991; and at Barcelona FC matches (Crexell, 1994: 96–100; Antich, 1994: 280).

On 8 May the nationalists – La Crida, COC, Acció Olímpica, Omnium Cultural and ERC – announced that their demands and actions would now be unified, and gave the IOC an ultimatum that if it did not accept their conditions by 10 June they would mobilise. This time they wanted: presidents of Catalan sports federations in the march past bearing the Catalan flag and the name of Catalonia; 'Els Segadors' to be played at a moment of maximum solemnity and not treated folklorically; use of the Catalan flag and hymn when a Catalan athlete mounted the podium; the march past to be organised according to the Catalan alphabet; and a declaration that there was no impediment in the Olympic charter to the IOC recognising COC (*El País*, 8 May 1992).

The conflict continued like this through the rest of May and into the beginning of June, but with the nationalists being put somewhat more on the defensive, as their opponents accused them of spoiling the Games. Miró was accused of going too far by the PSC secretary, Josep Maria Sala, who claimed that the object of those behind the Catalanisation campaign was nothing less than boycott, and that Pujol should prove his support of the Games by throwing Miró out of CDC (*La Vanguardia*, 9 May 1992). Serra, the vice-president of Spain, accompanied by Samaranch at Expo, played down the conflict and proclaimed, 'The prestige of Barcelona, Catalonia and Spain will be ensured by the good organisation of the Games, showing that we are a country which openly welcomes others with tolerance' (*La Vanguardia*, 11 May 1992). The day before, Javier Gómez Navarro, the minister of sport, had reiterated the Spanish government's total support for the Games. Rafel Ribó, president of Iniciativa de Catalunya, joined the attack on the nationalists, and referred stingingly to the recently formed platform for Catalanisation as a heterogeneous mixture of groups that created political and social confusion (*La Vanguardia*, 13 May 1992).

La Crida, in response to Sala's accusation, denied that they intended to boycott the Games (*La Vanguardia*, 11 May 1992). Colom continued the campaign by calling on the citizens of Catalonia to demonstrate with *senyeres* on the torch route when it arrived on 13th June 'to show the world we are a nation without a state'. The demonstrations were not to be confined to the principality of Catalonia, and he called on the citizens of the *communidades* of Valencia and the Balearics (i.e. regions that are Catalan-speaking and which the nationalists regard as 'Catalan countries') to fill the streets (*La Vanguardia*, 13 May 1992).

Meanwhile Pujol, sensitive to the effects of a possibly deepening conflict rebounding on Catalonia, and no doubt on himself as well, cautioned against confrontation, emphasising that a well-organised, successful Games was what would enhance Catalan prestige (*La Vanguardia*, 13

May 1992) and that a boycott would have to contend with the Catalan government. The language issue, he claimed, was resolved and the inaugural ceremony would present a good image of Catalonia to the world. The Generalitat had guarantees of an adequate Catalan presence. Without specifying any particular group he cautioned organisations capable of disrupting the Games, but when asked about Acció Olímpica (a group said to count on the support of CiU) and CiU's entry into an alliance with militants, he adroitly replied: 'If a gentleman goes about carrying the Catalan flag it should not provoke aggression, for he has the right to be anywhere he wants in what will be the Olympic showcase' (La Vanguardia, 13th May 1992). He thus simultaneously managed to distance himself from entities deemed to be disruptive, while nevertheless not entirely disassociating himself from them.

The possibility of confrontation was highlighted by press reports of the Office of Olympic Security's plans to 'avoid propaganda acts by radical groups' at Olympic sites (*La Vanguardia* 18 May 1992). With La Crida especially in mind, the plans were said to have been designed to avoid incidents like the one at the inauguration of Expo already referred to, when police clubbed demonstrators. The entry of *independista* flags was to be prohibited as 'unconstitutional', in spite of the fact that they represented a legal party (ERC). Unlike the inauguration of the stadium in 1989, when many spectators bearing *senyeres* were prevented from entering, *senyeres* were to be allowed, except for those with excessively long flagpoles. Acció Olímpica and La Crida announced that they would be giving away *senyeres* in the stadia, and that they would enter with placards and banners. The police were ordered to be somewhat permissive, so that nationalist slogans and COC paraphernalia would possibly escape police action, but they were ordered to act forcefully against insults to the king.

ERC now carried the campaign to project Catalonia as a nation without a state to Catalan municipalities with Republican councillors and sympathisers, using as their model the town of Vic, where they had some strength, and extending their activity to the Olympic sub-sites. Javier Gómez Navarro, the sports minister, and Kebe M'baye, the IOC vice-president, were called upon to reconvene the cancelled COE–COC meeting, and town halls in the sub-sites were urged to demand that COOB accept ERC's main demands for Catalanising the Games (*La Vanguardia*, 18 May 1992). COOB continued to try to convince the opposition of its good intentions on Catalanisation by releasing details of a *pubilla*, a Catalan girl dressed in traditional Catalan costume who, it was claimed, would be a central figure in the medal presentations (*La Vanguardia*, 20 May 1992).

On 25 May Terra Lliure, a small *independista* terrorist organisation, exploded two bombs at the National Employment Institute in Barcelona, injuring eighteen people (*La Vanguardia*, 26 May 1992). The incident occurred three days before a one-day general strike organised by the main trade unions, UGT and CCOO, concerning cuts in the social wage. Although not aimed at the Olympics, and by no means typical of *independista* actions, it served as a reminder to the authorities of the vulnerability of the Games to such action, and it would have repercussions later.

By this time the city was garlanded with *senyeres* and Barcelona flags, partly spontaneously, partly at the instigation of the various political interests with a stake in the Games, among them the Town Hall. The latter now came under criticism from PP for calling on citizens to display these two flags and for not mentioning the Spanish flag, an act which, the party claimed, discriminated against those citizens who felt it was their emblem (*La Vanguardia*, 28 May 1992).

It seemed then, at the beginning of June, that the pact reached earlier had broken down under nationalist pressure, and that efforts to reach agreement between the main political protagonists were proving to be nugatory. So the chances that the Games would be disrupted by the more militant nationalists now looked ominous. The response of the main decision-making bodies that were directly concerned, the COOB management and the Town Hall, had been cautious and firm, but also to an extent accommodating. They had persevered with assurances that there was a basic pact between the members of COOB, which guaranteed a satisfactory presence of Catalan symbols in the Games, but they still refused to give specific guarantees and full details, a policy that only served to fuel nationalists' suspicions and stimulated them to pursue their demands with more vigour and determination.

It was in this atmosphere of heightened tension that on 2 June the press carried the announcement of a total accord between Maragall and Pujol over Catalanisation. Pujol indicated that the details would be presented in a joint statement at a date before 13 June, when the Olympic torch was due to arrive in Catalonia from Greece. The delay was to enable 'final touches' to be made by the central government and COE (*La Vanguardia*, 2 June 1992). The sports minister, Gómez Navarro, confirmed it was '98 per cent complete'; COE president, Ferrer Salat, gave assurances that 'Els Segadors' would be played with due solemnity; and Abad, COOB's executive director, reiterated that the accord conformed with the Spanish constitution and the Olympic charter (*El País*, 3 June 1992). Pujol warned that it would not satisfy some sectors of Catalan society, 'who ask for impossible things'. Sources close to the Generalitat indicated that the agreement had been reached some time previously, but the parties to it had opted to make it known as late as possible, to avoid protests from the more radical sectors.[11] Pujol invited the population of Catalonia to 'explode *senyeres*' at the passing of the torch.

Colom, La Crida and another *independista* group, La Assemblea Unitaria per l'Autodeterminació welcomed the announcement, although it did not stop the latter organisation from announcing it had arranged a march for Catalan independence, to finish in Barcelona on the day the Games were due to open. Three days later, ERC's motion in the Catalan Parliament to Catalanise the Games was thrown out, opposed by both CiU and the PSC, who accused ERC of trying to split popular support for the Games.

Maragall, confirming the coming joint declaration, justified his position by reiterating that the issue had never been controversial, that the polemic had been artificial, and that what was important was not to know the moment at which the flag would appear and the hymn sound, but that the Games would go well and that prestige and political collaboration were thus gained. To his chagrin, no doubt, at the send-off ceremony for the torch at the Acropolis in Athens, the 'Freedom for Catalonia' banner was unfurled, and at the handover ceremony at the Panateneo Stadium, members of Acció Olímpica demonstrating with *senyeres* were ejected by the police for disruptive activity (*La Vanguardia*, 8 and 9 June 1992). At the same time Acció Olímpico placed large advertisements in the Catalan press calling for demonstrations at Empuries, where on 13 June the Olympic flame was to be received on Catalan soil, and at Montserrat, the nationalist shrine, through which it would pass on 19 June.

On 8 June, before the details of the latest accord were known, ERC decided to accept the existing level of Catalanisation in the opening ceremony and to renounce mobilisation for 25 July. The other groups – La Crida, COC and Acció Olímpica – were reported to be on the point of doing the same, but were waiting for the details. Colom claimed to have trustworthy inside information that the accord met his demands. The announcement of the pact had mollified much of the opposition; indeed, it split the nationalists, ERC's decision having been taken unilaterally, to the evident annoyance of the other groups (*La Vanguardia* 10 June 1992; *El País*, 11 June 1992).[12] COC, now fearing that further opposition might

---

[11] This unattributed admission of collusion between Generalitat and Town Hall tallies with what was later revealed by a Town Hall spokesman. He put it rather differently, saying that the Town Hall was reluctant to concede demands in the early stages in case this was perceived as weakness and encouraged more demands (interview with Rafel Llusà, Jefe de Gabinete (departmental head), Directorate for Sports and the Olympic Games of the Town Hall).

[12] Jordi Sánchez of La Crida confirmed the other groups' annoyance at Colom's actions in an interview.

jeopardise its relations with the Spanish sports federations and the IOC, which it was courting with long-term recognition in view, requested ERC to withdraw its motion that the Generalitat recognise COC. ERC refused to do so (*El País*, 11 June 1992). At the last moment before the joint announcement, Pujol again warned against actions that might damage the image of Catalonia and reiterated assurances about the level of Catalanity (*La Vanguardia*, 11 June 1992).

Finally, on the morning of 13 June, the day the Olympic flame would arrive in Spain, the details of the pact were revealed in a joint call from Maragall and Pujol for public support. The timing was plainly to forestall the possibility of embarrassing and possibly disruptive demonstrations, now that the reception of the Olympic flame on Catalan soil and the start of the torch relay around Spain were imminent. It revealed a capacity for brinkmanship on the part of the contending parties that continued right up to the start of the Games. The announcement confirmed that Catalan was an official language of the Games on a par with the other three official languages; that the Catalan symbols would be present in all the acts, at a level and with the dignity they deserved; that in the inaugural and closing ceremonies, when the king entered, both anthems would be played; and that before the king entered the Presidential box the Spanish, Catalan and Barcelona flags would be presented in the centre of the stadium (*La Vanguardia*, 13 June 1992). The population were exhorted to show their participation by garlanding the city with flags and banners as a sign of welcome.

Thus, the threatened nationalist mobilisation on 25 July was to a large extent averted, although it is important to emphasise that none of the groups renounced the right to demonstrate peacefully around the Games, which indeed they proceeded to do, and which contributed to further tension. Nor did the Maragall–Pujol accord completely clarify precisely how the symbols would figure in the Games, nor did it satisfy worries about civil liberties, with which La Crida in particular was concerned. What it did achieve was the substantial withdrawal of the threat of disruptive activity, which would tarnish the Games and the image of Spain and Catalonia.

Around this time other parts of the *paz olímpica* (Olympic peace) fell into place. In contrast to their one-day general strike in May against government expenditure cuts, now the trade unions guaranteed industrial peace during the Games (*La Vanguardia*, 15 June 1992). Spanish and Catalan TV announced an agreement in principle on transmission of the Games in Catalan. However, negotiations over the details dragged on until the beginning of July, when a 'historic pact' to share coverage of the Games was announced (*La Vanguardia*, 11 June and 3 July 1992).

Testing the *paz olímpica*

For the next six weeks until the opening of the Games, despite the *paz olímpica*, there continued to be tension, mutual suspicion and conflict between the more activist nationalists and the authorities (resulting in several incidents with potentially serious consequences for the success of the Games), and also between Pujol and Maragall, which precipitated increasing intervention from Madrid. The issues were: the civil liberties of the nationalists, Pujol's capitalisation on the Olympics, the relation between Pujol and Acció Olímpica's campaign; and the marginalisation of the central government. For the nine days the Olympic flame was in Catalonia the situation was particularly tense.

The reception ceremony at the ancient ruins of Empuries for the arrival of the Olympic flame by boat was to be an almost completely Catalan cultural feast. Under the guidance of the distinguished Catalan philosopher and cultural historian, Xavier Rubert de Ventós, the conception and design were completely Catalan, the performing artists and the works performed were predominantly Catalan, and the proceedings were conducted almost entirely in the Catalan language. In marked contrast to the programmes for the opening and closing ceremonies of the Games, which will be analysed later, this was a relatively exclusive affair with the accent on high, rather than popular or mass culture.

The torch bearer, a beautiful, graceful young girl dressed in ancient Greek costume, disembarked from a fishing boat, and while she ran slowly with the torch across the sand dunes to the ancient site, accompanied by four male dancers, at the site itself pieces of Catalan traditional music and Catalan songs were performed, interspersed with Greek music, in honour of the Grecian origins of the Olympics. Victòria de los Ángeles, the Catalan-born soprano, contributed to these sequences. The torch was welcomed with an oration in Greek, given by the Greek actress, Irene Papas. Nuria Espert, the distinguished Catalan theatre director and actress, gave an oration in Catalan based on works by Horace and by the Catalan poets, Joan Maragall and Eugeni D'Ors. She was accompanied by the music of Enric Granados, a composer usually identified simply as Spanish, but in fact a Catalan. There were readings on 'Admiration and Nostalgia' from Pal•lades, Schlegel, Pla, Schiller and D'Annunzio, on 'Games and Sports' from Huizinga, Aristotle, Philostratus and Soló, and on 'Fire and Criticism' from Heraclitus, Euripides, Xenophanes and Herodotus. There were Catalan litanies and poems from the work of Carles Riba, Joan Teixidor, Josep Carner, Victor Català, Miquel de Palol and Narcis Comadira, followed by Catalan baroque music. In keeping with the Olympic theme of peace, a long message from the imprisoned leader of the Burmese democracy movement and Nobel Peace Prize winner in 1991, Aung San Suu Kyi, was delivered by her son.

The ceremony was attended by a large invited audience of about 2–3,000 people, consisting mainly of Catalans, some of whom were important people in Catalan society. Many of the audience were bearing *senyeres*. Outside the enclosure many thousands more people had assembled in the immediate vicinity and on the adjoining beach. The ceremonial proceedings were projected on to a giant screen for the benefit of both those inside and outside the enclosure. Among the assembled dignitaries were the Spanish minister of education, Javier Solana; the minister of sport, Javier Gómez Navarro; the president of COE, Ferrer Salat; Jordi Pujol; Pasqual Maragall; Josep Miquel Abad, the director of COOB, the president of the Diputación de Barcelona; the mayor of the nearby town of Escala; and the president of the Catalan parliament. Felipe, Prince of Asturias, was also expected, but did not come, it was said, for security reasons. It was rumoured also that the king had been advised by Pujol not to come for fear of riots. The nationalists (ERC, La Crida, Acció Olímpica, etc.) were present in force all over the area, bearing *senyeres* and *independista* flags, and displaying 'Freedom for Catalonia' on their T-shirts and banners. Acció Olímpico had an air balloon and there was a 30-metre *senyera* pegged out, first on the beach and later, for better visibility, on the sand dunes nearby. The security forces were present in force with helicopters sometimes buzzing rather obtrusively overhead, but on the whole security was discreet.

When a group (reported to be ultra-rightist members of the Bloque Catalan) pointedly displayed a Spanish flag on the beach to salute the flame's arrival, it was regarded as a *franquista* provocation. The group was surrounded by a hostile crowd and pelted with sand, some stones were thrown and the flag was seized and burned. The police intervened and took the *'franquistas'* into custody, perhaps for their own protection. The incident showed the fine line between the expression of nationalist sentiment on an ostensibly festive occasion and overt violence (*El País*, 14 June 1992).

Angel Colom and four republican deputies in a boat attempted to follow the flotilla accompanying the flame towards the beach, but were obliged by the *Guardia Civil* to move away (*El País*, 14 June 1992). La Crida claimed to have got closer by actually getting three boats of theirs, with placards and *independista* slogans, into the flotilla (*El País* 17 June 1992).

On this strongly Catalan occasion when the majority of the notables' speeches were in that language, the Spanish minister of education, Javier Solana, although he is said to have opened his address in Catalan before

switching to Spanish, was virtually drowned out by the chorus of whistling and shouting (from both inside and outside the official enclosure)
that commenced as soon as he opened his mouth. Speaking in Spanish
was taken as a mark of disrespect to Catalan culture. Some said his voice
sounded unpleasant, like an authoritarian *franquista* politician. Reference
to anything Spanish was greeted with whistles from outside the enclosure.
As time progressed a division between the audience outside and inside
the enclosure had grown, with more vociferous, noisier manifestations of
Catalan nationalism outside, but the two audiences were as one in ridiculing the Spanish minister. Nevertheless, the atmosphere was, on the
whole, relatively good-natured, with people commenting on how stupid
the minister had been, when all he had to do was to use Catalan.

The centrepiece of the torch's arrival was a solemn ceremony for the
reception of the sacred flame at the Greco-Roman remains of Empuries,
in which Irene Papas and Nuria Espert, dressed in ancient Greek
costume, delivered their orations. At this most dramatic moment in the
whole ceremony, when the flame had just been received and the 'Cant de
la Senyera' was being played, a young La Crida militant, who had
somehow concealed himself at the centre of the enactment, emerged displaying a large 'Freedom for Catalonia' banner, which he then draped
around the stand on which the sacred flame was burning, where it
remained for the rest of the ceremony. Spanish television edited out the
incident, but the photograph showing the slogan held aloft appeared on
the front pages of the national newspapers (*La Vanguardia* and *El País*, 14
June 1992).

The central authorities, who were responsible for the elaborate and
massive Olympic security operation, were alarmed and embarrassed by
the ease with which security had been breached. The central government
was offended by the audience's hostile reaction, by what it regarded as
excessive Catalanisation and by the marginalisation of Spanish symbols.
La Crida boasted in the national press that 'security is always vulnerable',
announced its determination to carry on as at Empuries, and to campaign
against the security deployment as an occupation of Catalan territory by
alien forces (*El País*, 14 June 1992).

As the Olympic torch carrying the flame traversed Catalonia during the
next eight days, the socialists became incensed at the nationalists' campaign and Pujol's apparent complicity in it (*El País*, 17 June 1992). Pujol
rejected PSC accusations that his party was allied to Acció Olímpica and
that he was playing a double game by signing the accord with Maragall,
while militants of his own party were actively involved in what PSC
spokesmen termed 'boycotting actions'. The Generalitat rejected criti-
cisms emanating from Spanish government circles, claiming instead that

Catalan symbols also represented Spain, and that the country was a pluri-national and pluri-lingual state. COC President Miró Ardèval character-ised Empuries as a good example for the rest of the Olympic acts to follow. As the torch set off around Catalonia, a well-organised Acció Olímpica preceded the official caravan, inundating the local population with flags, banners and nationalist placards, which were collected up afterwards for use elsewhere. What was perceived as an oppressive secur-ity presence caused strong local resentment in certain localities, and deep concern among activists about civil liberties. They were determined to take advantage of the opportunities afforded by the progress of the torch relay to agitate in favour of the nationalist cause, and they continued with their attempts to appropriate it symbolically by surrounding it as much as possible with all the paraphernalia of Catalan nationalism – flags, banners, slogans and so on. Pujol's son, in fact, was photographed running with a 'Freedom for Catalonia' banner along the route (*El País*, 13 March 1994).[13] In terms of the extent of media coverage, particularly in Catalonia, the nationalists' efforts were highly successful.

It was to the political advantage of the authorities, of course, that the torch proceeded smoothly along its route, and like many others along the route, they were not averse to capitalising on it personally as well. Thus, leading actors on the politico-Olympic scene like Josep Miquel Abad, the director general of COOB, Samaranch, the IOC president, Maragall's wife, Diana Garrigosa, Jordi Solé Tura, the Spanish minister of culture, and Joan Gaspart, the vice-president of Barcelona Football Club, seized the photo opportunities offered and took a turn themselves with the torch (*La Vanguardia*, 16 June 1992).

The secretary of state for security, Rafel Vera, after attending a meeting of the Commission for Olympic Security in Barcelona and talking with Maragall, stated his determination that firm control would be taken. The apparently hardening attitudes on both sides contributed to the increase in tension. As the torch passed through Empordà to the nationalist stronghold of Banyoles, an Olympic sub-site of 13,000 inhabitants, where local *independistas* and 400 *Guardia Civil* stationed there for the Olympics co-existed in a state of cold war, tanks and helicopters were deployed. La Crida declined to mobilise here, apparently for fear of violence, but it hardly needed to, given the local nationalists' capacity to do so (*El País*, 7 June 1992).[14]

---

[13] Antich alleges that Pujol's son, Jordi, was one of half a dozen key personnel given the task of masterminding the Acció Olímpica campaign (Antich, 1994: 279).

[14] The *independista* body responsible was La Candidatura d'Unitat Popular (CUP).

Appearing before the Catalan Parliamentary Commission on the Games, Maragall sought to minimise the impact of the demonstrations. He stated that he understood those who wanted to express their opinions, and pleaded for consideration and a sense of proportion, claiming no one should make party politics out of a phenomenon that belongs to everyone, to humanity. This was to be increasingly Maragall's line to counteract nationalist capitalisation on the Games (*El País*, 18 June 1992). He wanted a minimal security deployment, and stressed that the level of deployment had been necessary and was normal on such occasions in a democracy.

The arrival of the torch in the nationalist shrine of Montserrat, where the nationalists had made their maximum effort to mobilise, witnessed bitter confrontation between them and Maragall. The official welcoming of the flame as a symbol of fraternity and peace by the abbot of Montserrat had to compete with a chorus of nationalist and *independista* slogans, and Maragall, who was present but did not speak, was subjected to catcalls and insults while being interviewed for TV. He reacted vehemently against those 'whose disproportionate and stupid acts put in jeopardy the spirit of peace, festivity and universality of the Olympic Flame' (*El País*, 21 June 1992), and against Pujol, accusing him of supporting Acció Olímpica's campaign and of acting against the spirit of their accord (*La Vanguardia*, 20 June 1992). He refused a debate with Pujol on Catalan TV, from which Serra had been excluded, because of his disquiet over the marginalisation of the central government. This counterattack by the socialists put Pujol on the defensive.

While still refusing to judge the 'freedom for Catalonia' campaign and denying he was playing a double game, saying it was a matter of freedom of expression, Pujol nevertheless issued a warning against whistling or the barracking of anthems, flags or institutions, including the king, and against violence, provocation of the security forces and interference with Olympic acts like that perpetrated by La Crida at Empuries (*El País*, 24 June 1992). Colom, however, blamed the tension unequivocally on the Madrid-controlled security forces, claiming it was they who were acting outside the pact and they who intended to provoke the Catalans to break the Olympic peace, because Españolisation was not succeeding (*El País*, 24 June 1992).

The most serious episode concerning security and civil liberties which threatened to jeopardise the *paz olímpica* came on 29 June, when the *Guardia Civil*, under the direction of a leading judge, Baltazar Garzón, began a pre-Olympic sweep to detain the remnants of Terra Lliure. This extremist Catalan nationalist organisation had perpetrated small-scale acts of terrorism in the past, been marginalised, and had disbanded itself two years previously. Over thirty suspected members and collaborators were rounded up, some of whom were members of, or among the local leadership of, legitimate nationalist parties, like CDC and ERC (*El País*, 8 July 1992). The majority were eventually not charged and later released, but the arrests immediately fuelled suspicion among nationalists that the central state apparatus was up to its old tricks, and intended to intimidate them into desisting from campaigning around the Olympics.

The round-up provoked an outcry among Catalan nationalists, particularly because those arrested claimed to have been tortured under interrogation. Carles Campuzano, a Catalan parliament deputy and secretary general of the CDC youth wing (some of whose members were among those detained), denounced the arrests as indiscriminate and told *Europa Press* that it did not create a climate of normality for the Games. Rafel Ribó, president of IC and not a nationalist sympathiser, said it was a put-up job in terms of pre-Olympic politics, aimed against ERC (one of those detained was Carles Buenaventura, ERC president of Gerona). Colom accused the government of breaking the Olympic peace, petitioned the president of the Catalan parliament, called for the resignation of the minister of the interior, Corcuera, telephoned Pujol urging him to make a statement, and went to complain to the king who was visiting Barcelona. He was told by a member of the Catalan government that Pujol had already complained. The mayor of Banyoles sent a telegram to Garzón to release three Banyoles detainees, and a telegram campaign from all over Catalonia followed. Translators and interpreters at the Autonomous University of Barcelona went on strike, in sympathy with one of their members who was among those arrested. A platform of support for the detainees was formed by La Crida and other *independista* organisations. Other prominent political figures expressed their concern (*La Vanguardia* and *El País*, 9 July 1992).

Pujol declared he did not think the arrests were indiscriminate, but to do with the investigation of terrorism, and called for clarification, adding that it must not affect the Olympics. Addressing a CDC summer school, some of whom were wearing 'Freedom for Catalonia' insignia, he accused the socialists of criminalising nationalism. Angel Colom, leader of ERC, called for an official investigation into the matter, claiming it was a constitutional, as well as a civil liberties issue, but did not think it convenient to demonstrate about this during the Olympics. He secured talks with Rafel Vera on the understanding that ERC would not boycott the inauguration (*El País*, 29 and 31 July 1992).

Colom's anxieties were apparently assuaged in these well-publicised talks. La Crida also approved, but the political counterpart of Terra Lliure, Catalunya Lliure, denounced them as 'opportunist'. Colom presented a denunciation of Carles Buenaventura's 'torture' in the Gerona courts and threatened to break off formal relations with the PSC for blocking his proposition on the issue in the Catalan parliament. Buenaventura, who had been released, intended to take his 'illegal' detention and torture to the highest authority, including the European Court at Strasbourg (*La Vanguardia*, 15 July 1992). The local CDC in Berga, a nationalist stronghold in the north, went so far as to say that it was treason to collaborate with the government over the Terra Lliure arrests. At a meeting attended by a thousand people, a declaration subscribed to by, among others, ERC and JNC was made opposing the 'Spanish Olympics', and called instead for COC to be the officially recognised body (*El País* and *La Vanguardia*, 20 July 1992).

The PSC, on the other hand, expressed its strong approval for the police operation and blocked ERC moves to debate the matter in the Catalan parliament, accusing ERC of calumniating the PSC. The latter's spokesman, Sala, said 'We cannot permit this small minority to stop us taking the opportunity of showing the world in the next few weeks how tolerant and co-habiting we are.' (*El País*, 19 July 1992). The PSC leader in Catalonia, Raimond Obiols, accused Pujol of criminalising the socialists with his accusations, and called for an investigation of TV3, the Catalan channel, for allegedly misrepresenting what had occurred by using film footage of the Franco era to report it (*El País*, 18 July 1992). Corcuera and the *Guardia Civil* rejected the accusations of torture, and the latter had the matter remitted to the State Fiscal General as a defamation campaign.

In the two-week period before the opening ceremony, the success of Pujol's and the nationalists' efforts to capitalise on the Games, particularly their success in marginalising the central government, worried the socialists increasingly. On 10 July, Maragall announced that the government would have a major presence at the social events around the Games, and called for a major recognition of its economic support (*La Vanguardia*, 11 July 1992). Tense negotiations were held between the Town Hall and the Generalitat over Maragall's and Pujol's roles at the ceremony for the arrival of the torch in Barcelona. A week later the Town Hall changed the location for the reception for the Olympic flame in Barcelona, from the Palau de la Generalitat, in the centre of the old city, to the port. The Town Hall is situated opposite the Palau de la Generalitat in the Plaça de San Jaume, but the latter has greater historical resonance for Catalans than the Town Hall and Maragall was unwilling to allow Pujol the opportunity to take advantage of this historic setting to further capitalise on the Games.

At this point the Generalitat placed large two-page advertisements in major European, American, Far Eastern and Australian newspapers, pin-pointing Barcelona on a blank map of Europe and inviting readers to guess in which country it was located. The second page gave the answer – 'In Catalonia, of course'. It provoked a furious reaction in the Madrid press, around the country and across the political spectrum for its exploitation of the Games without a mention of Spain and its contribution (*El País*, 20 July 1992; *El Periodico*, 21 July 1992). The Generalitat used the same tactics earlier in publicity aimed at visitors to Catalonia.

By 19 July, a week before the Games were due to open, Pujol's political impact on the Games, according to the results of a national opinion poll, caused *El País* to comment that the socialists were stupefied by the success of the nationalists in using the Olympics (*El País*, 19 July 1992; *La Vanguardia*, 21 July 1992). For in Spain the Games were perceived as Catalan and more saw the Generalitat as the main contributor to the work, with the city second and central government third. In Catalonia more people saw the Games as Barcelona's, with the Generalitat making the second-biggest contribution and central government ranked an even poorer third. Thus the central government's contribution, which had been the largest in financial terms, was discounted in both Catalonia and in the rest of Spain. In a separate poll of Catalan opinion, however, Maragall received a higher rating than Pujol for his contribution to the Games (*La Vanguardia*, 20 July 1992). Pujol also caught the limelight, taking on the mantle of international statesman by playing host on the eve of the Games to a number of prominent foreign politicians, the British prime minister among them (*El País*, 25 July 1992).

The socialists hit back in various ways. They continued to criticise Pujol's ambiguous relationship with the militant nationalists. On 15 July Acció Olímpica had initiated a campaign placing large advertisements in the Catalan press that only *senyeres* should be displayed on balconies during the Games (*La Vanguardia*, 22 July 1992). When CDC, Pujol's own party, recommended the same it was rounded upon by Maragall, who countered with his 'The Games Belong to Everyone' line (*El País*, 19 and 23 July). Also, he insinuated that CDC intended to disrupt the Olympics (*El Observador*, 24 July 1992).

On 18 July, at the first of two full dress rehearsals for the opening ceremony attended by the public, and one week before the Games were due to start, there was, to the consternation of Samaranch who was present, loud whistling in the stadium when the Spanish flag appeared and the Spanish national anthem was played. It was said to have come from some of the many young volunteers, thousands of whom had been recruited to help with the tasks necessary for the Games to function, and whose presence in the stadium as an offstage army of helpers was absolutely essential. The nationalist activists had thus, as they had warned, managed to infiltrate the main stadium and were poised, if they so determined, to demonstrate and disrupt the Games. It was obvious to the authorities on the spot that something more concrete needed to be done to allay remaining suspicions about their intentions *vis-à-vis* Catalanisation and restraints on civil liberties. The young militants had shown considerable imagination, initiative and daring already, were rather numerous, and obviously quite fearless and determined. Representatives of the city administration and of COOB, who had over the weeks maintained informal contact with their nationalist adversaries in La Crida, attempted to further reassure its spokesman by inviting him to the final dress rehearsal, now only two days away from the opening, so that he could verify for himself the extent to which the nationalists' demands had been taken into account. The day beforehand La Crida threatened that their Olympic volunteer members would intervene. La Crida wanted permission to have its stalls in the Olympic zones and other parts of the city. It was reported that it also wanted a 'Welcome Everyone to Barcelona' banner in Catalan (*Benvinguts tots a Barcelona*) to lead the march past in the opening ceremony, or for it to be shown on the stadium big screen (*La Vanguardia*, 23 July 1992; *El País*, 25 July 1992; *El Observador*, 24 July 1992).

On 24 July the press carried the news that La Crida had agreed not to demonstrate or stage a boycott, although its demands for stalls had not been granted, and that it was satisfied with the ceremony, although the demand for Catalan symbols had been diluted. Sánchez invited spectators to bring *independista* flags and 'Freedom for Catalonia' banners, and he warned that if the authorities went back on their assurances they were ready to cause disruption, as the volunteers did, at the rehearsal on 18 July (*La Vanguardia*, 23 July 1992; *El Observador*, 24 July 1992). They were said to possess many tickets for the inaugural ceremony and their propaganda materials could be readily deployed. Their plans to disrupt had included flying a light aircraft into the stadium.[15] The telephone call agreeing definitely not to disrupt the Games came just one day before the Games opened.[16] As a precaution La Crida smuggled their materials into the stadium anyway, in case the authorities went back on their word.[17]

The security forces were still worried, however, because Juntas Españolas, an extreme right-wing organisation which was flying an air balloon over the city with a Spanish flag, intended also to bring Spanish flags around the Olympic ring in order to Españolise the Games (*El Observador*, 24 July 1992; *El País* 25 July 1992).

---

[15] Interview with Jordi Sánchez.   [16] Interview with Rafel Llusà.
[17] Interview with Jordi Sánchez.

According to one source, unknown to Pujol himself, the leadership of the 'Freedom for Catalonia' campaign which, included his eldest son, Jordi, had planned, with the help of a mole inside the TV network, to disrupt the Games by cutting the TV transmission at the point when the king was to declare the Games open. At the last moment the mole got cold feet and another collaborator could not be found in time (Antich, 1994: 283). This would have been an audacious and spectacular act with untold consequences.

A volunteer is reported to have unfurled an *independista* banner during the opening ceremony and the police to have confiscated 'Freedom for Catalonia' banners and *independista* flags unfurled in the stadium (*La Vanguardia*, 29 July 1992). A member of La Fura dels Baus, the theatrical group responsible for the Mediterranean Sea sequence in the opening ceremony, is reported to have 'streaked' in the middle of it with a 'Freedom for Catalonia' banner (*La Vanguardia*, 31 July 1992).

The day before the Games opened COC expressed its satisfaction with the symbols and advised against protests, adding that the central government and COE were responsible for the IOC rejecting its recognition, that Samaranch had not been helpful, and that COC would be recognised by the next Games in Atlanta in 1996. ERC, although not in favour of protests at the Games, asked for respect for those who might whistle at the king. Colom himself refused to go to the king's reception. He also announced that 200,000 *independista* flags would be distributed in Barcelona and 100,000 in the sub-sites, and claimed that the absence of Spanish flags, in contrast with the massive presence of *senyeres*, was a plebiscite for Catalanisation (*El Periodico*, 24 July 1992). In the Olympic sub-site of Banyoles tension between the security forces and the local population was reported to be still acute: the *Guardia Civil* was socially ostracised to the extent that girls associating with members were subject to sanctions (*La Vanguardia*, 27 July 1992). The search for the presumed leader of Terra Lliure, Carles Castellanos, was still going on; the campaign against the security forces having lost some of its sting since a number of the detainees were reported to have made damaging admissions, agreed to cooperate with the investigation and denounced Castellanos (*El País*, 25 July 1992).

Meanwhile, the torch had completed its journey around Spain, and had finally arrived in Barcelona by ship from Majorca the evening before the opening ceremony. Symbolising their unity over the Olympics, Maragall and Pujol jointly received the torch at the port in a euphoric atmosphere (*El País*, 25 July 1992). Huge crowds in festive mood assembled at every point in its passage through the different districts of the city that evening and all through the night. There were firework displays and music and dancing in the squares. In each district the torch relay was framed by the flag displays – on the buildings, on passing vehicles and enthusiastically waved by massed onlookers.[18] Although the atmosphere was of virtually undiluted festivity, the press did report some isolated outbreaks of hooliganism and one incident in Gracia, a nationalist stronghold fairly close to the centre of the city, was instructive. After the torch passed in a melée of cheering spectators, revellers and the police cordon, there was a sudden commotion and loud, angry shouting as a man was suddenly set upon by half a dozen *independistas*, including women, who were trying to seize his bag, verbally abusing him and demanding to see the contents. The rough manhandling went on for some time while the victim clung grimly on to his bag, resisting attempts to open it and protesting his innocence. Finally, the bag was pulled from his grasp, a camera was opened and the film removed. His attackers were apparenty convinced he was a police spy. Nothing further seems to have happened to him and he disappeared. In a matter of seconds a festive scene had been transformed at this spot into an ugly, menacing incident, a further illustration of the thin line between festivity and violence where nationalist sentiment is concerned.

The war of the flags: an analysis

Up to the eve of the opening ceremony, the outcome of the conflict was a substantial Catalanisation of the Games. Flags were the key symbols in this conflict and played a crucial part in its outcome. In the increasingly acrimonious atmosphere of mutual suspicion that built up over the months before the opening, a 'war of the flags' broke out all over Barcelona, as the nationalists and the socialist municipality mobilised support over the political meaning of the Games. In Catalonia to an extraordinary degree, equalled by nowhere else in Western Europe except perhaps Northern Ireland, flags are a ubiquitous aspect of popular culture, so when people feel a need to declare their political allegiance it is quite usual to do so by displaying flags. In the weeks before the Games and during the event itself, Catalan, Barcelona and Olympic flags, singly or in different combinations, signifying the range of reactions and political allegiances in this situation, festooned the city. To ascertain what in precise detail the different flag displays meant to those deploying them is problematic, and would constitute an investigation in its own right,

---

[18] I closely observed the torch relay on its way from the port through the central districts and also in two contrasting districts, the working-class, socialist-dominated district of Nou Baris, and the more middle-class nationalist stronghold of Gracia.

requiring time and resources beyond the scope of this study. The received meaning of the flags, who displayed them, the nature of the display, the display's location, and how they were acquired, are all relevant factors helping to explain the part played by the war of the flags in the struggle between nationalists and their opponents.

The Catalan flag consists of four red bars on a gold-yellow background. The *independista* version is the same with the addition of a large blue star at the leading edge. The city flag is quartered, with two diagonally opposed red crosses of Sant Jordi on white backgrounds and two diagonally opposed Catalan flags (the Town Hall's version has only two red bars). The Spanish flag has two broader red bars, one at the top and the other at the bottom, enclosing a gold-yellow middle section. The Olympic flag has five interlinked coloured rings on a white background.

Catalans are well aware of the legend recounting the origins of the Catalan flag, which they learn at their mother's knee and in the schools. Louis the Pious, son of the great Emperor Charlemagne, dipped his fingers in the blood of Guifre El Pelós, the first count of Barcelona, as the latter lay wounded, following the Frankish–Catalan reconquest of Barcelona from the Saracens. Drawing his bloody fingers across Guifre's golden shield, he gave him his new coat of arms and Catalonia its flag. Plainly, there are strong connotations here of Catalonia's resistance to external domination.

The red cross in the Barcelona flag is the cross of Sant Jordi, the patron saint of Catalonia. The flag with only two red bars is the Town Hall's version of the Catalan flag. There is also a strong reference to Catalonia here. The nationalists dispute the authenticity of the Town Hall's version of the Catalan flag, claiming that there should be four bars in the Catalan flag, and that the Town Hall has a reason for preferring the two bar version – because it more closely resembles the Spanish flag.[19] Apparently the Town Hall promised to change it, but interestingly did not seem to be taking any active steps to do so. The Catalan, *independista*, Barcelona and Spanish flags are thus quite similar, so much so that it is easy for the non-cognoscenti to confuse them. The first three share the Catalan flag in various ways and all four share its red and yellow colours and the bar design. Yet they each signify quite different things. The five-ringed Olympic flag, designed by the founder of the modern Olympic Games, de Coubertin, is of course indisputably a well-recognised symbol of internationalism and non-partisanship.

---

[19] The four-bar version seems to be more firmly embedded in Catalan history and cultural tradition. For example, the altar of the Catedral de la Mercè (St Mercè, referred to as la Mercè, is the patron saint of Barcelona) is decorated with an escutcheon which shows the four-bar flag of Catalonia.

The flags were sometimes accompanied by slogans, the most common of which were 'Freedom for Catalonia' and 'Welcome to Catalonia'. Flags were displayed on public buildings, monuments, business premises (office blocks, stores, shops, restaurants, etc.) and residents' balconies.

Official flag-flying and the commercial appropriation of these symbols were important, but they were not necessarily indicative of the population's allegiance. Such displays were often in place before the population was explicitly called upon to show their allegiances. The Spanish constitution makes it mandatory to fly the Spanish flag at certain locations during visits by the head of state, and it is normally flown on public buildings – the civil and the military governors' offices, army barracks, the *Guardia Civil* and police stations, etc. Otherwise it is not usually seen and one is frequently told by Catalans that it is not a popular symbol, but rather one of oppression and past humiliations. Prestigious business and commercial enterprises, like banks, large expensive hotels and department stores, routinely display national symbols and during the Olympics were in a position to put on elaborate, impressive displays featuring the Catalan, the Barcelona and sometimes the Spanish flag. Such displays tended to be more characteristic of the more frequented, fashionable centre of the city, and the public spaces where people (many of them visitors) tended to congregate. While in many cases they give the impression of strong support for Catalan nationalism, what probably lay behind them was the rather more mundane desire of business to promote public relations by cashing in on the general air of festivity.

In contrast to large institutions, owners of small neighbourhood enterprises, such as shops, bars and restaurants, could give vent to more individual expressions of their allegiances, although they may have felt pressure to conform with local feeling or risk unpopularity. This is the case of course for residents of local communities in general (there were isolated instances reported of flags being torn down from balconies) and it brings us to one, if not the best indicator, of popular feeling with regard to nationalism and the Olympics – the balcony displays put up by individual residents. Barcelona is the most densely populated major city in Europe. Most people live in blocks of flats, whether in the more middle-class Eixample central district, the working-class suburbs, or adjoining towns of the metropolitan area, and it is usual for a flat to have some kind of balcony. It was the more solidly residential districts that were most implicated in the war of the flags between nationalists and the Town Hall.

The nationalist groups appear to have been well financed, and able to deluge the city and the region with propaganda both directly and via the media. The Town Hall, put on the defensive by this agitation, responded by distributing the Barcelona flag free of charge for display on balconies.

A spokesman claimed it also distributed the Catalan flag and it may well be that the Catalan government in one way or another also made the Catalan flag available.[20] Both sides accused the other of subsidising propaganda.

Overall, in the city of Barcelona covering a population of about a million and a half, in terms of single flags displayed, the dominant symbol numerically was the Catalan flag. The Barcelona flag, though numerically second, nevertheless registered a significant presence. A considerable number of balconies displayed both, and the Olympic flag was often added, while a small number incorporated the Spanish flag as well. The distribution in the metropolitan area covering the total conurbation of about four and a half million people (constituting most of Catalonia's population) is more difficult to gauge. In both the city and the metropolitan area the nature of displays varied with the character of the district. Where Castilian was the predominant language, that is, in working-class *barrios* populated mostly by immigrants from the rest of Spain and where socialist sympathies were stronger, Barcelona flags tended to predominate, whereas in the more middle-class districts like Gracia, nearer the centre, the flags were overwhelmingly Catalan, with a good proportion of these in this particular case being *independista*.[21]

It might be unwise to assess the success of nationalist appeals simply by relying on a count of the types of flag displayed, without qualification. Probably the most unequivocal message is conveyed in the extremely rare instance where the Spanish flag appears on its own, which in this context could signify defiant allegiance to *franquismo*, or the kind of loyalty to the idea of Spain, and hostility to any hint of separatism, that is characteristic of the conservative Partido Popular, the party that tends to give voice in the loudest terms to Spanish nationalism. It is significant that such gestures were rare, but as an indicator of the strength of this type of allegiance their absence is, perhaps, rather misleading. To display them at such a time of Catalan nationalist celebration would have been to court unpopularity. Sometimes sporadic expressions of opposition to perceived Catalan triumphalism would occur. In one incident I witnessed, two young men passing the office of COC in a fashionable, busy part of the city at midday, and from which the COC/Catalan banner was hanging, screamed abuse up at the first-floor windows.

The *independista* flag most clearly signifies militant Catalan nationalist allegiance, but additional elements can enter into its signification. When

---

[20] Interview with Rafel Llusà.
[21] Gracia has a very strong tradition of political activism, currently strongly nationalist and socialist, and in the past anarchist.

worn or carried by the young it seems to be a fashionable part of their apparel, a factor which cannot be discounted as at least part of the motivation to display. Although this flag was much in evidence, especially in the proliferating graffiti, it was always in a minority in balcony displays and was only really prominent when and where *independistas* congregated.

The 'mixed' type of display incorporating both the Catalan and Barcelona flags seemed to indicate a rejection of the attempt to polarise the issue along nationalist lines. It could have indicated a political commitment to the Town Hall's line, namely, as Maragall claimed, one could be simultaneously a good 'Catalanist' and reject nationalism. In other words, the PSC attempted to accommodate the existence of a distinct Catalan identity with its moderate socialism, while rejecting what it categorised as the opposition's chauvinism. Therefore, it is likely that this type of display expressed what the addition of the Olympic flag to such a display seemed to be indicating unequivocally, namely, that the Olympics were primarily a festival not a political issue. This was a theme that Maragall had been pushing increasingly to neutralise nationalist propaganda. In both these cases the message seemed to be one of communal and civic pride rather than support for nationalism.

The Barcelona flag displayed by itself would seem to indicate unequivocal support for the PSC line versus the nationalists. However, the fact that it was distributed free by the Town Hall may mean that some people were as much entering into an apolitical festive spirit as demonstrating support for the Town Hall's socialism. After all, Maragall's slogan, 'The Games Belong to Everyone', was not so much an attempt to appropriate Olympism for socialism as a species of populism: it traded on humanist, internationalist sentiment associated with Olympism, with the objective of defusing Catalan nationalism. In the more working-class districts the tendency for the Barcelona flag to predominate indicates that the appeal worked. Here the flag signified, at the very least, passive resistance to the nationalists' appeals, or otherwise active rejection of their attempts to politicise the issue for nationalist ends.

The most difficult symbol to interpret is the Catalan flag which, like the Barcelona flag, was distributed free of charge. It could have been on display for a number of reasons, ranging from nationalist sentiment, local patriotism and civic pride to convention, conformity to pressure and expression of the festive spirit.

In terms of the impact of such displays for the ongoing struggle between nationalists and their opponents, clearly politicians and activists in both camps did regard them as important weapons in their arsenals and regarded their successful deployment as a crucial part of their campaigning strategies. The flag displays mediated a reciprocal relationship between them and their respective publics. Perhaps one way of understanding the impact of the war of the flags is to imagine what would have been the effect if, say, the only flag displayed had been the Catalan flag. It seems inconceivable that this would not have been interpreted on all sides as an exhibition of nationalist strength, a victory for Catalan nationalism and an advance of its cause. Also, whatever the intended meaning may have been to those displaying their flags, there are likely to have been unintended effects. The colour code and design of the Catalan flag is important here. The four evenly spaced red bars on an ochre-yellow background are strong, striking, primary colours, connoting primordial elements like blood and sun, and they are arranged in a very simple design. This uncluttered, instantly recognisable flag is easy to reproduce in versions differing in length and breadth so that, for example, it could be deployed horizontally, draped across the breadth of a balcony, a section of a building or a whole building. It was also deployed vertically, suspended from balconies, roofs, gateways, monuments, etc., hanging down over a considerable length of tall buildings and other large edifices. In such ways Catalan flags were easily the most in evidence: they were usually the biggest, there were more of them, since they figured both on their own in large numbers as well as in mixed displays, and in their coloration and design they were the most striking.

Flags were the main weapons in the conflict: they were the most potent expression of political loyalties and identities, and thus the extent of their presence on the political scene and the manner in which they were deployed was of crucial importance in mobilising the local population. Mobilisation was not just a matter of renewing and reinforcing established loyalties by successfully getting existing supporters to express their predetermined allegiances with the relevant symbol. To a significant extent, also, it was in the deployment of flags that those very loyalties and identities were constructed, that support was won – especially among the younger sections of the population who were being inducted into politics. Thus, a significant dimension of the conflict consisted of a battle over the meaning of the flags.

Because their meaning remained open to interpretation, these symbols were subject to appropriation in different ways by the contenders for power and influence. In this sense the flags – and most evidently the Catalan flag – were themselves stakes in the conflict and not just reflections of pre-existing interests and loyalties with fixed meanings. This can be seen in the fact that, as in any democratic system, the conflict was fought out in a war of words, but this particular war of words was concentrated to a great extent on what the Catalan flag signified – Pujol's pragmatic nationalism, *independismo*, or Maragall's pluralism – and what constituted its legitimate form and its legitimate deployment.

On balance, on the eve of the opening ceremony, in this particular kind of street battle, the nationalists gained the edge in the sense that nationalist sentiment was very successfully mobilised, nationalist morale was raised, and a good deal of pressure was thereby brought to bear on those responsible for the Games. In particular, Pujol's brand of nationalism benefited from the preponderance of the Catalan flag, an outcome to which the *independistas* had unintentionally contributed. Pujol had not anticipated this degree of success. However, the strength of Catalan nationalism symbolised by the displays was itself rather deceptive: for the actual result of the war of the flags was, after all, a compromise – the *paz olímpica*.

The *paz olímpica* was an achievement that allowed the Games to go ahead without disruption and enabled tension between Spain and Catalonia to be expressed in more symbolic terms as the Games proceeded. What remains to be ascertained is how the political competition between them was mediated symbolically during the Games themselves and what was the ultimate effect of the Games on the relationship between the centre and the region.

5 Catalanisation versus Españolisation

Introduction

This chapter analyses the way the relationship between Catalonia and Spain was vividly represented in, and mediated by, the Games through the manner in which national symbols were deployed throughout the two-week proceedings. The focus of the analysis is the ceremonial aspect of the Games, particularly the ceremonies that took place in the Montjuic Olympic stadium, because these were at the forefront of this symbolic work process. Even on the eve of the Games, despite the existence of a *paz olímpica* that had been negotiated after much effort between the national-ists and the authorities, and in which the authorities made major conces-sions, there was still tension. The possibility that there might still be disruption could not be dismissed. The conduct of the Games consti-tuted the arena in which the compromise arrived at by the contending parties was put into practice, tested out, worked on and perfected. It was by no means guaranteed to succeed. That would depend on a combina-tion of factors.

COOB's preferred strategy had been to present an image of the Games that departed from the stereotypes of Spain as an indolent land of sun, sea, sex, blood and sand. The objective instead was to create an image of a Mediterranean city with an ancient cultural heritage, as well as being in the artistic avant-garde, situated in a modern country that could get things done efficiently.[1] However, cross-pressured by Catalan nationalists on the one hand and by Spanish interests on the other, it became increas-ingly imperative to produce a pluri-national show that would mollify the political combatants by incorporating, in addition, highly Catalanised and Españolised elements. The most important way in which this was accomplished was in the structure and content of the opening and closing ceremonies. The former was more important in this respect because it set the tone for all that was to follow.

[1] Interview with Josep Roca, Director of the Ceremonies.

To appreciate fully the significance of these occasions one has to bear in mind that they lasted for many hours and that they comprised, in fact, a multilayered series of ceremonies, acts and spectacular shows, which directly or indirectly involved thousands of performers. The Spanish king and royal family, the political and other dignitaries, the IOC officials, the 'Olympic family', the performance artists (singers, dancers, actors, musicians, etc.) the athletes, and even the spectators in certain respects, were active participants. This was all acted out, not only to the packed audience in the Olympic stadium, but via television to the rest of the world.

The intention here is to show how both political and cultural nationalism were woven into the proceedings in specific ways to achieve an overall effect. There are, of course, many other fascinating aspects of the Games' proceedings that might equally deserve attention from a sociological or other points of view, but which fall outside our scope. Political nationalism most clearly manifested itself in the deployment of the Catalan flag, the use of the Catalan national anthem and in the official status accorded to the Catalan language. Less obviously and more subtly, cultural nationalism underpinned the proceedings in the more informal, more entertaining aspects, notably in the great spectacular sequences designed to show off Catalan and Spanish culture to the whole country and the rest of the world.

Catalanisation

The opening ceremony began with a strikingly colourful and melodious amalgam of traditional and modern Catalan culture. The Olympic fanfare, composed by Carles Santos, was delivered by a group of eighty musicians playing on the *tenora*, a reed instrument, whose distinctive wailing sound can be heard leading the *coblas* (bands) which traditionally accompany the national dance, the *sardana*. Their costumes (leopard-skin jackets and red caps of liberty) were inspired by the celebrated Catalan surrealist, Salvador Dalí, and designed by the leading Barcelona costume designer, Antonio Miró. They performed in the closing ceremony also. A 17,000 square metre expanse of blue fabric, symbolising the sea and the sky of the Mediterranean, covered the floor of the stadium. Eight hundred performers in gay, brightly coloured costumes formed a bouquet of flowers representing the Rambla de les Flors in Barcelona and a flock of birds. They recombined to form the greeting ¡Hola!, a welcome to Barcelona and the Games.[2]

---

[2] Unless otherwise stated, this chapter is based upon my own observations in the Olympic stadium, supplemented by COOB (1992a, b).

The *pièce de résistance* of the opening sequence came when the 800 dancers regrouped themselves to fill the centre with the shape of the Games logotype. The abstract brush-stroke design in the Catalan, Spanish and Mediterranean colours of red, yellow and blue evoked Barcelona's important contribution to modern visual art, in the work of figures such Joan Miró, Salvador Dalí, the early Picasso, and Antoni Tapies. This image of a modern, cultured city and nation (designed by a Catalan, Josep Trias) had become instantly recognisable long beforehand throughout the world, due to the formidable efficiency of the COOB publicity machine (Trias, 1992; Moragas, 1992).

At the beginning of both the opening and the closing ceremonies the Catalan national anthem and the Spanish national anthem were played. The impact of this act in the opening ceremony was much the more important of the two. The first sequence of the opening ceremony, just described, was followed by the entrance of the king and the royal family into the presidential box to the music of the Catalan national hymn, 'Els Segadors'. Simultaneously the Spanish, Catalan and Barcelona flags were paraded into the stadium by the three flag bearers, marching abreast down the running track, in their scarlet military tunics and cockaded helmets, the Spanish flag in the middle. They halted and swung around to face the presidential box, filled by dignitaries, and which the royal family had just entered. All attention was focused first on the Catalan symbols: the television cameras broadcasting the scene to the nation and the whole world, and to the stadium audience on the large stadium screen, showed the *senyera* in close-up, to the stirring music of 'Els Segadors', the song chosen as the Catalan national anthem by Catalonia's esteemed poet, Jacint Verdaguer. The Spanish national anthem followed immediately after, this time with the focus on the Spanish flag. The two sets of national symbols were thus accorded equal status. The only difference was that the king stood to attention throughout 'La Marcha Real' and waved to the crowd when 'Els Segadors' was played. For the first time for centuries, Catalan national symbols ranked equally with Spanish ones, in an official act. The significance of the act can, perhaps, be gauged if we consider that 'Els Segadors', is a call to revolution, recalling memories of the revolt of the Catalans in 1640 against Philip IV during the war with France, and in which the peasantry played a leading part (hence the reference to sickles as weapons in the anthem) (Elliot, 1963). This vivid reminder of the blood spilt between the two nations, expressed in the anti-Spanish sentiments of this song, could not have been easy for the central authorities to swallow, especially on a supposedly diplomatic occasion like this and, of course, it could not but also evoke memories of the civil war.

Catalunya, triomfant,	Triumphant Catalonia
Tornarà a ser rica i plena!	Will once again be rich and full!
Endarrera aquesta gent	We must not be the prey
Tan ufana i tan superba	Of those proud and arrogant invaders!
Bon cop de falç!	Let us swing the sickle!
Bon cop de falç,	Let us swing the sickle!
defensors del la terra!	Defenders of our land!
Bon cop de falç!	Let us swing the sickle!
Ara és hora, segadors!	Now is the moment, oh reapers,
Ara és hora d'estar alerta!	Now is the moment to be alert!
Per quan vingui un altre juny	Awaiting the arrival of another June
Esmolem ben bé les eines!	Let us sharpen our tools!
Que tremoli l'enemic	May our enemy tremble
En veient la nostra ensenya:	On seeing our noble flag:
Com fem caure espigues d'or	Just as we reap the golden corn
Quan convé seguem cadenes!	May we also cut free of the chains!

(Puigjaner, 1992: 11)

The king was castigated by the Esquerra Republicana leader, Angel Colom, for showing disrespect to the Catalan symbols by waving to the crowd when 'Els Segadors' was being played, instead of standing to attention as he did during the Spanish national anthem. This was to underrate the significance of the act. Just six days before the Games, the king and Maragall had taken part in a ceremony signifying the healing of wounds between Spain and Catalonia. It was the inauguration of a replica of the Republican Pavilion that had been at the Paris Exhibition of 1937, and in which Picasso's painting, *Guernica*, was exhibited. The painting depicts the destruction of that Basque town in an air raid designed to terrorise the population, which was carried out by Franco's German allies. The ceremony was timed to take place on the same day, 19 July, on which fifty-six years previously, the civil war broke out in Barcelona, and on which the anti-fascist alternative to the Berlin Nazi Olympics, the *Olimpiada Popular*, was aborted. This 'discreet and profound gesture', as Maragall put it, referring to the king's participation, symbolised the reconciliation of the Spanish nation (*El País*, 20 July 1992). The only other noteworthy reference to the civil war came in Maragall's speech later in the opening ceremony, which had been approved by central government beforehand,[3] when he briefly alluded to the connection between this setting and the former president of the Generalitat, Lluis Companys, who was shot by the Franco regime in 1940. At one point, prior to his execution, Companys had been kept in the stadium and it may eventually be named after

---

[3] Interview with Fernando París, special adviser to the Spanish minister of sport.

him. There is a commemorative plaque to him at the main gate. The crowd applauded appreciatively at this reference and Maragall quickly passed on.

Since the Catalan anthem was played first, it might have been seen as taking precedence. On the other hand, the Spanish flag was in the middle, flanked by the other two, which thus could have been seen as signifying its precedence. What the deployment of the flags in this instance undoubtedly did indicate was the strong desire on the part of the authorities to give them equal status and to avoid any slight to nationalist sensibilities.

It is worth noting that the Catalan national symbols resonate more strongly for Catalans than the Spanish flag and anthem do for the Spanish people as a whole. The relatively late and feeble efforts of the Spanish state to 'nationalise' the country in Castilian–Spanish terms meant that there was no national flag until 1843, and even then the Carlists and Republicans contested it in subsequent civil wars. Neither was there a national anthem until the twentieth century; and even today there are no agreed words, which makes it rather difficult to express feelings of national solidarity by singing it (Junco, 1996).

Throughout the Games the Catalan flag was given the same status as the Spanish flag: they flew together with the Barcelona and EEC flags from the top of the stadium, they were raised inside the stadium for the Olympic oath ceremony, paraded together in the closing ceremony, and flown on all the many Olympic installations and sites throughout the Games.

As previously discussed, language is the main marker of Catalan ethnic distinctiveness and identity (Barrera-González, 1995; Woolard, 1989; Laitin, 1989; Conversi, 1997). As such, gaining official status for Catalan as one of the four official languages of the Games alongside Spanish, French and English was absolutely vital. Catalan figured prominently in every aspect: throughout the long opening and closing ceremonies, every award ceremony, the official speeches, the continual public announcements for all aspects of the Games, in song as well as speech, in signposting and other kinds of visual information. Perhaps most significant of all in this connection was the moment when the Games were officially declared open by the king, in which the Catalan language was privileged, for his first words were in Catalan: '*Benvinguts tots a Barcelona*' ('Welcome Everyone to Barcelona'). The effect of the king's words on the crowd was electric. The remainder of his words in Spanish was drowned out by wild applause in appreciation of the fact that he had opened in Catalan. This single brief act seems to have won over the Catalan audience at the outset.

The traditional national dance of Catalonia, the *sardana*, followed the national anthems, performed by six hundred *sardanistes* dressed in white from associations all over Catalonia and accompanied by the Catalan opera stars Montserrat Caballé and Josep (José) Carreras (Carreras was also the Games' musical director). They sang a specially composed 'Sardana of Official Welcome' in honour of 'the first Olympic athlete from Barcelona', Lucius Minucius Natalis, a rich Roman praetor (Hughes, 1992: 65), who is reputed to have won the chariot race in the Games of 129 AD. The choreographer was the professor of dance at the Dance Institut del Teatre de Barcelona, Raimon Àvila. The *sardana* was created during the *Renaixença* by the Andulusian immigrant, Pep Ventura, on the basis of a folk tradition dating back to the Middle Ages and documented since the sixteenth century. It is said to have originated in the region of Empordà in north-eastern Catalonia (Hall, 1986: 129). Launched in 1859 at the Liceu Theatre in Barcelona, it thereafter acquired increasing popularity throughout the region, until by the turn of the century it was the most characteristic of Catalan dances. Together with choral societies, rambling clubs and other professional and leisure associations, it formed an important part of the social basis of Catalanism by that time, and thus was closely associated with nationalist politics (Balcells, 1996: 52–4; Hall, 1986: 41; Conversi, 1997: 216). Associations of *sardanistes* formed an integral part of the semi-clandestine social networks that circumvented Franco's proscription of Catalan culture at the micro level, and the dance thereby played an especially important part in helping to sustain Catalan sentiment and political identity. One can readily see it performed in village, town and city squares all over Catalonia today. Its contemporary political significance can be gauged from the fact that the Generalitat and the main nationalist party, CiU, promote the dance, and it is not uncommon to see hundreds of dancers on, say, a Sunday morning in the Parc Joan Miró, or a festival day in Poble Nou, dancing under the CiU banner.

As Torras i Bages, ideologist of Catalan nationalism at the turn of the century, emphasised, the *sardana*'s sedate, serious quality is almost the exact opposite of the sensual southern Andalusian flamenco, whose growing popularity in Catalonia he excoriated: 'Nothing could be more antithetical to the Catalan character, or be more damaging to the severity and restraint of our race.' (Hughes, 1992: 321). Dancers link hands held at shoulder height and form a circle. Movement is confined mostly to small, intricate steps in unison, requiring mathematical precision and carried out at the direction of a leading dancer. A great deal of concentration is required and the highly disciplined nature of the movements is reflected in the usually rather serious facial expressions of the dancers. Possibly more than most aspects of Catalan culture the *sardana* expresses what has been popularly depicted as the Catalan national character. Catalans like to think of themselves as disciplined, hard-working, efficient, and possessed of that quality they call *seny*, meaning something like good commonsense. They are often seen in the rest of Spain in less flattering terms, that is, as rather cold, calculating, mean and selfish.

At the opening ceremony the dance was choreographed so that the circles of dancers formed the five Olympic rings, conjoining a key symbol of Catalanity with a powerful symbol of peace and internationalism. The dancers re-formed themselves into the shape of a gigantic human heart, while the orchestra played the 'Cant de la Senyera' ('Song of the Flag'), a popular, strongly emotive, patriotic song with words by the patriot–poet Joan Maragall, who happened to be the grandfather of the mayor, Pasqual Maragall:

Oh, bandera catalana	O flag of Catalunya
Nostre cor t'es ben fidel.	our hearts keep faith with you.
Volaràs com au galana	You will fly like a brave bird
per damunt del nostre anbel.	above our desires.
Per mirar-te sobirana	To see you reigning there
Alcarem els ulls al cer.	We'll lift our eyes to the sky.
	(Hughes, 1992: 19)

The music was by Lluis Millet, founder of the famous Orfeó Català, and initiator of a choral and musical movement that was at the heart of the efflorescence of Catalanism at the turn of the century. The Orfeó Català was also one of several renowned Catalan choirs performing at the ceremonies. The rich Catalan musical tradition, and in particular folk song and choral music, has provided one of the major ways in which Catalan consciousness has been fostered and sustained; and the many song societies and choirs have played an important part in this process (Conversi, 1997; Giner, 1984).

Barcelona and Catalonia were in the foreground for fully fifteen minutes in a spectacular performance, 'The Mediterranean, Olympic Sea', written and directed by the avant-garde Catalan theatre group La Fura dels Baus, and employing 1,200 actors. The origins of Western civilisation and the founding of Barcelona and the Olympic Games were all linked together in an epic drama, drawing on Greek and Roman mythology, which seems to have been based upon Verdaguer's epic poem, 'Atlàntida', probably the most outstanding literary work of the *Renaixença* (Hughes, 1992: 311). Hercules' heroic exploits, the creation of the Mediterranean Sea, and an Odyssey featuring the triumph of good over evil culminating in the foundation of Barcelona, made up a stunning, spectacular, and technically brilliant cultural performance. At the finish, the mythological foundation of the city by Hercules was celebrated with a song of thanksgiving to music based on the Virolai, a mediaeval form of ballad and a traditional Catalan tune dedicated to the Virgin of Monserrat. Simultaneously, 10,000 spectators formed two mosaics designed by the Catalan artist Antoni Miralda. The first was inspired by the work of Catalonia's most renowned architect, Antoni Gaudí; the second reproduced some of the principal monuments of the city: Gaudí's extraordinary Sagrada Familia church, the column to Columbus, and the Collserola communications tower, specially constructed for the Olympics. It must be said that the mosaics were not very effective, partly because they were too dependent on the vagaries of the spectators' participation.

Other spectacles on the same scale, designed to advertise the Catalan flare for design, production and performance and embodying features of Catalan culture at all levels, figured in the opening and closing ceremonies. One such was the 'Festival of Fire' in the closing ceremony, devised, directed and coordinated by another Catalan avant-garde multi-media artistic group, Els Comediants, who based their performance on traditional Catalan festivals like the Festa de la Mercè, Barcelona's main festival of the year. This is celebrated on a grand scale with thousands of costumed participants. The huge, noisy, seemingly chaotic procession moves slowly from the port up the Via Laietana, an avenue which cuts a swathe through the old city, enveloped in smoke, firework explosions and flames. The flames emanate from the huge mouths of numerous dragons and all along the route men, boys and girls vie to see who dares to stay in the path of the dragons for as long as possible.

The 700 actors and technicians turned the stadium first into a planetarium, in which the Earth, the Moon and Sun danced, the stars and planets rose above the stadium, and shooting stars crossed the sky in a pyrotechnical display depicting the creation of the world. The scene was transformed when a volcano belching fumes and fire appeared and a host of devils raining fire descended from the terraces down to the stadium floor, which had been transformed into a macabre, subterranean 'garden of fire and mischief', in which 250 devil dancers, tumblers and circus artists cavorted. Beautiful beasts and monsters mingled with dragons emitting fire, as the *festa* culminated in the terrifying appearance above the stadium of an enormous red dragon amid shattering explosions, bolts of lightning, thunderclaps and fires.

Catalan folk culture was also represented in the opening ceremony by the spectacular *castells de xiquets* (human towers), a traditional sport in which teams of men and boys compete to build the highest tower. Like the *sardana* they are popularly seen as an expression of typical Catalan virtues: 'those manly symbols of the strength and aplomb of our people', as Torres i Bagès put it (Hughes, 1992: 322). Today, *castells* are raised during the spring and summer festivals in the main squares of many towns in Catalonia. It requires both strength and intelligence to erect these towers, which rise normally to seven or eight levels, and in competition to even greater heights. The pyramid is topped by an '*anxaneta*', a six- or seven-year-old boy, who climbs to the top and waves to show the *castell* is completed. Towards the end of the opening ceremony sixteen teams, or *collas* numbering in total 2,174 *castellers* from all over Catalonia, erected twelve towers at intervals around the track, so enclosing the 15,000 competitors and officials assembled in the arena. The intention was not only to represent the strength of Catalan culture, but also to stress Catalonia's status as a region in a 'Europe of the regions', an association the Catalan government uses as a counterweight to Spain – hence twelve *castells* for the twelve members of the EEC at that time. We will take up the significance of the European theme in the next chapter.

Perhaps the most poignant moment of the Barcelona Olympics came in the closing ceremony, at the point when the Olympic flame was quenched and just after the Olympic flag had been ceremoniously lowered and the Olympic hymn sung by the Orfeó Català. Then, as the flame grew dim against the night sky, the soprano Victòria de los Ángeles, yet another celebrated Catalan artist, accompanied by Lluis Claret on the cello, sang the beautiful Catalan folk song the 'Cant dels Ocells' ('The Song of the Birds'), made popular by the cellist Pau (Pablo) Casals, in a version by the composer Xavier Montsalvatge. The song, the music, the performing artists past and present, were all Catalan (Casals, the world-famous cellist, whose memory was recalled by this song, vowed he would never return to Spain as long as Franco remained in power). Before the whole world the rich inheritance and current vitality of Catalan culture was being proudly asserted.

The elements of Catalanisation discussed so far were augmented spontaneously in enthusiastic displays on the part of spectators. For example, in the main stadium, despite the plethora of flags on display among the foreign visitors, *the senyera* made an impressive showing and was easily the predominant flag on the terraces throughout, although its presence was not as strong as in the streets of the city. Young Catalan activists tried to gain TV exposure by getting their flags in camera shot at every opportunity. Two or three would hold a largish conspicuous length of flag in close proximity to an event that they knew was being screened, and by checking the large stadium TV screen they could monitor the effect of their own performance. This was a hit-and-miss tactic, for while appearing to have the advantage of frequently getting the flag in close-up shots (the TV camera otherwise is incapable of showing this kind of detail), the camera was actually focused on the competitor. Consequently, the flag was very fleetingly on camera as the competitor was in motion, or it tended to be out of focus when the competitor was static. The tactic was most effective where events took a length of time and where athletes stood still in preparation, such as the long jump and high jump. Here there was more opportunity to simply display the flag in shot behind the competitor, and this was quite often successful.

Some nationalist militants claimed that the police seized their 'Freedom for Catalonia' banners and *independista* flags at the opening ceremony. This is unlikely, given the understanding between the authorities and the nationalist opposition, but it may have been so in isolated instances. Certainly an attempt to display such material from trees overlooking the main gate of the stadium was, in fact, prevented. If there was an attempt to prohibit the more radical nationalist symbols from the main stadium during the rest of the Games, it was not very effective, for *independista* flags, for example, were readily to be seen in the stadium throughout the Games, although their number was small compared with the ordinary Catalan flag.

There was no animosity towards the Spanish team among the Catalan spectators, and it would have been difficult to express it anyway, given the fact that the team had a large Catalan contingent. It was noticeable that during the march past of the different countries' teams, an event in itself lasting almost two hours, the Catalan audience gave an especially warm welcome to small nations that had recently gained their independence like the Baltic states, Croatia and Bosnia. In fact, the Catalan Olympic Committee (COC), the body which played a leading part in the Catalanisation campaign, established relations with the Baltic republics precisely to show solidarity with fellow oppressed nations, as they saw them. The director general of COC, Xavier Vinyals, became an official representative of the Lithuanian team in Barcelona. As such, he circumvented the official protocol by marching with the Lithuanian team in the opening ceremony past the tribune and in front of the world's cameras, waving the only Catalan flag in the whole parade.[4]

Catalan identity also found expression among the Catalan members of the Spanish team. One of the first members to win a gold medal for Spain

---

[4] Interview with Xavier Vinyals, director general of the Catalan Olympic Committee.

and at a relatively early point in the Games, was a Catalan, Daniel Plaza, the twenty-kilometre walk winner, who proudly paraded himself around the track after his victory carrying a large *senyera*. The team quickly adopted the custom whereby medal winners celebrated their achievement with the customary victory lap wrapped in, or carrying, not only the Spanish flag but also the flag of their autonomous community. Since Catalan athletes won more medals than athletes from other regions, the Catalan flag was quite salient in this way. Whether this practice was spontaneous or officially sponsored is unclear, but when all Spain's gold-medal winners started to carry both the national emblem and the emblem of their region the effect was somewhat to reduce the impact of the Catalan flag. A factor complicating the signification of Catalonia as the salient nation in this case was the fact that the flags of the *autonomías* of Aragon and Valencia are the same as Catalonia's.

Few Catalan athletes went so far as actually to articulate any support for the nationalist cause. At the start of the Games, the tennis player Sergi Bruguera, declared himself to be Catalan rather than Spanish, and said that it would give him more satisfaction to carry the Catalan flag than the Spanish one. Valentí Massana who had entered the twenty-kilometre walk, declared that there was no such thing as Spanish athletics and that Spain did not gain medals; they were won by individuals and he would like to see Catalonia triumph. In contrast, some Catalan athletes, such as the waterpolo player Manuel Estiarte, the walker Mari Cruz Díaz and the runner Gaietà Cornet, when asked for their opinion in a COC survey, preferred to be members of a Spanish rather than a Catalan team (Antich, 1994: 286). Nor could COC muster the support of more than a minority among the Catalan sports federations for its campaign.

Alongside the Games, there was a very ambitious cultural programme, the *Olimpiada Cultural*, whose objectives were to provide platforms for dialogue and cultural exchange; to promote maximum participation in the Olympics by citizens, creators and artistic and cultural bodies and institutions; to express cultural tradition and strengthen cultural life; and to promote the image of the Games internationally. The programme included arts festivals, popular festivals, exhibitions, educational activities, historic landmarking of the city, scientific and cultural debates, music, opera and the performing arts, work in audio-visual arts, and six prizes for outstanding recent achievements in a variety of cultural fields. The *Olimpiada Cultural* does not seem to have fulfilled its potential as a means of projecting Catalan culture in parallel with the Games. It was overshadowed by them, ran into financial problems and its top management had to be changed.

Españolisation

While Catalanisation was much in evidence, there was also clear evidence of Españolisation. Outside Catalonia, the torch relay carrying the Olympic flame progressed slowly through each region, from Galicia in the north to Andalucía in the south, and thence to the Canaries and the Balearics, before finally returning to Barcelona five and a half weeks later. Apart from some isolated incidents where the occasion was taken as an opportunity to demonstrate a local grievance, the torch passed through local communities in a fiesta-like atmosphere. Local and national dignitaries took full advantage of the publicity opportunities afforded by its progress and participated prominently in the accompanying ritual and ceremonial. A steadily increasing national euphoria was thus generated as the weeks wore on. In Madrid even the king himself took an 'institutional turn' with the torch, that is, in a dignified, ceremonious manner as befitting a monarch he received the torch and directly passed it on to the next runner. The relay was thus turned into a warm celebration of Spanish national unity.

Indeed one of the most important aspects of Españolisation was the role played by the king and the royal family. As a head of state tutored by Franco, Juan Carlos may not be as popular in Catalonia, which Franco treated so badly and where there is a strong republican tradition, as in the rest of Spain; but he is appreciated and respected for his effective opposition to the 1981 attempted coup, and it would be a mistake to underestimate his popularity in the region.[5] The royal family, and the king in particular, are avid sports enthusiasts: throughout the Olympics the king and his family were present, obviously enjoying and, at times, in raptures over the proceedings, especially when Spain won medals. The king reacted like a typical overjoyed fan when Fermin Cacho crowned Spain's achievements by unexpectedly winning the blue riband event of the Games, the 1,500 metres. The presence of the royal family at the Games and their reactions were a constant focus of attention in the media. Thus the king and the royal family were able to associate themselves closely with what was a heavily Catalanised occasion, not only because the king was present as the head of state symbolising Spain's sovereignty over Catalonia, but because the king and the royal family are active, enthusiastic adherents of the very activity that on this occasion was doing symbolic work celebrating the unity of the two nations. Without the royals' sporting image, this symbolic appropriation of the proceedings would not have been as effective.

[5] See Preston (1986) for an account of the king's crucial role in aborting the coup.

We have already noted that the king in his first act of opening the Games injected a distinctly Catalan element by using Catalan. The enthusiastic response on the part of the Catalan audience indicated, however, that this gesture had also succeeded in unifying it symbolically with Spain. What followed next in the line of symbolic work was little short of a stroke of genius. As host nation, the place of the Spanish team in the march past of nations, according to Olympic protocol, is last. After an hour and a half of watching teams from 172 countries parade by, the crowd waited with anticipation for the entry of the Spanish team. Finally, the largest Spanish contingent ever to participate in an Olympics entered the stadium, dressed in the red and gold of Spain, led by the king's son, Felipe, the Prince of Asturias, bearing the Spanish national flag. The Prince is young, tall, athletic and handsome – and in this Olympics had been selected for the Spanish yacht team. The entry was greeted deliriously by the crowd and by the royal family. As the smiling prince led the national team past the tribune, his sister Elena could be seen on the huge stadium TV screen, and of course by everyone on TV, with tears streaming down her face. The king and royal family and everyone around them on the tribune had leapt to their feet waving and clapping, while those around them turned to shake hands with the king and congratulate him, and then congratulate each other warmly. At that moment the TV cameras focused on each of the major players on the tribune in turn – the king, Maragall, Felipe González, Narcis Serra and Jordi Pujol – waving, clapping and looking extremely pleased with the moment. The wild enthusiastic reaction continued unabated as the team continued around the track and the prince ascended the stage to deposit the Spanish flag there.

The music specially written for this moment by Carles Santos played a major part in stimulating the reception of the Spanish team. Before its entry the athletes' parade had trundled by to the relatively undifferentiated refrains of a medley based on Spanish classical and folk music, which, in fact, was not readily identifiable as Spanish and was comparatively muted in volume. At the entry of the Spanish team the music changed abruptly as the Spanish team sauntered into the stadium to the refrains of Santos' 'España'. The title belies the style of this piece, which was not at all Spanish in character. This was a Hollywood-style fanfare, an exuberant musical firework display, a richly orchestrated, loudly amplified paean of triumph, which filled the stadium with warmth, colour and excitement. The piece reached a crescendo as the prince reached the stage.

It was rumoured that the team uniforms, which for the first time were designed in the red and gold national colours of Spain, had been purposely designed that way so that the team could be seen as representing not only Spain but Catalonia as well (Catalonia's national colours are the same), thus making it difficult for Catalan malcontents to demonstrate against the team. Whether intentional or not, it worked extremely well and there was no dissent whatever from the vociferous acclamation for the Spanish team.

This team contained a greater proportion of members from Catalonia than from any other part of Spain, for Catalonia led the development of sport in Spain and has always been at the forefront. On the other hand, it was the Spanish team as such in which they paraded past the tribune before the Spanish head of state and with a Spanish prince at their head. When a Catalan won a gold medal it was a Spanish victory, for which the Spanish national anthem was played and the Spanish flag was raised at the victory ceremony. Catalonia was thus symbolically subsumed within the greater Spanish state-nation.

The great success of the Spanish team surprised everybody. They won medals right across the board, from the victory of their women's hockey team to Fermin Cacho's victory in the 1,500 metres for men, one of the last events of the Games – a total of twenty-two medals, including thirteen gold, giving Spain sixth place in the medal table (*El País*, 10 August 1992). Had Spain done badly, Españolisation would not have been so successful and the latent tension between Spain and Catalonia could well have surfaced.

Victory ceremonies at the Olympics are often seen as the quintessence of nationalism and it would be tempting to interpret the victory ceremonies for Spanish gold-medal winners in this light. However, they cannot reasonably be construed as expressions of Spanish nationalism, even though they deployed the Spanish national symbols, because the Spanish government was not playing nationalist politics. The national symbols in this instance signified a non-nationalist, civic conception of the nation. On the other hand, these ceremonies could hardly promote Catalan nationalism when the only symbols of Catalan culture incorporated in these ceremonies were Catalan as one of the official languages and the *pubillas*, the girl attendants dressed in Catalan national dress.

The Spanish state was also represented on the tribune throughout by key figures in the government. The most important of these, the president, Felipe González, was only present at the opening and closing ceremonies and his absence for the remainder of the time provoked some criticism in the media. Catalan nationalists were prone to interpret it as a slight on the part of a pesident who was more interested in Andalucía, his power base, which had been favoured by costly projects like Expo 92 in Seville and the high-speed train link between Saville and Madrid. The government's friends thought it might have been a tactical error to seem to be distancing himself from what was turning out to be such a successful affair, and Maragall, the socialist mayor of Barcelona and president of the Organising Committee, had to defend his absence. The second most important figure in the government, the vice-president Narcis Serra, a Catalan and former mayor of Barcelona who had been instrumental in getting the bid together for Barcelona, was, however, in constant attendance, and there were plenty of other ministers prominently in attendance as well, to show central government solidarity. It is important to understand that González's unpopularity in no way negated the function of the theatre of the great as a unifying symbol of the Spanish state: the criticism was directed not at the latter but at González himself and, to an extent, at the government over which he presided.

This theatre of the great played out on the tribune before the crowd and the television audience importantly, included parts for the Catalan political elite as well. The presence of Jordi Pujol, the Catalan president, and of Maragall, together with the head of state, the president and members of the national government, amid the foreign dignitaries, strongly signified the harmonious integration of Catalonia within the Spanish state.

Just as Catalan culture was prominently represented in certain spectacular sequences of the opening and closing ceremonies, so an image of Spain was presented in music, song, costume, dance, tableaux and drama. The 'Land of Passion', a sequence lasting a full fifteen minutes, followed the 'Sardana of Welcome' in the opening ceremony. Three hundred and sixty drummers from Aragon descended the steps of the stands and were joined by 300 musicians from Catalonia and the Levant, and 200 *bailaoras* (flamenco dancers) in the centre of the stadium. Simultaneously a giant tableau was mounted, created by Javier Mariscal, the designer of the Games mascot, Cobi. It depicted the achievements of Spanish painting in the form of figures from Velaquez's *Las Meninas* and from Goya's paintings, and of Spanish literature with figures from Cervantes' *Don Quixote*. On stage Placido Domingo, Spain's best-known opera singer, rendered a passionate Spanish love song, a *jota*, to a mysterious woman dressed in red, who entered the arena on a black stallion. It was Cristina Hoyos, Spain's most celebrated flamenco dancer and choreographer in theatre and film, and she gave a bravura performance on the vast stage, joining twelve pairs of dancers in the gay *Sevillanas* and the passionate *jaleo*. The sequence ended with Alfredo Kraus, another world-famous Spanish tenor, singing a well-known, nostalgic, popular air. At such points the cultural codes were switched abruptly, interrupting the pronounced Catalanity of the proceedings in keeping with the organisers' strategy of taking account of sensibilities in the rest of Spain, in order to achieve a cultural balance. The performance was well received. Though Catalans perhaps do not care to broadcast it, such aspects of Spanish popular culture as flamenco are popular in the region and Andalucía is a favourite holiday destination.

The closing ceremony contained a sequence lasting eight and a half minutes: *Love, the Magician*, pursuing the same hispanic theme. To Manuel de Falla's exhilarating, haunting and intensely emotional music, Cristina Hoyos and her troupe of flamenco *bailaoras* danced the bewitching 'will o' the wisp', while in the background Teresa Berganza, the Spanish mezzo-soprano, sung of the mystery of love. The sequence culminated in Falla's *Ritual Fire Dance*, a piece of music which probably more than any other in the popular imagination celebrates the hispanic soul.

For about thirteen minutes prior to the farewell speeches of the mayor of Barcelona, Pasqual Maragall, and the IOC president, Juan Antonio Samaranch, Spanish symbols were at the forefront once more, this time in the 'Salute to the Athletes' and the 'Raising of the Flags'. The Olympic fanfare heralds the last time the athletes will be acclaimed and the final parade of the flags of all the competing countries. In the spotlight at the head of the parade, advancing abreast, were the flags of Barcelona, Catalonia, Spain, and the European Community, together with the Olympic flag. The Spanish flag, in the centre of these five flags, was the focus of attention as the TV cameras picked it out and held it in close-up. 'The Ode To Joy' from Beethoven's ninth symphony (adopted by the European Union as its anthem) gave way to the upbeat, populist and exhilarating tones of the signature tune 'España' that had orchestrated the entry of the Spanish team in the athletes' parade at the opening ceremony. Taking their cue from the music, the Spanish TV commentators went into a eulogy on the theme of the Spanish team's performance, reciting 'Twenty-two medals'. The flags trooped past, by now as many as twelve abreast, until finally one solitary flag appeared a long way behind the others – the Spanish flag, carried by a female representative of the Spanish team in her red and gold costume. Walking alongside her was one of the girl attendants, also in red and gold. While the TV cameras focused exclusively on this image, Spanish TV commentators once more recited the Spanish team's success, 'Twenty-two medals, thirteen of them gold', and went through a roll call of their successful athletes. As the Spanish flag arrived on stage, 'España' reached its climax, signifying in true Hollywood style the perfect happy ending to the story of the past fortnight.

As the host country, Spain was one of three countries who were specially honoured by having their flags raised and their national anthems played. The others were Greece as the cradle of the Games in antiquity, and the United States, as the host country of the next Games to be held in Atlanta in 1996.

Crowd behaviour in the Olympic stadium and other venues is a further indication of the presence of influences at work tending to counteract the impact of Catalanisation. Audiences were composed not only of Catalans but of visitors from the rest of Spain as well as from abroad. What was noticeable as the Games progressed was the gradual emergence of the Spanish flag among the crowd, whereas it had hardly made an appearance in this context at the beginning. There was, in other words, a creeping manifestation of pride in the Spanish flag, after years in which it was anathema in Catalonia. It even made its appearance in that temple of Catalan nationalism, the Barcelona Football Club stadium, when Guardiola, one of the Spanish team's Catalan players and a Barça star well known for his Catalan patriotism, draped himself in the Spanish flag. Maragall's niece, a member of Spain's winning women's hockey team, did the same (*El País*, 10 August 1992). Such expressions of loyalty to Spain would have been hardly thinkable, let alone tolerated, just a short time before.

6   Symbolising the international dimension

Clearly the rich symbolic content of the Games was not confined to the representation of Catalonia and Spain. Alongside, and interacting with these processes, there were other forces pulling the Games, at least potentially, in quite different directions. Four aspects need to be considered in this respect: Olympic internationalism, Europeanisation, Americanisation and the question of global culture.

Olympic internationalism

A species of internationalism constitutes the chief rationale of the Olympic movement: it is implicit in, and permeates every aspect of, the language and symbolism of Olympism. De Coubertin sought to revive in the form of the modern Olympic movement what he saw as the spirit of the ancient Greek Games – a spirit which sanctioned the pursuit of excellence in sporting competition, while setting aside quarrels and rivalries between the different city states. Participants came from all over the Greek world and the suspension of armed conflict during the Games gave the competition the character of a truce (Finley and Pleket, 1976). In the ideology of Olympism this noble ideal is elided with the claim that the Olympic movement in fact functions to bring diverse nations and peoples together: that it facilitates communication, cultural interchange and a growth in mutual understanding, and thereby makes an important contribution to world peace. We are interested not so much in the truth of this dubious claim but in how Olympic internationalism was registered in the Barcelona Olympics and to what extent, if at all, it is likely to have impinged on the process of Catalanisation which was proceeding in parallel.

According to the Olympic charter, certain acts must take place during the opening and closing ceremonies. The athletes in their 'delegations', that is, the teams, greet the head of state of the host country and the president of the IOC as they file past them; the president of the games Organising Committee and the president of the IOC make speeches of welcome; the Olympic flag enters and is raised to the strains of the

Olympic anthem; the Olympic flame is lit; the Olympic oath is taken by representatives of the athletes and officials; the president of the IOC makes the closing speech, symbolically hands over the Games to the next Olympic city and calls on everyone to assemble in four years time for the next Games. The majority of these acts take place in the opening ceremony and they are among the most highly ritualised acts of the Games. Powerfully charged with Olympic internationalist ideology, they transmit it in the main in the way that the Olympic flag, the key symbol of Olympic internationalism, is deployed. Designed by de Coubertin himself, the five interlocking, coloured rings – blue, yellow, black, green and red on a white background – represent the unity of the five continents. It is the most prominent flag in the Games: it constitutes the main focus of attention in specific ceremonies and ritual acts devoted to celebrating Olympic internationalism. Also, it is flown over the main stadium and at the Olympic sub-sites of which, in the case of the Barcelona Games, there were fourteen spread over Catalonia.

The athletes' parade in the opening ceremony was projected by the organisers as representative of all races, religions and ideas in the 'Games of peace and reunion'. More countries were represented than at any previous Games: 172 teams from 183 countries, all distinctively clothed, many in their national costume, speaking seventy different languages filed past the tribune. Each team was preceded by one of COOB's young women attendants carrying a placard with the country's name followed by a team standard bearer carrying its national flag. The carnival tone was set for the 'March of the Heroes', as the programme described it, when eighty young girl rhythmic gymnasts entered at the head of the parade, weaving patterns in the air with their coloured ribbons and performing acrobatics, as they jauntily moved along to a medley of Spanish classical and folk tunes. There was no hint of militarism here. An immediate and continual interaction between parade and audience ensued: athletes waved, smiled, laughed and gesticulated in response to the enthusiastic reception each section of the crowd gave them, as they moved at a leisurely pace around the stadium (the officials, who tended to be older, were somewhat more staid). Groups supporting individual teams and bearing their national symbols in the form of flags, placards, banners, painted faces, clothing or whatever, expressed themselves volubly and good-naturedly, rather than in a partisan manner. The multicoloured parade, the music, the happy relaxed demeanour of the athletes and the carefree manner in which the audience participated generated, above all, a festive atmosphere for the hour and a half or more it took for the 15,000 athletes and officials to file past the tribune and finally assemble in the centre of the arena.

A number of smaller third world countries were represented in the parade by token teams of a few members or, in some cases, by a few officials. Such countries have few opportunities to attract the world's attention, except perhaps, in the context of some disaster or other, and as competitors they were unlikely to do so. Therefore their chief objective was to use the parade as a way of being seen on the world stage.

Some notable examples of countries that had been split by conflict and had come together for these Games, and of others which had emerged from independence struggles, were on display. South Africa, which had been excluded from the Games and treated as a pariah state for thirty years because of its apartheid regime, now appeared transmogrified into the new post-apartheid South Africa, represented by a smiling, relaxed, racially mixed team, led by a black standard bearer. The team, and a beaming president-to-be, Nelson Mandela looking down from the tribune from among the many foreign dignitaries, were received warmly by the audience and together they provided one of the main foci of attention in TV coverage. German reunification after the collapse of the German Democratic Republic in 1989 and the ending of the cold war was signified by the appearance of a truly united German team in an Olympics for the first time since 1936.[1] The twelve republics of the former Soviet Union, still in the chaotic aftermath of the break-up, had nevertheless managed to unify themselves into a single team for these Games. In contrast, the three new Baltic states demonstrated their newly won independence by fielding separate teams. A newly united Yemen was represented for the first time. The appearance for the first time of teams representing Bosnia Herzegovina, Croatia and Slovenia poignantly reminded the audience that their independence came at a price and that conflict in Yugoslavia was continuing. Their appearance was warmly received.

In the above ways the parade was an impressive expression of peace, friendship and international solidarity. At only one point was this celebration of fraternity interrupted, and that was when the Iraqi team was briefly whistled at by the audience. Iraq's recent invasion of Kuwait had incurred widespread international opprobrium, so far from departing from the internationalist spirit of the occasion, this reaction to the Iraqis served to confirm the spirit of internationalism.

From a platform which revolved over a mappa mundi placed in front of the grandstand, the mayor of Barcelona and president of the Organising

---

[1] Because the IOC refused to recognise a separate East German team, a single team represented the two Germanies from 1956 to 1960 in the summer Games and in 1964 in the winter Games.

Committee, Pasqual Maragall, and the president of the IOC, Juan Antonio Samaranch, made their speeches of welcome. Both strongly emphasised the internationalist spirit of the occasion. Maragall carried a message from the secretary of the United Nations stating his wish and his hope that the agreement of 17 July relating to the Olympic truce would be implemented, and good sense and civilised behaviour would be restored in Europe. This was a reference to the war in Yugoslavia. Samaranch talked of the occasion as a dream come true, of which de Coubertin would have been proud: the youth of the world was assembled in Barcelona; the Games were the greatest festival of contemporary society; the large number of foreign heads of state in attendance signified the Games' importance for peace and understanding; thanks were due to the many in Spain and throughout the world who had contributed.

The Olympic flag now made its official entrance, accompanied by a musical tribute composed by Mikis Theodorakis and sung by the Greek mezzo-soprano Agnes Baltza. Theodorakis in person conducted the orchestra of ninety-six musicians and a choir of 120 singers, as the flag was carried around the stadium in the horizontal position by six Spanish athletes and two volunteers dressed in white, the colour symbolising peace. Theodorakis had been imprisoned for three years under the miltary junta that had seized power in Greece in 1967. The presence of these Greek celebrities and Theodorakis' music symbolised the Greek origins of the Games and also, in a more subtle way, a contemporary triumph of peace over conflict, for a democratic regime succeeded the junta in the mid-1970s, in which Theodorakis became a government minister.

The music was rather unmelodious, somewhat ponderous and set to a pounding rhythm. Agnes Baltza was to be seen on rear centre stage in silhouette, a stark priestess-like figure dressed entirely in black, shrouded in stage mist, and making her delivery with exaggerated dramatic gestures, to all intents and purposes a phantom in full cry. The festive atmosphere was having to give way at that moment to what, clearly, was being signalled as sacred ritual. The flag having now arrived at the side of the stage, where it would be raised on an eighteen-metre pole to fly for the duration of the Games, the occasion now reached a point of great solemnity. To the strains of the Olympic anthem, the flag was raised. The music, by another Greek, Spiros Samara, dated from 1896, the first Games of the modern era, held appropriately enough in Athens. The three verses were sung from the stage by Alfredo Kraus, the well-known Spanish tenor, one verse in Catalan, one in Spanish and one in French. The words by Costas Palamas were adopted in 1957:

Immortal Spirit of antiquity,
Father of the true, beautiful and good,
Descend, appear, shed over us thy light
Upon this ground and under this sky
Which has first witnessed thy unperishable fame.

Give life and animation to these noble games!
Throw wreaths of fadeless flowers to the victors
In the race and in the strife!
Create in our breasts hearts of steel!

In thy light, plains, mountains and seas
Shine in a roseate hue and form a vast temple
To which all nations throng to adore thee,
O immortal spirit of antiquity.

It is doubtful whether the sentiments expressed here in this rather over-blown language accorded with those of the audience. In any case, since the words were hardly familiar, the main effect was conveyed by the rousing and again rather strident sound of the music and by the visual image of the flag spotlighted in the evening light, as it was slowly hoisted. In this part of the ceremony the continuity of the Games with Greek antiquity, and the universality of what the Games purportedly represent in these terms, was very heavily emphasised.

In contrast to this traditional, ritualised format constrained by Olympic protocol, the next sequence played on the internationalist theme in an entirely different show business fashion, celebrating the history of the modern Games and how it blended with the present and future. Twenty-five model girls, each one wearing a costume inspired by the landscape, culture and symbols of the city of Barcelona, which had been created by twelve leading Spanish designers and entitled the 'Barcelona Collection', strutted on stage to music, with the great Marathon Gate in the back-ground. From the opposite end of the stadium twenty-four young men, each representing one of the previous Olympic cities, ran at short inter-vals through a narrow gap between the assembled athletes to the stage carrying an Olympic flag, while the date and city that each represented was announced dramatically, in chronological order, from 1896 to 1992. Symbolising the fact that the 1916, 1940 and 1944 Games were cancelled due to the two world wars, and that the Games are only held in peacetime, the three flags representing those years bore the emblem adopted by the peace movement in the 1960s, Picasso's dove of peace. Picasso, of course, was a leading light in Barcelona's artistic avant-garde before moving to France. The provenance of the music to this sequence, composed by Angelo Badalamenti, who also wrote the music for the film *Blue Velvet* and the TV crime soap opera *Twin Peaks*, was unequivocally the mainstream pop music industry. The total effect of the sequence was to glamorise internationalism. We will return to this point in a moment when we discuss the arrival of the sacred flame in the stadium and the lighting of the cauldron that preceded the oath-taking ceremony.

With the Olympic oath ceremony which followed, the proceedings reverted once again to a solemn ritual act. On stage, beneath the sacred flame, with the Olympic flag flying at the side of the stage and over the stadium, and in the presence of all the flag bearers as witnesses, one of the Spanish athletes holding the Olympic flag in his left hand and with the right hand raised, swore:

In the name of all the competitors, I promise that we shall take part in these Olympic Games, respecting and abiding by the rules which govern them, in the true spirit of sportsmanship, for the glory of sport and the honour of our teams.

A Spanish judge adopting the same stance, swore:

In the name of all the judges and officials, I promise that we shall officiate in these Olympic Games with complete impartiality; respecting and abiding by the rules which govern them, in the true spirit of sportsmanship.

The qualities upheld here – respect for the rules, sportsmanship, the glory of sport, the honour of the teams, and complete impartiality – through the imagery of the Olympic flag, were explicitly linked to the ideal of peace and friendship between nations.

One of the most striking expressions of internationalism occurred imme-diately after the oath-taking had finished, when sixty-two volunteers unfurled an Olympic flag of 114 metres in length, with which they com-pletely covered the 15,000 assembled athletes in the centre of the arena, to the accompaniment of the instrumental and choral version of the official slogan 'Friends for Life' (*Amigos Para Siempre*), composed by Andrew Lloyd Webber for the Games. 'The Great Flag of Friendship' astonished, enchanted and amused audience and athletes alike and brought once more the festive element to the forefront. The TV coverage carried an aerial view from directly above the brightly illuminated stadium, showing the entire centre filled by the flag literally covering the nations of the world. It was an extraordinarily vivid image flashed across the world and to the stadium audience via the large stadium screen. The cameras also moved about among the athletes, who were jostling and laughing together in the space underneath the flag, some helping to hold the flag up and all evidently thoroughly enjoying the sensation.

The orchestral and choral version of what was a typical catchy, senti-mental Lloyd Webber melody certainly contributed significantly to the creation of the carefree atmosphere of friendship. Curiously the lyrics, which were not sung until the closing ceremony, revealed that the song was not only about friendship, but a love affair, no less, between Barcelona and Olympism, which was to be consummated, at least in the minds of the organisers, in the closing ceremony. Olympic internationalism was being made sexy. Hyperbole apart, the moment constituted a most spectacular image of international fraternity and identity and of universal humanity.

The aura of internationalism was strongly reinforced by the presence of so many foreign dignitaries on the tribune, enacting their subsidiary parts in the theatre of the great. In his opening speech Samaranch had referred to their presence as evidence of the international importance of the Olympic enterprise and, indeed, as president of the IOC he must have had contact with more heads of state, great and small, than almost anyone else alive. Thirty-two heads of state, or other dignitaries representing their countries, were present for the opening ceremony. Some, like John Major, had come before; others were due to attend later. It was an impressive number, but hardly representative of the 183 countries parading past the tribune. Of the thirty-two, half represented Latin American countries, due no doubt to the fact that Latin America has close historical and cultural ties with Spain, and also in all probability because Latin Americans play the game of international sports politics rather well and are strongly represented in the network of international sport. Just over a third were from Europe and the majority of these were from Western Europe. Five were from Asia, the majority being from the Far East. Only one was from Africa. Obviously some were taking advantage of the occasion to deal with a particular problem on the diplomatic front. Fidel Castro, for example, to be seen seated just below the Spanish king, beaming and waving as his team passed the stand, was desperate for Cuba to make the most of this opportunity to escape its increasing isolation in the new world order. No doubt Nelson Mandela was present at this prestigious event as part of the good public relations work his racially mixed team was doing for the new South Africa.

The internationalist theme provided a thread for the Games from start to finish. Strongly trumpeted in the opening ceremony, it was re-addressed and reinforced during the second part of the closing ceremony – in Maragall's and Samaranch's farewell speeches, in the handover to the next Olympic city, Atlanta, and with the lowering of, and farewell to, the Olympic flag.

Maragall, in his closing speech, once again characterised the Olympic spirit as a force for peace and friendship and expressed his disappointment that war was still going on around the world, despite recent international agreements and the Pope's message of peace on the occasion of the Olympics. He hoped that sport would not have to suffer from the arrogance of culture (a covert criticism, perhaps, of the nationalists' attempts to Catalanise the Games), nor culture suffer from the arrogance of power and money, nor the cities from the arrogance of commercialisation. These rather terse, enigmatic remarks seem to have been aimed at upholding the Olympic ideals against the economic and political tide they had encountered, but coming from the president of COOB, which had done so much to connive at commercialisation and political intervention, it sounded rather hollow. Samaranch managed to convey the impression, by the way he effusively thanked all those who in his opinion had made these the best Games ever (he decorated Maragall with the Olympic Order for his special contribution), that the whole world was thereby united. Once more he referred to the peace and friendship the Games expressed.

The moment for the handover had arrived. The Olympic fanfare sounded. On the great stage stood Maragall, the mayor of Barcelona and president of the Organising Committee, the mayor of Atlanta, the American city of the next Games, and Samaranch, the president of the IOC. Maragall, in his capacity as mayor of Barcelona, took the Olympic flag with its staff and through the hands of the president of the IOC passed on the Olympic heritage to the mayor of Atlanta. This act, according to the Olympic charter, is the central event of the closing ceremonies and symbolises the continuity of the Olympic movement. Samaranch then called on the youth of the world to meet in Atlanta in four years time.

Great effort was put into making the lowering of the Olympic flag a memorable last solemn ritual act of the Games. As the Olympic anthem played, softly and more sweetly than in the opening ceremony, the flag was gently lowered. Sixteen children dressed in white, the symbol of peace, received the flag in the horizontal position, and as they conveyed it away across the stadium Placido Domingo, centre stage, began to sing, accompanied by the rich sound of the combined choirs of the Orfeó Català, the Coral Sant Jordi and the Coral Càrmina, three of the foremost Catalan choirs. As the flag was carried along it passed directly over the TV cameras, leaving viewers at home and in the stadium with a final close-up image of international fraternity.

The sacred flame, symbol of life itself, burning in the huge cauldron next to the classical portico of the Marathon Gate, was then gradually extinguished to the music of 'El Cant dels Ocells' ('The Song of the Birds'), a song symbolising universal peace played on the cello by Lluís Claret and sung by Victòria de los Ángeles. These were nostalgic, emotional moments which subtly, yet powerfully, invoked the ideals of peace and universal brotherhood at the core of modern Olympic ideology, and which had been orchestrated in so many different ways throughout the previous days.

Europeanisation

In 1984 the governments of the twelve member states of the European Community formed an *ad hoc* committee to find ways of strengthening European identity. In 1985 the resultant Adonnino Report, among other things, charged the European Commission with encouraging sport and supporting sporting activities as an important element in European integration. In 1989 the Commission launched its Olympic programme to develop the Community's presence at the 1992 Olympic Games, a programme which had the full backing of COOB and the IOC. The rationale at that time was that they would be the last Games in the twentieth century to be held in Europe and they would coincide with the completion of the Single Market and the elimination of internal barriers to trade. A more long-term consideration was that sport and sport-related activities were estimated to make up 2.5 per cent of the value of world trade, a fact that the Single Market could not afford to ignore (European Commission, 1992). There was, however, a more pressing reason for the European Community to take a keen interest in the Olympics: its image had been rather badly tarnished, as a result of the loss of momentum to European integration caused by the mounting opposition in several member states to ratifying the Maastricht Treaty on political and monetary union.

The Community Olympic programme spent fifteen and a half million ECUs on the Games (four million went to the Winter Games Organising Committee in Albertville, six million to COOB, one million to the Paralympic Games, and four and a half million for an information and communications campaign). The information activities included special campaigns about the Community in the host cities; a travelling exhibition about recent Community initiatives; the promotion of Europe's high-definition television, including continuous broadcasts of the Games; an advertising campaign; the promotion of a Europe-wide anti-doping code; and finally, a visual presence for the EEC in the Olympic opening ceremonies.

The most explicit ways in which there was an attempt to articulate a form of European identity occurred in the concluding part of the opening ceremony, which was specially devoted to 'Music and Europe'. It was also articulated in the way the EEC flag was deployed in general, during the

'Salute to the Athletes' in the second part of the closing ceremony and, finally, in the well-publicised appearances of Jacques Delors, the president of the European Commission, in the theatre of the great on the tribune.

Arguably some element of 'Europeanism' was also implicit in other aspects, for example in the Hellenism of the second part of the opening ceremony and in the Mediterranean, Olympic Sea sequence, where the Graeco-Roman origins of Western civilisation were narrated. While it is the case that ritual symbols have many referents and they may thereby be made to signify more than one thing simultaneously, it would be stretching credulity to maintain that Europeanism was the dominant meaning of these two sequences, or indeed, as thirdworldist ideology would have it, that European ethnocentrism dominated the proceedings as a whole. Earlier we argued that the Hellenistic sequences articulated internationalism; and in the previous chapter we argued that the Mediterranean, Olympic Sea epic articulated Catalanism. The issue here is what constitutes the dominant meaning of the symbol and how this depends upon its configuration. The 'Sardana of Welcome' at the beginning of the opening ceremony illustrates the point well. The five rings of the Olympic flag form a well-recognised international symbol: however, when it was modified by the *sardana* being danced in a formation of five interlinking rings to Catalan music and Catalan song its meaning was transformed so that it became predominantly a symbol of Catalanism.

The concluding part of the opening ceremony began with the *castellers* or human pyramids which we previously categorised as an aspect of the process of Catalanisation, but it was also clearly intended to signify identification with Europe in the shape of the EEC. Here is an example of symbolic work conveying two meanings simultaneously without any contradiction between them. The twelve pyramids constructed by sixteen teams from all over Catalonia represented the twelve countries of the European community at the time. Building one of these pyramids is fraught with risk, and requires strength, intelligence, precision, unity and solidarity – qualities which, as the organisers maintained, were required for the construction of Europe. This Europe, according to the publicity material, was the largest market in the world and the cradle of democracy and liberty, reflecting the richness of its cultural diversity (COOB, 1992a: 59–60). This was the message that its EEC sponsor had paid COOB to project.

The main way in which Europe was represented during these Games was through its great musical tradition. Opera symbolised Europe in a sequence entitled 'Opera, Music for the World' in which seventeen familiar well-loved arias were sung, solo and in chorus, by six world-famous Spanish opera stars – Placido Domingo, Montserrat Caballé, Teresa

Berganza, Joan Pons, Jaume Aragall and Josep Carreras. This 'universal music' was presented as the product of the world's greatest opera composers: these turned out to be Bizet, Verdi, Offenbach, Puccini, Leoncavallo, Rossini and Bellini. There is an artistic sense in which opera is universal, so the organisers could, with some plausibility, claim that the European theme was compatible with Olympic universalism, although it was difficult to escape the thought that this particular selection represented not so much Europe's openness to the world, as Spain, France and Italy's openness.

The most spectacular way in which an image of Europe was projected was in the 'Ode to Joy' sequence that followed the opera sequence. Beethoven set verses from Schiller's poem, 'Ode to Joy' to the prelude of the final movement of his ninth symphony, and it was adopted by the EEC as its anthem. Schiller's poem and Beethoven's music express the Enlightenment ideal of universal brotherhood. What the EEC was interested in primarily, however, was European unity and identity. The organisers contrived to bridge the gap by asserting that the anthem signified the unity of the peoples of Europe with the other peoples of the world (COOB, 1992a: 64).

The 'Ode to Joy' is among the most moving passages of music that have ever been written, and it was performed by the City of Barcelona Orchestra, the three Catalan choirs mentioned previously, and the six opera singers. The voice of a boy soloist began the anthem, a child's innocence signifying peace. He was dressed in blue and on his chest bore the emblem of the EEC, a circle of twelve gold stars on a royal blue background. This flag was adopted in 1986 and is said to have a connection with de Coubertin's Olympic flag, in that each of the circles in the latter stands for one of the continents and, by chance, the blue one stands for Europe. It was this colour that was chosen as the colour of the background to the EEC flag. The twelve gold stars represent the heraldic symbol of perfection and have nothing to do with the number of countries in the EEC.

The verses were sung in Catalan, Spanish and German, and as the sublime sound of Beethoven's music filled the stadium, the night sky above exploded with a myriad of shining stars to represent the stars of Europe. Simultaneously members of the audience, who had been given blue or gold lights according to where they were sitting, held them up to form a gigantic EEC flag. The performance culminated in a stunningly brilliant fireworks display. The grand finale of the opening ceremony thus gave the last word, as it were, to Europe and the EEC. Catalan TV picked out Jordi Pujol clapping enthusiastically. Why he, in particular, should be doing so we will come to in a moment.

The EEC anthem and flag also occupied a privileged place in the closing ceremony in the 'Salute to the Athletes' sequence. In the second part of the closing ceremony all the national and the other flags were paraded in a column which advanced the length of the stadium from the south end towards the stage on which they were finally to assemble. The flags were borne by team representatives and COOB's costumed young women standard bearers. Representatives of the athletes and officials were seated with the public in the stands at the sides of the stadium. It was dark, and as the parade advanced the standard bearers were picked out by powerful lights. At the head of the column five flags advanced abreast of each other: those of Barcelona, Catalonia and Spain, together with the Olympic and the EEC flags. The parade advanced to the EEC anthem, the 'Ode to Joy', rendered once again by the mass choir and full orchestra. It was an emotional occasion and the Spanish TV commentary continually alluded to the emotional impact. To have the parade starting with the music of the EEC anthem and to include the EEC flag among the five that led the whole parade at this juncture, towards the close of the Games, was indeed, a coup for the EEC, as if to say that Europe leads the world.

The EEC connection was concretised by the presence of Jacques Delors, the president of the European Commission, on a five-day break from Brussels 'watching the Games . . . [where he was to be seen taking a prominent part in the theatre of the great on the tribune] . . . and meeting international leaders' (*City of Barcelona Daily Newsletter*, 30 July 1992). The highly publicised presence of Delors not only signified the importance the EEC attached to the Games but, like the EEC flag and anthem, the person of Delors symbolised their European identity.

There was a further connection. Delors was there to confer with Maragall, to whom the Community made a 'symbolic contribution' of 780,000 pesetas, about the role of municipalities and regions in Europe's progress towards unity. The talks were said to be part of the frequent rounds of conversations that they had with each other about the creation of a more integrated Europe and the role that cities played in it. They discussed the constitution of the Committee of the Regions, set up at the Maastricht summit. Maragall's close interest in this stemmed from the fact that he had been elected president of the Council of European Municipalities and Regions, and the question of who was to represent Spain on the new committee involved his rival Pujol, who was soon to become its president. Maragall, in his closing speech already referred to, returned to the European theme when he declared, in rounding off his speech, that Barcelona was the capital of Catalonia, an ancient capital in a new pluralistic Spain and in a new united Europe – a Europe in which cities have a future.

What of Delors' talks with international leaders? No details emerged about these, but given the presence of a good proportion of representatives from EEC countries (France, Italy, Germany, Belgium, Luxembourg and Spain) and the British prime minister having also visited close to the opening of the Games, it is perhaps not beyond the realm of possibility that some conferring on the tensions over implementation of the Maastricht agreement did occur.

In these Games there was a symbiotic relationship between Catalan nationalism, Olympic internationalism and Europeanisation. Catalan nationalism, as a species of minority nationalism, typically seeks to legitimate itself externally beyond the confines of Spain. It needs allies in its struggle against the state to maximise its degree of independence. The Olympics, therefore, provided a golden opportunity to publicise the nationalist cause, to differentiate Catalonia from Spain, to step on to the international stage and enthusiastically to embrace internationalism. In particular Catalan nationalists, like their counterparts elsewhere in Europe such as Scotland, look to the EEC's regional policy as a way to create a 'Europe of the Regions' which will enable them to loosen their ties with their host states, and give them an increasing voice in a reshaped Europe in which the larger, more powerful states have been weakened. For Catalan nationalists the EEC is thus looked upon as a counterweight to the host state.

Americanisation

Americanisation pervaded the Barcelona Games. It was readily identifiable in pure form, as it were, at certain points in and around the Games, but mostly it was so embedded in their general character that it was difficult to pinpoint and to categorise as a specifically American influence. The main problem here is that of differentiating American from global culture. The former in many ways merges with the latter and this is not fortuitous, for Americanisation, while not synonymous with globalisation, is at its leading edge, and this being the case, we would expect the Games as a global enterprise to exhibit Americanisation to a significant degree.

Perhaps we can best illustrate the difficulty here by taking a key instance from the opening ceremony – the entry of the Olympic flame into the stadium and the lighting of the Olympic flame. By now it was night time. An athlete would enter the stadium at the south end carrying the Olympic torch. It was to be handed over to a second athlete to take the final stage of the relay to the Marathon Gate and then up the central steps on to the stage. There an archer waited for his arrow to be lit from the torch; the arrow would then be launched to light the cauldron carrying the sacred flame for the duration of the Games. The cauldron, twenty-one metres high, with a dish of four by three metres, rose twelve metres above the stadium and was some distance away from the archer, so it required great skill and precision on the archer's part to light it in this way. The manner in which this was staged was in pure Hollywood style, a classic show business dramatic spectacle. The method of lighting had been kept a secret. For the first time an archer's arrow would light the sacred flame. The athlete carrying the torch entered the stadium to the strains of music one associates with Hollywood films like *Ben Hur*. The composer Angelo Badalamenti's compositions had been performed by a string of show business figures – Liza Minelli, Roberta Flack, George Benson, Dusty Springfield and Shirley Bassey among them – and this music was redolent of those characteristic moments in show business when the audience is induced by every trick in the book to gasp at the sensational spectacle before its very eyes. The archer's arrow had been designed by a special-effects artist, Reyes Abades, who had worked not only with leading film and TV directors in Spain, but with the Hollywood directors Ridley Scott and Richard Lester. The music built up the tension as the spotlight followed the torch around the stadium and finally reached the archer highlighted on the stage. The arrow was lit, the bow pulled back, and the flaming arrow launched at its target. The cauldron sprang into life with a flame three metres high, which could be seen from virtually all over the city. The audience loved it. What they did not know was, as in the best Hollywood show business tradition, that the success of the illusion was guaranteed: if the arrow had missed its mark it had been arranged that the cauldron would have been lit at that moment by an alternative method.

An American team was responsible for the choreography of various pieces in the opening ceremony. They had worked on large-scale choreography projects around the world directing, choreographing and producing the Superbowl shows, the opening of the Disney Studios in Orlando and a British Airways spot for the Los Angeles Games. Consequently, although the various pieces on which the team had worked in the opening ceremony did convey specific meanings, the fact that it was done in what was, to all intents and purposes, an American idiom, was also not without significance.

In these two examples of American influence, it was the packaging rather than the content that was American. In the closing ceremony, where, near the end, the handover to Atlanta was made, we had an example of American mass culture inserting itself into, and temporarily taking over, the Barcelona Games in terms of its content as well. The handover ceremony to the mayor of Atlanta was followed by a show put together by the Atlanta Games Organising Committee, presenting Atlanta as the next Olympic city. A video of the modern city was shown, and its history was evoked with reference to the film *Gone with the Wind* and a music and dance spectacular whose central theme was sport. It drew on the popular music and dance of modern America, particularly black America, to present a lively, colourful and energetic jazz ballet. The racial mix of the performers reflected the racial mix of the city, the headquarters of Coca Cola, one of the biggest sponsors of the Olympic Games. The Atlanta Games mascot 'What is it', a Disneyesque concoction, was the focus of the final part of this presentation.

The American presence was also registered in the great number of gold medals won by American athletes: in winning these Olympic Games, America made them in a sense its own. The stars and stripes was the most visible flag to be raised at the victors' podium and the American national anthem was the one most frequently played in the victory ceremonies that punctuated the proceedings throughout the two weeks of competition.

The most overt sign of Americanisation was the way in which the city and the Spanish mass media, especially the TV channels, were saturated with symbols of American capitalism – that is, with American corporate advertising. American companies had bought into the Olympics in a big way: they were cleansing their profane images with the spirit of Olympism and associating themselves to the maximum degree possible with images of youth, vitality and Olympic idealism to promote themselves and sell their products. They were not the only ones: European and Japanese companies did the same, but the important thing to note is that they were imitators: capitalising in this way on the Olympics was pioneered by American companies, notably at the 1984 Los Angeles Olympics. Symptomatic of American commercial opportunism, that doyen of American fast food, MacDonalds, opened a branch that was strategically located immediately adjacent to the newly developed Olympic village and marina area. Indeed, one could argue that the whole process of commercialising the Olympics was American-led, if we also bear in mind, the role of the American TV companies as the major source of revenue for the IOC and the Games' organisers. The role played by NBC, which had successfully secured the American rights for the last three Olympics, was crucial in this respect. It was also in part a covert role, for as purchaser of the rights to broadcast the Games for the benefit of the largest audience in the world, it was in a position to negotiate the scheduling of the events, so that they would coincide as far as possible with American peak viewing times and thus attract the maximum amount of advertising revenue.

Global culture

In cultural terms these Games were a pot pourri: a mixture of diverse elements and influences. Taken as a whole, they were neither one thing nor the other: riddled with hard-bitten commercialism, they were yet full of high ideals; they were sacred as well as profane; authentic in some respects, and quite artificial and false in others; politicised in key ways and apolitical in others; a mixture of the festive, the carnivalesque and the spectacular on the one hand, and of solemn ritual and ceremonial on the other; inflected with nationalism, yet also with internationalism; European, yet American; rooted and rootless. What was true of the Games as a whole was often true of its composite elements, most of which cannot simply be slotted into a single category. That is why in the foregoing analysis some aspects, such as the athletes' parade, fall into several different categories: it was internationalist and Españolised, it was festive and spectacular. Some aspects do not seem to fit easily into any category. In other words, the Games encapsulated the emergent global culture.

Take the Mediterranean, Olympic Sea spectacle, which we have examined previously in terms of the way it projected Catalan cultural nationalism. The accompanying music was extremely important in creating the exciting and exotic atmosphere of this sequence. The composer was Ryuichi Sakamoto, a Japanese artist, not based in Japan, but living in New York, who has worked with Bernardo Bertolucci, the Italian film director, on the music for his films *The Last Emperor* and *The Sheltering Sky*. He had just made an LP of his music, has been an actor and produces videos. His music here was not recognisably Japanese or Spanish; neither was it Western, as such. The nondescript character in cultural terms, it seems, admirably suited it to its task, for it was cast in a form familiar to, and appreciated by, a global audience.

The performers' costumes in the overture sequence of the opening ceremony, as well as certain other designs, were the work of Peter Minshall, an artist who has worked in the theatre, sculpture and painting. He was born in Guyana, brought up in Trinidad, and had taken part in shows all over the world: for example, he had worked for the Trinidad Carnival and with Jean Michel Jarre on one of his big performances in Paris. Clearly there was a global market for his kind of work.

The Olympic song 'Friends for Life' has already been examined in terms of the way it projected the theme of internationalism in the opening ceremony, when the orchestral and choral version accompanied the unfurling of the Olympic flag over the heads of the assembled athletes and officials. In the closing ceremony it was performed as a duet between Josep Carreras and Sarah Brightman. Here was Josep Carreras, a leading tenor from the world of opera and the serious concert platform, and Sarah Brightman, from the world of the popular light musical show, singing an Andrew Lloyd Webber love song to each other. At that moment pure pop entertainment culture took over, internationalism was superseded, and we could have been at a pop concert almost anywhere; that is, we were transported into the depthless, context-free realm of global culture.

In these three examples the artists work on the global stage. The culture in which they are involved is rootless – Sakamoto's music, Minshall's designs and Lloyd Webber's song could be at home almost anywhere. The Olympics, as a quintessentially global phenomenon, had sucked into its orbit artists like these and many other cultural professionals and specialists operating on the world stage, and what was produced as a result was a characteristically cosmopolitan, and in some ways quite bizarre addition to the emerging global cultural repertoire. It is not difficult to find other aspects exhibiting the same features. As the Games unfolded, their global cultural character became more evident. In the celebratory third part of the closing ceremony, the Games mascot Cobi was whisked off into space in a giant shining boat, accompanied by the planets and the Sun, while a hundred musicians and a choir played him on his way. The technical specialists and artists in this case were Spanish, but there was nothing especially Spanish about it. Technically brilliant as it was, it was also the stuff of theme parks all over the world. The Games were concluded on a note of fiesta with a rumba medley played by three bands. The vibrant rhythmic music was said to be authentically Catalan and to combine *mestizo*, gypsy and flamenco roots, but when audience joined athletes in the dancing and the stage was invaded, to the consternation of the organisers, whatever authenticity this music may have possessed seemed to be dissipated in the cosmopolitan jamboree that ensued.

Internationalism, Europeanisation, Americanisation and global culture were not imposed on the Olympics. The organisers positively embraced these influences because there were advantages to be gained by doing so. And they were no impediment to Catalan nationalism: they did not cut across it, divert attention from it or cancel it out. They stimulated it, not in the sense that nationalism manifested itself in opposition to them, but rather in the sense that the character of the Games offered the nationalists opportunities to exploit the Games to their advantage. How this finally worked out is the subject of the next chapter.

7   The outcome

There was almost universal agreement that these Games were successful, if not the most successful Games ever held. None of the fears held
before the Games – about whether the organisation would be up to standard, the threat of terrorism, and disruption by Catalan nationalists –
materialised. Neither were there any boycotts or international incidents
or major drug scandals. The whole operation was excellently organised,
COOB made a profit, even the weather improved in time, and Spain
won an unprecedented number of medals. How and why was serious
conflict avoided? What does the outcome reveal about the state of relations between Catalonia and Spain, the nature of Catalan nationalism
and the state of Spanish democracy? Also, what does it reveal about the
relationship between nationalism and global culture in the form of
Olympism?

Getting the Games for Barcelona fused the local and the global: it
rather abruptly intensified exposure to global culture and processes of
globalisation while projecting Catalonia on to the world stage. The
linkage presented the protagonists with enormous opportunities in terms
of legitimation and enhanced prestige and power, and in terms of the economic activity the Games would stimulate. But globalisation was a
double-edged sword: in the aforementioned ways it was a gift, but it also
presented a potential threat. Spain could lose prestige if something went
wrong: disruption by the Catalan nationalists, an attack by ETA, poor
organisation, and a weak performance by the national team were the main
threats. From the Catalan point of view the main threat was that the
Games would be used to tighten the political and cultural links to Spain:
the culture would be further homogenised and there would be more
interference in, and control over, her affairs from Madrid. It also meant
that both Spain and Catalonia would be dependent upon the global institution with strategic control over the Games, the IOC, and its president
Juan Antonio Samaranch.

As the situation developed it became clearer to the contending
parties that everyone could gain, provided they did not overstep certain

mutually agreed limits. Agreement on what constituted these limits emerged out of the process of conflict, rather than being stipulated at the outset. All sides came to recognise that it was in their interests to compromise, and by the end of the Games each could plausibly claim that they had achieved their objectives and, in a sense, had won. The outcome of this process in turn rested upon, first, the extent to which the *España de las Autonomías* was pluralist; second, how well the pactist political culture of Catalonia functioned under stress; and third, whether exclusive or inclusive sentiment was to predominate. It would be wrong to understand the outcome purely and simply in terms of how a consensus was generated on the fundamental issues. Rather, there was consensus on some issues, and continuing tension and polarisation over others, but the tension and polarisation were kept under control and not allowed to escalate into open conflict. Last, the outcome was never guaranteed by these structural and cultural determinants – contingent factors also played an important part.

In what follows we will show how each of the major agents – the central state apparatus and the central government, the Catalan government and Pujol, the municipality and Maragall, and the *independista* nationalists – were able to make specific gains by working within an emergent framework of compromise, so that none of the protagonists were able to determine the outcome unilaterally.

Pluralism

The above view is in contrast to the alternative interpretation offered by Cardús and some of the more radical nationalists, namely, that allowing the Olympics to be Catalanised was a highly effective strategy (*'una estrategia de la condescendencia'*) on the part of Spanish ruling circles, aimed at reinforcing Spanish hegemony over Catalonia (Cardús, 1992). Spain's acquiescence in the Catalanisation of the Games, from this point of view, was a form of tokenism, a ritual obeisance to Catalan sensibilities that in reality legitimated the status quo. Olympic sport functioned as a form of cultural capital, or an ideological apparatus, enabling the Spanish elite to set the political agenda, absorb challenges to the existing political order, and totally to nullify the efforts of opposing forces. According to this interpretation, Catalan nationalism was actually incorporated within a wider frame of reference, which rendered it relatively meaningless and harmless.

Thus, the Catalan national anthem, 'Els Segadors', was included in the opening ceremony, and at that particular crucial point when the king's party entered the stadium, as a way of preventing the crowd from whistling at the king as they had done in 1989 when the stadium was inaugurated.[1] Similarly, the massive security operation was cleverly planned in order to avoid any confrontation with nationalists. The respect for Catalan sensibilities and for civil liberties was more apparent than real. The security forces were tactfully deployed out of sight of the public; plain-clothes police were disguised as volunteers; propaganda material that was considered dangerous was quickly and efficiently confiscated, and after all there were arrests beforehand. It was Spain that became increasingly the focus of attention as the Games progressed and the evident public euphoria accompanying the Games was encouraged, in particular by the media which is controlled in the main from Madrid.

What this interpretation of events fails to appreciate is that the authorities were forced to capitulate to nationalists' demands to accommodate their key symbols on an equal basis with the Spanish symbols by sustained and growing nationalist pressure, to which, ultimately, they wisely gave way. Had this pressure not been applied, the evidence is that COOB would have adhered to the model they preferred, the 1984 Los Angeles Olympics, a show which highlighted the host city and the multicultural character of the nation, and where the primacy of the host state's symbols could be taken for granted. However, the planners were realists and had plans to Catalanise the Games to the extent that would prove to be necessary.[2] The timing of the king's entry, then, was actually determined by the fact that the nationalists had already secured the presence of a key symbol, despite the strong initial resistance of the authorities.

The same point applies to the security operation. It was indeed massive – 45,560 security personnel were deployed – and it was mostly discreet and very efficient. The central authorities who were in overall command could not act just as they wanted, because they knew better than to react to breaches of security and considerable provocation by being heavy-handed. Instead, they worked in close cooperation with COOB and the municipal government. Guidelines on how to treat Catalans and their culture with respect were issued to the police, many of them tough paramilitaries drafted in from other parts of Spain. Their conduct around the progress of the torch relay in the metropolitan area of Barcelona, where the majority of the population is located, was exemplary. It was at Banyoles, again an extreme nationalist stronghold where the rowing competition took place, that the opening was marked by considerable tension and hostility between the security forces and an *independista* faction. But

[1] Interview with Salvador Cardús.
[2] Interview with Josep Roca, Director of the Ceremonies. As late as 3 July the designers of the opening ceremony, Ovideo Bassat, were reported to be still awaiting instructions about the national flags (*La Vanguardia*, 3 July 1992).

this was an exceptional situation due to special local circumstances. Around the main Olympic installations in the metropolitan area of Barcelona, which were not policed by the *Guardia Civil*, security was discreetly implemented and not overbearing. For example, the work of searching and electronically frisking spectators as they entered the stadium was left to the young and usually friendly volunteers, with only a few uniformed police looking on in the background. It is quite likely, as it was rumoured, that some police were dressed as volunteers and others were in plain clothes, but this kind of precaution is standard practice in any democracy where there is a threat of terrorism. Earlier in the year, with the cooperation of the French authorities, the effectiveness of ETA as a terrorist organisation had been very much reduced, so there was less to be fearful about and the security forces could afford to be more relaxed. This operation must surely have been carried out at least in part to pre-empt possible ETA terrorist attacks on susceptible and attractive targets like the Olympics. Most Catalans were more than satisfied with the security operation, if the Opinion Institute survey conducted for *La Vanguardia* is anything to go by. It found that the majority of Barcelona's citizenry thought not only that the Games were highly successful, but that security was the most successful aspect of all (*La Vanguardia*, 11 August 1992).

The point is that the central authorities were forced by nationalist pressure to desist from taking their customary heavy-handed measures. If the Games were to serve their purpose as a showcase for a modernised democratic Spain, they could not afford to be seen behaving otherwise before the rest of the world, which was observing Spain on the television screen. The nationalists were well aware of this and took advantage of the situation accordingly to enforce the protection of civil rights. The round-up of thirty-four terrorist suspects and their supporters by the *Guardia Civil* in June should be seen in this light. The *Guardia Civil*'s controllers seem to have been panicked by the potentially serious breach of security that occurred at the ceremony to welcome the arrival of the Olympic flame at Empuries, and by the successful show of nationalist strength. These arrests, and the heavy security presence around the progress of the Olympic Flame through Catalonia, rather than intimidating the nationalists, threatened to provoke precisely the kind of confrontation the centre was anxious to avoid, and there were no such further measures.

As for the part allegedly played by the media, the fact that it is mainly controlled from Madrid did not prevent the Spanish public at the time from seeing the Games as predominantly Catalan rather than Spanish, and from discounting the central government's great financial contribution to the Games. Nor did it prevent Spanish television (TVE) from giving the specifically Catalan character of the Games full attention. Some nationalists, recognising this, claimed that the media had exaggerated the Catalan character of the Games in order to create anti-Catalan feeling. There is little evidence to support this claim: the only sectors of the mass media it applied to were organs of the right-wing press such as the newspaper *ABC*. In fact, television edited out the Empuries incident featuring the 'Freedom for Catalonia' banner, while influential sectors of the press, like *El País* and *La Vanguardia*, were critical of the perpetrators rather than of Catalan nationalists in general. Furthermore, the one analysis of Spanish TV coverage of the Games conducted so far concludes that it tended to be apolitical.[3]

Cardús' interpretation tends to treat powerholders as omniscient, and it neglects the difficulties they have in achieving unity among themselves and in resisting those who challenge them. Consequently in this instance he exaggerates the degree to which Catalonia was subordinated to the centre and underestimates Catalan power and the gains Catalonia made. Crucially, he underestimates the capacity of a pluralist democracy to learn from previous mistakes and to facilitate genuine compromise. The furore created by the nationalist demonstration at the inauguration of the Olympic stadium in 1989, and the heavy-handed way the demonstrators were treated by the security forces, seems to have been a key factor in making all parties to the conflict realise the need to compromise.

Our view also differs from that put forward by the mayor of Barcelona and president of COOB, Pasqual Maragall, namely, that the outcome represented a turning point in the development of Spanish democracy. While we would argue that the Games were a significant event in the relationship between Spain and Catalonia, it would be an exaggeration to suggest that they constituted a turning point as such. Following the transition period, from Franco's death in 1975 to the abortive military coup in February 1981, Spain had been a functioning pluralist democracy for at least a decade by the time of the Games. Indeed, had it not been so, it is difficult to see how such a successful outcome of the Games could have occurred. However, the Games did constitute a significant test for Spanish democracy that it came through rather well.

Rather than exercising hegemony in Cardús' sense, as we will see, the state, the central government and the people of the rest of Spain showed a willingness to compromise and in some ways a surprising openness to Catalonia. From July 1990, two years before the Games, public opinion polls were indicating the existence of a consensus in Spain that Barcelona,

---

[3] I owe this information to Miquel de Moragas, director of the Centre d'Estudis Olímpics at the Autonomous University of Barcelona, which carried out a comparative study of TV coverage of the Games.

Catalonia and Spain would all benefit, but that Barcelona with Catalonia would do so the most and Spain the least (García Ferrando, 1990). In Catalonia the extent to which Barcelona and Catalonia would gain tended to be played down. In contrast, opinion over who ideally should benefit was sharply polarised between the rest of Spain and the region. In Spain as a whole, a big majority (70 per cent) wanted Spain to benefit and only 12 per cent and 6 per cent wanted Catalonia and Barcelona, respectively, to do so. In Catalonia only 33 per cent, i.e. less than half the proportion in Spain, wanted Spain to benefit, while 36 per cent wanted Catalonia and 20 per cent wanted Barcelona to benefit, i.e. a majority favoured the region over the centre. The contrast with other regions is much starker. In every region except the Balearics, where Catalan is spoken and there is a strong regional identity, a very large majority favoured Spain and a very small minority Catalonia. However, from 1986 when the Games were awarded to Barcelona, to 1990 with two years to go to the Olympics, Spain as a whole was becoming more optimistic and confident about the prospect. Although it went against the grain, the rest of Spain realistically accepted that Barcelona and Catalonia would benefit most.

The state contributed significantly to the success of the Games through the important role taken by the king and in the generous financial support the central government gave, as we will see in a moment. The latter would not even countenance any criticism emanating from influential sources within its own party, PSOE, to the effect that Catalonia was exploiting the Games at the expense of the rest of Spain (*El País*, 25 July 1992).[4]

Pactism

The conflict that developed around the Games was very skilfully handled by the two main protagonists, Maragall and Pujol, who are not only immensely talented individuals, irrespective of the context, but are also highly skilled practitioners of the political art of 'pactism', a longstanding characteristic of Catalan political culture (Giner, 1984). As one informant, a local government official with some responsibility for the Games put it: 'We don't fight, we get what we want by other means.'[5] As members of the Catalan political elite, Pujol and Maragall have something in common. Pujol was sentenced to seven years in prison in the early 1960s, and served three of them, for his association with a public act of defiance

---

[4] Such criticism came, for example, from the leader of the party in Extremadura, Rodriguez Ibarra.
[5] Interview with Montserrat García, *head of sports* services, Diputación de Barcelona.

against Franco's regime. During one of Franco's rare visits to Barcelona with his ministers in May 1960, the ministers attended the centenary celebration of the Catalan patriotic poet, Joan Maragall, mayor Maragall's grandfather, at the Palau de la Musica. The celebration included a musical setting of the 'Cant de la Senyera', the patriotic poem by Maragall and, as such, banned by Franco. To the *franquistas'* fury, a group of nationalists stood up and sang along with the orchestra. Maragall, with his family background and as a socialist, was of course opposed to Franco. He has said that 'A Catalan who claims to be a Catalanist but does not like nationalism finds himself in a difficult position. But it is my position' (Hughes, 1992: 35).

Pujol protected his flank against the radical wing within his party and against the *independistas* by publicly pressurising Maragall on the question of Catalanisation and through his covert support of Acció Olímpica, around which the nationalists as a whole had cohered. In this way he could kill two birds with one stone: achieve his objective of Catalanising the Games, and at the same time exert control over the more radical nationalists and *independistas*. Pujol's pactism was devious to say the least. Throughout the period when the nationalists were applying the pressure, he never repudiated the existence of some kind of pact, although he was himself pressurising the Town Hall and COOB for more Catalanisation. When the final details of the *pacto olímpico* were agreed, it was very close to the press announcement in mid-June, only six weeks before the Games were due to start, and only days before the Olympic torch was due to arrive. He was, then, perfectly capable of issuing a solemn warning against excessive demonstrations: there was to be no whistling or jeering at national anthems, flags, institutions and especially the king; no acts of violence; no provocation of the forces of public order; and no disruption of Olympic ceremonies. He cooled down nationalist tempers if they threatened to get out of hand or became politically embarrassing. For example, he persuaded local nationalists in Banyoles to defer to the IOC's wish and not exhibit a 'desiccated negro' in the local museum during the Olympic Games, for fear of a possible 'racist scandal' (*La Vanguardia*, 5 June 1992). He was also prepared to defer pushing any further the question of gaining recognition for the Catalan Olympic Committee (COC) until after the Games were over. But at the same time the tacit support for Accío Olímpico's agitation around the torch relay continued, and his son Oleguer even ran a stage of the torch relay, accompanied by his fiancée and a friend displaying, respectively, the Catalan flag and a 'Freedom for Catalonia' banner (Antich, 1994: 282).

When in 1993 González lost his majority, Pujol's party was invited to participate in a coalition government. Pujol carefully distanced himself by refusing to join a coalition as such, but he did agree to support the government and keep it in power, and justified this move as a contribution to maintaining political stability in Spain. More to the point, it was a bargaining counter with which he hoped to increase Catalonia's control over its affairs. It is difficult to see how this arrangement could have been made if the Games had resulted in confrontation between the two. The arrangement continues under the new conservative government formed by Aznar's Partido Popular, for this government also lacks an absolute majority in the Cortes and relies on Pujol's party's support to stay in power. There could hardly be a better illustration of the nature of pactism than the fact that Pujol is willing to support either of his main political opponents at the centre, as long as it increases the chances of greater independence for Catalonia.

Maragall responded to the nationalists' and to Pujol's provocations by refusing to concede specific demands until it became expedient to do so. He would claim that he himself had planned to Catalanise the Games as they turned out to be anyway. The Games Organising Committee, of which he was president, in fact had contingency plans to include whatever elements of Catalanisation would be finally required. He could always hide from the nationalists behind the IOC, arguing with some plausibility that the IOC had the final word on Olympic protocol and therefore over the degree to which the Games could be Catalanised. And he was adept at counteracting nationalist propaganda with the internationalist slogan 'The Games Belong to Everyone'. Maragall's socialism, which is internationalist and Europeanist, and emphasises the role of cities and civitas as opposed to the role of 'nation-states' and nationalism, was in sharp contrast to Pujol's emphasis on Catalanism and its folklore (*castellers*, the *sardana*, *festes*, devil dancers, etc.). At what the two leaders deemed to be the critical moment, only ten days before the torch was due to arrive at Empuries, they proclaimed the existence of a *pacto olímpico*, which was left for the central government to ratify. It took the government virtually the whole of that time to make its decision, for the actual concession on the inclusion of the key Catalan symbols was not announced in the press until 13 June, the day the Olympic flame was due to arrive on Catalan soil. It would be reasonable to assume that Maragall's close relations as a socialist with the central government made it possible for him to convey the necessity to ratify Catalanisation in the nationalists' terms and that a sensitive handling of security would avert trouble.

The *independistas* could afford to look upon the outcome of the Games with some satisfaction, for it was to a great extent due to their energetic pursuit of the campaign that such a prominent place in the Games had been won for the key Catalan national symbols. Angel Colom, the ERC leader, could claim with some justification that Catalan identity had been strengthened as a result. While the *independistas* threatened until the last moment to disrupt the Games, and continued to agitate (for example, ERC threw its weight behind Pujol's call for 'Els Segadors' to have equal status with 'La Marcha Real' in future whenever the king was received in Catalonia, and protested that the six medals won by Catalan athletes belonged to them and not to Spain), they refrained from actually boycotting or disrupting the Games, even when provoked by arrests. Colom, in particular, despite his sour grapes, was quick to accept the *paz olímpico* even before the other radical groups. Ultimately the other radical nationalist organisations – La Crida, Acció Olímpica and COC – also acted quite pragmatically, accepting concessions and realising they could not completely achieve all their objectives. La Crida, indeed, showed its own goodwill by revealing to the Town Hall that it had been passed some tickets by an *agent provocateur* to disrupt a civic reception at the Liceu Theatre. La Crida refused to be used in this way and handed over the tickets instead.[6] The apparent political recklessness in the way negotiations were pushed to the brink of conflict, only finally reaching agreement at the last moment as the Games were due to start, far from being incompatible with the practice of pactism, only serves to confirm it.

The role played by the IOC president, Juan Antonio Samaranch

The outcome of the Barcelona Olympics has been characterised so far in terms of the character of Spanish democracy and Catalan pactism – factors that can hardly be said to be contingent. Neither is the role of the IOC, with the exception of one aspect – the crucial part played in these particular Games by its president, Juan Antonio Samaranch. He is a Barcelonese, from a family successful in the textile business, whose wealth he inherited. He rose to prominence in Spanish sport as a successful trainer and administrator of the Spanish roller hockey team, which under his guidance won the world championships in 1951. He simultaneously pursued a political career and was one of Franco's appointees to the Barcelona City Council in 1954. Thereafter his careers in sports administration and politics were thoroughly entwined. In 1966 he became a member of the IOC and was appointed as Franco's minister of sport. In the following year he became president of the Spanish Olympic Committee. By 1970 he was on the Executive Committee of the IOC and was made vice president in 1974. Meanwhile, from 1973 until 1977, he

---

[6] Interview with Jordi Sánchez, spokesman for La Crida.

served Franco as president of the Diputación de Barcelona, the most important of the four provinces of Catalonia, a post he remained in after Franco's death for a year or so during the transition period to parliamentary democracy. Like many others who were once loyal to the Franco regime, he successfully reconstructed himself during this period, and in 1977 departed from Barcelona for Moscow as the Spanish ambassador. Not surprisingly, his political past did not make him a particularly popular figure with the nationalists in Catalonia. In 1980 he succeeded his powerful patron, Avery Brundage, as president of the IOC. In 1987 he became president of the largest Catalan financial institution, La Caixa, and in 1990 president of La Caja de Ahoros de Barcelona, with which it merged. Here is a man who occupies the world's top position in sport and is equally at home as a top diplomat, politician and businessman (Boix and Espada, 1991).

It was surely a stroke of luck that the president of the IOC, the man in the best position to swing the IOC's decision in favour of giving the Games to Barcelona, and who has responsibility for overseeing the arrangements for the Games and monitoring their preparation and their progress, was none other than one of the Spanish political elite and, furthermore, a prominent Catalan. No other president of the IOC, by virtue of his national origins, has been able to play the kind of role that Samaranch did at the Barcelona Games. As president of the IOC he was the bearer of an external global force that threatened in some ways to exacerbate conflict between Spain and Catalonia, and within the Catalan political field. Yet he was also an insider who was able to mediate between the protagonists and contribute to resolving the conflict between them.

There can be little doubt that Samaranch used his position as president to procure the Games for Barcelona and thus to benefit Spain and Catalonia. Given his Spanish and Catalan background and the politics of the IOC, any other decision would have been inconceivable. We can be almost as sure as to his motivation: he wanted to wipe out residual memories of his *franquista* past and to enhance his personal standing in Spain and Catalonia. He knew he would be constantly in the public eye as one of the key figures, alongside the king and other members of the political elite. As an accredited, reconstructed member of the Spanish political elite and with his Catalan connections, he could present himself to both the centre and the Catalans as having their interests at heart. An indication of the confidence that Samaranch enjoyed was that when he was stigmatised by British journalists as a former fascist (Jennings and Simson, 1992), both Pujol and Maragall rescued him from a possibly embarrassing scandal by publicly defending him, pointing out what a good job he was doing. At the same time, his position as president of the IOC, an important international position, meant that he could be perceived by the protagonists as exercising a degree of detachment from the issues at stake. He could thus be seen to be acting as an honest broker in any conflict that might break out.

Samaranch's policy was necessarily Janus-faced. As the Catalan nationalists' campaign mounted, he associated himself with their demands; and the IOC even arranged a meeting between COC and COE in Lausanne, which seemed to hold out the possibility of the IOC recognising COC. However, when it became apparent that these moves were too much for Maragall and the central government to take, a *rapprochment* with Maragall was engineered that enabled them to make a joint declaration aimed at placating the nationalists, while deferring any further concessions. Meanwhile, although the meeting that Samaranch had promised to chair between COC and COE was aborted, the possibility of the IOC recognising COC was still not explicitly rejected. It was only after these Games (by which time he had achieved his objective) that Samaranch finally closed the door to COC obtaining recognition from the IOC. He had the IOC charter amended to ensure that recognition could only be given to a National Olympic Committee (NOC) if it represented an independent state, which of course ruled out Catalonia. Throughout the Games he took centre stage alongside the king, Maragall and the other dignitaries. He emerged from the Games just behind Maragall, with the second-highest opinion poll rating among the various personalities involved in the Games – concrete evidence indeed that he had achieved his objective of improving his standing in Spain and in Catalonia (see tables 11 and 12 p. 152).

Once the Games had been awarded, he harried and encouraged the Organising Committee and used his position to ensure support from Madrid. He managed simultaneously to support further Catalanisation of the Games and, to an extent, placate the nationalists while lending his weight to Maragall and COOB's efforts to resist their pressure. In the months leading up to the Games, Samaranch shuttled between Madrid and Barcelona monitoring the preparations and ironing out problems.[7] There can be little doubt that he played a significant part in the negotiations that went on over the inclusion of Catalan national symbols, and that he approved the measures that were taken to achieve a balance between the representation of Catalonia and Spain in these Games. He seems to have made a significant, if not crucial, contribution to the integration process that went on around the Games.

[7] Interview with Fernando París, special advisor to the Spanish minister of sport.

Inclusive nationalism

There is a further reason why pactism worked well in this situation and why the conflict over the Games was resolved amicably. As was shown in chapter 2, the majority of Catalan nationalists are not separatists: the phenomenon of dual identity, i.e. the feeling that one is both Catalan and Spanish, is common. Consequently, Pujol's nationalism, in contrast to the 'exclusive nationalism' of his *independista* rivals, takes the form of 'inclusive nationalism': that is to say, he seeks recognition of Catalonia's right to independence as a nation within the existing Spanish state. On the other hand, Pujol and those who sympathise with inclusive nationalism would, perhaps, adopt a separatist strategy and be more confrontational if the conjuncture was judged to be appropriate. At the present time CiU hopes that Catalan 'sovereignty' will be gained as a result of further erosion of the Spanish state, both upwards by the further development of the European Union, and downwards by further devolution of power to the Generalitat.

The nature of the Catalan political field, particularly the predominance of dual identity and the fact that roughly half the population are of immigrant origin from the rest of Spain, means that none of the political actors can afford to stray too far outside certain parameters. The socialists and the communists (between whom there is a pact which keeps the former in power in the Town Hall) must steer a course between the scylla of centrism and the charybdis of nationalism: too much of the former alienates leftward-leaning Catalans, and too much of the latter risks losing support among the Spanish-speaking, working-class population of immigrant origin. Pujol's nationalism, on the other hand, walks a tightrope between separatism, which frightens off those who want to remain part of Spain, and being too moderate, which alienates his more radical followers and runs the risk of driving them into the arms of his separatist critics. Since political fields are not fixed entities, but rather a series of shifting positions, in his circumstances especially it pays to be flexible. Hence his politics often appear disingenuous and lead to accusations that his inclusive nationalism is actually the Trojan horse of separatism, or that his nationalism is mere opportunism. His majority in the Catalan parliament was reduced in the next election as a result of his accommodation with the socialist central government.

Table 1 (p.32) shows that Catalan sentiment reached a peak at the end of the 1980s (at the time of the big nationalist demonstration at the inauguration of the Olympic stadium), and that six years later it had fallen considerably. In 1990 a bigger proportion of the Catalan population identified with the *Autonomia*/region (45 per cent) than identified with Spain (16 per cent) or had a dual identity (36 per cent). By 1996 these proportions had changed: the proportion identifying with the *Autonomia*/region had reduced to virtually the same as those having a dual identity (37 per cent and 36 per cent respectively) and the proportion identifying with Spain had risen to 24 per cent, reflecting the election of a conservative government in Madrid. This is the kind of fluctuation that Pujol has to take account of. The period from 1986 when Barcelona was awarded the Games, until the Games opened in 1992, coincided with an expansive phase of Catalan nationalism during which Pujol could afford to ride the crest of a nationalist wave and push for Catalanisation almost as vigorously as the separatists.

The separatists could not go too far in their struggle for independence. There is no significant support for violent 'liberation struggle', and excesses can frighten away support. Thus, the manner in which the radical nationalists disrupted the inauguration of the Olympic stadium in 1989 seems to have been rejected rather than applauded by the majority of Catalans, and made them more amenable to a compromise solution to the issue of how the Games were to be Catalanised. Nevertheless, for the radical nationalists, Pujol's kind of pragmatic nationalism had to be outdone continually in order to mobilise support among those impatient for change, especially among the younger generation.

This is a richly textured, sophisticated political field in which the nationalists and their opponents who came into conflict over the Olympics skilfully mobilised support, fought the conflict out energetically, and ultimately managed to resolve it in a way that ensured that all made significant gains.

The gains made by Spain

Spain gained from its willingness to compromise with Catalan nationalism over the Games in three ways: it was able to enhance its prestige internationally, by demonstrating its efficiency, modernity and maturity as a democracy; second, Spanish identity and national integration were strengthened in certain respects; and third, Spain as a whole benefited from the economic growth which the Games stimulated.

To organise successfully a global event of this magnitude and importance is certainly a test of a country's efficiency, if not its maturity as a modern 'nation-state'. A late moderniser when compared with the rest of Western Europe, still burdened in some ways with an image of backwardness, a country somewhat isolated from the mainstream of advancing

Europe in the last two centuries, and having only relatively recently emerged from Franco's dictatorship, Spain has tended to suffer somewhat from a national inferiority complex. Doubt existed in the country as to whether it could successfully stage a well-organised, efficiently run Olympic Games and thus live up to its claim to be, at last, an integral part of modern Europe. Spain would be on trial also, of course, in terms of the performance of the Spanish Olympic team. In the last sporting event on this scale Spain had organised, the football World Cup in 1986, the poor performance of the Spanish team was widely interpreted as a national humiliation and the relevant authorities were determined this should not be allowed to occur again.

The enhancement of Spain's prestige abroad can be inferred from the very success of the Games as outlined so far. The country was the centre of non-stop world attention for two weeks and had attracted continual and growing attention in the long build-up to the Games. It was well positioned to show itself off in a most positive light as a country to which the world and a large number of its leaders had flocked: a modern, unified Western European country, which had proved itself capable of successfully organising the largest festival in the world and of performing better than most in the sports competitions.

As far as the effects on national identity and national integration are concerned, we have the detailed evidence of the survey of public opinion conducted shortly after the Games by the Centro de Investigación Sociológicas (CIS) on which to base our conclusions (Hargreaves and García Ferrando, 1997). This is the most comprehensive evidence there is to date of the effects of the Games on public opinion in Spain, and it allows us to compare the effects in Catalonia with the rest of Spain.

Modern states employ powerful symbols that encourage the population to identify themselves with the 'nation-state' and that cut across local, regional and sub-national sentiments and identities. As we saw in chapter 5, the king and royal family played a pivotal role in the Games' proceedings and table 2 reveals the effect on public opinion – virtually unanimous positive evaluation of the king's and the royal family's role during the Olympics. That is, there is a consensus here embracing the whole of the country including Catalonia.[8] The significance of this evaluation has to be seen in the light of the fact that the king is the head of state and the monarchy is the single most important symbol of the unity and integrity

[8] *La Vanguardia,* 11 August 1992, gave the results of a poll of 8 August of 800 Catalan residents, in which the king and Maragall, mayor of Barcelona and president of the Organising Committee, are given the highest evaluation.

Table 2 *Evaluation of the role of the king and the royal family during the Barcelona Olympic Games (%)*

Evaluation	Total	Catalonia	Rest of Spain
Very good	48	49	48
Good	40	40	40
Average	4	4	4
Bad	1	2	1
Very bad	–	–	–
Not important	4	4	4
Don't know/no answer	3	1	3
	(2,495)	(396)	(2,099)

Source: Hargreaves and García Ferrando (1997).

Table 3 *Evaluation of the success of the organisation of the Games (%)*

Evaluation	Total	Catalonia	Rest of Spain
It has been an organisational success	87	94	83
It was not well organised	2	2	2
Don't know/no answer	11	4	13
	(2,495)	(396)	(2,099)

Source: CIS, Estudio Barometro 2018 (1992).

of the Spanish state. In this respect the Games reinforced Spanish national identity and fortified national integration.

Table 3 shows that there was also general agreement among respondents that the Games were successfully organised. A higher proportion of Catalan residents are convinced of this (94 per cent as opposed to 85 per cent in the rest of Spain), indicating a heightened sense of local pride in the achievement. Catalans have long differentiated themselves from the rest of Spain in terms of their superior organisational and entrepreneurial capacities and their work discipline, so their higher evaluation of the organisation seems to be a function of this aspect of their particular sense of national identity. The proximity of the Games and greater media coverage in the region no doubt contributed to this heightened awareness of their achievements as well.

A consensus also existed that the Games exceeded expectations, as Table 4 shows. The lack of self-confidence and the fear that the Games would be marred by poor organisation, or be disrupted by nationalist

Table 4 *Evaluation of the results of the Games in relation to previous expectations of the outcome (%)*

	Total	Catalonia	Rest of Spain
Better	67	79	65
Same	17	15	17
Worse	1	–	1
Don't know/no answer	15	6	17
	(2,495)	(396)	(2,099)

Source: CIS, Estudio Barometro 2018 (1992).

animosity or by terrorism, proved to be groundless. These Games were remarkably successful from almost every point of view, not least from the Spanish point of view, because of the completely unexpected degree of success of the Spanish athletes in winning so many gold medals. As we have seen, this success produced a growing euphoria among spectators and in the Spanish media, to the extent that the Spanish flag, which is not a popular symbol in Catalonia, manifested itself increasingly in the stadia and on the streets, while the salience of dissonant symbols, like the flag of the *independista* party, Esquerra Republicana, tended to be reduced. We come back to the fact that contingency played a great part in the resolution of the conflict around the Games. Had this gold-medal success not occurred, the latent animosities between Catalonia and the rest of Spain might have broken out and resulted in a very different kind of ambience. The fact that expectations were exceeded by a greater margin in Catalonia than in the rest of Spain (79 per cent compared with 65 per cent in the rest of Spain) articulates a distinct sense of national identity once more.

Tables 5–7 reveal a similar pattern of response on the question of what kind of image of Spain, of Catalonia and of Barcelona was projected abroad by the Games. There is virtual unanimity that the Games projected a positive image of all three, and this unanimity expresses, perhaps, a new-found self-confidence that Spain is a modern country that can take its place alongside the others. Again, there is a gap between Catalonia and the rest of Spain. Catalans are more strongly inclined to assert that all three levels of government were successful in projecting their images abroad, and the discrepancy is sharpest with respect to the image of Catalonia (Table 6). The rest of Spain is considerably more reluctant to concede that Catalonia was successful in projecting its image abroad (in

Table 5 *The image of Spain that the Games projected abroad in terms of efficiency, security and modernity (%)*

Characteristics of the image	Evaluation					
	Great/Average			Little/Nothing		
	Total	Catalonia	Rest of Spain	Total	Catalonia	Rest of Spain
Efficiency	81	93	79	3	3	3
Security	81	94	79	2	2	2
Modernity	81	94	79	2	2	–

Source: Hargreaves and García Ferrando (1997).

Table 6 *The image of Catalonia that the Games have projected abroad in terms of efficiency, security and modernity (%)*

Characteristics of the image	Evaluation					
	Great/Average			Little/Nothing		
	Total	Catalonia	Rest of Spain	Total	Catalonia	Rest of Spain
Efficiency	80	93	77	3	3	3
Security	80	93	77	3	3	3
Modernity	81	94	78	2	2	2

Source: Hargreaves and García Ferrando (1997).

Table 7 *Opinion concerning the contribution of the Games to improving the international image of Barcelona (%)*

	Evaluation					
	Great/Average			Little/Nothing		
	Total	Catalonia	Rest of Spain	Total	Catalonia	Rest of Spain
Improved the international image of Barcelona	84	95	81	3	1	4
Helped to make Barcelona a more modern city with better services	82	92	81	3	3	3

Source: Hargreaves and García Ferrando (1997).

the case of images of efficiency and security the gap is as wide as 93 per cent compared with 77 per cent). This perception gap reflects, on the one hand, the sense among the Catalan population of having closer ties and having more in common with Europe and abroad than the rest of Spain. On the other hand, as far as the rest of Spain is concerned, it reflects a suspicion that Catalonia selfishly tries to promote itself and to discount the benefits it receives from being a part of Spain.

The gap between the two in the perception of the security measures is also of interest, because of what it reveals about the effectiveness of the more radical nationalists' campaign on this issue. The latter agitated vociferously that the massive security operation threatened freedom of expression and civil liberties. Yet despite their well-orchestrated campaign, 93–94 per cent of respondents in Catalonia evaluated the international image of security in quite contrary terms. The difference in perceptions of security, then, is not a matter of antagonism between Catalonia and the rest of Spain, but of relief in Catalonia that the Games went peacefully, and a sense of pride that, after all, good Catalan commonsense (seny) prevailed. On the other hand, the activities of the radical nationalists around the Games, which included breaching security and disrupting the reception ceremony for the arrival of the Olympic flame on Spanish soil, as well as making a good deal of threatening noise, seems to have had the effect in the rest of Spain of somewhat lowering the evaluation of security.

The evidence presented so far suggests that the Barcelona Olympics generated a significant degree of consensus in Spain as a whole on the king's role, on the success of the Games, and on the positive image of Spain, Catalonia and Barcelona that was projected. With respect to these aspects, therefore, the Games strengthened a sense of national identity and fortified national integration – an outcome that was not vitiated by the differences between respondents in Catalonia and the rest of Spain. Rather, these differences reflect a relatively mild Catalan national sentiment that is not at all incompatible with feeling part of a larger unit, and also, a relatively mild resentment in the rest of Spain that Catalonia had benefited more.

There is no doubt also that Spain as a whole benefited from the impetus the Games gave to the flagging Spanish economy in the period 1987–92. Associated infrastructural investment is estimated to have accounted for between 0.9 per cent and 1.6 per cent of growth. If the increased tax revenues are taken into account, then only approximately 16 per cent of central government expenditure on the Games was a cost to the state and ultimately to the tax payer (Brunet, 1992; Vegara and Salvador, 1992).

Table 8 *Opinion concerning the level of effort that was made by public institutions in order to achieve the successes of the Games (%)*

| | Level of effort | | | | | |
| | Great/Average | | | Little/Nothing | | |
	Total	Catalonia	Rest of Spain	Total	Catalonia	Rest of Spain
Central government	73	70	73	8	20	6
Catalan government	76	88	74	5	4	5
Barcelona Town Hall	78	93	76	3	1	4

Source: Hargreaves and García Ferrando (1997).

The gains made in Catalonia

Catalonia benefited from the Games in terms of a reinforced sense of Catalan identity, an enhanced reputation abroad, an improved status *vis-à-vis* Spain, and from the associated growth in economic activity. Consequently the nationalists, especially Pujol and his party, could justifiably claim that the Games had worked to their advantage. Maragall and the socialists also benefited considerably.

The responses of the Catalan respondents in table 6 (the image of Catalonia projected abroad) indicate the strong sense of Catalan identity the Games stimulated among Catalans. Similarly, although table 7 concerns the image of Barcelona specifically, we can be reasonably certain that the very positive image that the Catalan respondents attribute to the city is also an indication of a strong Catalan identity.

When asked to evaluate the level of effort made by public institutions (table 8), their economic contribution towards the Games (table 9), and how the Games strengthened their public image (table 10), that is, when respondents are asked to make more explicit political judgements, Catalan identity manifests itself more strongly. The rest of Spain does not see much difference in the efforts made at all three levels of government, although it is significant that the central government gets the lowest rating. In Catalonia the central government's effort is rated slightly lower but essentially the same as in the rest of Spain (70 per cent compared with 73 per cent), but the efforts of both the Catalan government and the Barcelona Town Hall are rated much more positively (88 per cent and 93 per cent respectively); and a significant proportion (20 per cent) perceive the central government's efforts in very negative terms. These differences are to some extent the result of media influence and they are a great deal

Table 9 *Opinion concerning which governmental institutions made the biggest economic contribution to the organisation of the Games (%)*

	Total	Catalonia	Rest of Spain
Central government	36	16	40
Catalan government	12	16	11
Barcelona Town Hall	9	19	7
All the same	19	26	18
Don't know/no anwer	24	23	24
	(2,495)	(396)	(2,099)

Source: Hargreaves and García Ferrando (1997).

Table 10 *Opinion concerning the public institutions that improved their image the most because of the Games (%)*

Public institutions	Total	Catalonia	Rest of Spain
Barcelona Town Hall	23	37	21
Catalan government	18	16	19
Central government	14	5	16
All the same	22	31	20
Don't know/no answer	23	11	24
	(2,295)	(396)	(2,099)

Source: Hargreaves and García Ferrando (1997).

to do with the different public relations strategies adopted by the central government, the Barcelona Town Hall and the Catalan government. The Catalan regional press is strong, there are also Catalan-language TV channels, and image consciousness is highly developed. Consequently, the efforts of the Catalan government and Barcelona Town Hall, personified respectively by Jordi Pujol, the Catalan president, and Pasqual Maragall, the mayor of Barcelona, who were not averse to taking full advantage of the opportunities afforded for favourable publicity, were constantly to the forefront, and Madrid's contribution tended to be side-lined in Catalonia. In the Madrid-based media the Games did not enjoy the same salience, although no doubt the efforts of central government were highlighted more. Also, it must be said that central government did not seem to concern itself so much with publicising its efforts. It is well established that media and audiences mutually influence each other, so

the apparent resentment against central government in Catalonia registered in (table 8), cannot simply be attributed to the media. It is rather a
reflection of a long-standing feeling in the region that central government
neglects Catalonia.

The more specific question as to which level of government contributed most to the Games in economic terms produces a quite polarised
response. In the rest of Spain 40 per cent rank the central government as
the highest contributor, 18 per cent think they all contributed equally,
and the rest rank the Catalan government above the Town Hall (11 per
cent and 7 per cent respectively). In Catalonia, however, 26 per cent say
they all contributed equally, and among the rest, 19 per cent see the Town
Hall as the main contributor, and equal proportions (16 per cent) rank
the central government and Catalan governments highest. At this point it
should be noted that the central government was, in fact, by far the largest
public contributor (37 per cent), the Generalitat was second (18 per cent)
and the Town Hall third (16 per cent), with the rest coming from a variety
of sources.[9] So it looks as if there was widespread misapprehension of the
facts among the general public in Spain. The rest of Spain tended to give
credit to the central government and to downgrade, in particular, the
Barcelona Town Hall administration, but also the Catalan government's
contribution. And in Catalonia there was a reluctance to recognise the
greater financial role of central government and a somewhat greater propensity to give credit to the Town Hall and the Catalan government. It is
worth noting that in mid-July 1992, in Spain as a whole the greatest proportion of people (33 per cent) saw the Catalan government as the major
contributor and the vast majority discounted the central government's
contribution. In Catalonia a majority credited the Town Hall (35 per
cent) and the Catalan government (32 per cent) with being the biggest
contributors, almost completely discounting central government's contribution (*El País*, 19 July 1992; *La Vanguardia*, 21 July 1992). Circles in
Madrid were staggered by the Catalan government's propaganda success
in gaining credit for the Games at the expense of central government. A
few days before the opening of the Games, Madrid reacted furiously to
the Catalan government's campaign to promote Catalonia in the foreign
press, which highlighted Catalonia to the exclusion of any mention of
Spain (*El País*, 20 July 1992; *La Vanguardia*, 18 July 1992; *El Periodico*, 21
July 1992).

By September the polarisation had become less and public opinion
seemed to be better informed on who paid for the Games, although there

[9] The calculation is immensely complicated and hinges on the assumptions made. See *El
Pais*, 19 July 1992 for a simplified breakdown.

was still widespread misapprehension, particularly it would seem in Catalonia, where there was still a tendency to discount the central government's economic role. Here, what was almost certainly being asserted was the nationalist view: since Catalonia contributes more in taxes to the central government than any other part of Spain and receives less in return from the centre, the region itself really paid for the Games over the years (Cabana *et al.,* 1998). Conversely, in the rest of Spain, where Catalonia is seen as well off, the latter was seen as benefiting at the expense of the rest, and the Town Hall and Catalan government's contributions tended to be discounted. If we correlate voting choice with respondents' replies to this question, this interpretation tends to be confirmed. Those who vote for nationalist parties, like Convergencia i Unió (CiU) heavily discounted the central government's contribution compared with other voters (Hargreaves and García Ferrando, 1997).

Opinion concerning which governmental institutions improved their image most with the help of the Games is in some ways less polarised. In the rest of Spain central government was thought to come off worst and the Barcelona Town Hall best, but in Catalonia the difference that is seen between them is much greater, and this indicates a tendency among some Catalans to nationalist triumphalism. In the rest of Spain there is a significant degree of agreement that they all did equally well. It is noticeable, also, that apart from the largish proportion of those in Catalonia who thought the Town Hall benefited, there does not appear to be any strong opinion as to who else did so. This is more marked in Catalonia where nearly a third of respondents thought all levels of government benefited equally. Catalan opinion appears to have been split between a moderate section, which saw the outcome in terms of a compromise, and the more partisan nationalist elements, which saw the outcome in terms of winners and losers. Care is needed here, because it is not entirely clear what the latter are being partisan about, for it has to be remembered that the majority of respondents in Catalonia are from the Barcelona metropolitan area, and therefore may be expressing civic, rather than Catalan national pride, as such.

If we consider the outcome in terms of winners and losers, our data confirms that the main loser was the central government, personified by its leader, the Spanish president, Felipe González. Tables 11 and 12 show that his role in the Games was not only lowly rated but also negatively rated, both in the country at large and especially in Catalonia. This is indeed ironic given the fact that the central government did most for the Games in economic terms. In the rest of Spain he receives far fewer accolades ('very good'/'good') than Maragall and Samaranch, and even Pujol

Table 11 *Evaluation of the role of the various personalities involved in the Games (rest of Spain) (%)*

Personalities	Very good	Good	Average	Bad	Very bad	Don't know/no answer
Samaranch, IOC president	26	27	5	2	3	37
González, president, central government	8	24	17	11	10	30
Pujol, president, Catalan government	10	28	14	8	6	34
Maragall, mayor of Barcelona	29	27	6	3	3	32
Gómez Navarro, minister of sport	5	18	7	3	3	64
Ferrar Salat, president, Spanish Olympic Committee	7	20	7	4	3	59
Serra, vice-president, central government	6	20	16	12	7	39

Source: Hargreaves and García Ferrando (1997).

Table 12 *Evaluation of the role of the various personalities involved in the Games (Catalonia) (%)*

Personalities	Very good	Good	Average	Bad	Very bad	Don't know/no answer
Samaranch, IOC president	50	28	4	1	–	17
González, president, central government	10	27	20	15	15	13
Pujol, president, Catalan government	25	43	11	3	1	17
Maragall, mayor of Barcelona	63	21	2	–	–	14
Gómez Navarro, minister of sport	4	24	7	2	1	62
Ferrer Salat, president, Spanish Olympic Committee	12	29	9	3	1	46
Serra, vice-president, central government	12	36	15	10	1	26

Source: Hargreaves and García Ferrando (1997).

exceeds him; and he receives scarcely more than his minister of sport and the president of the Spanish Olympic Committee. He also receives more 'bad' and 'very bad' evaluations than anyone else. In Catalonia only his minister of sport receives fewer accolades and González far outstrips everyone else in unpopularity.

The low perception of González is understandable in that, unlike the others listed, he did not have an Olympic role as such, so respondents would not be inclined to rank him high anyway; and there were other reasons for his low rating in the rest of Spain. There was resentment there that the government had let Catalanisation go too far; we will come to this in a moment. Spain was already feeling the effects of the economic crisis for which González's government was receiving much of the blame. And there was the sheer success of the Catalan propaganda machine that masked the government's contribution.

During the Games González was castigated in the media for staying away from the Games after attending the opening ceremony, when virtually everyone else of note in the government was in attendance, and his absence had to be publicly defended by Maragall. This appears to have been a political error. It was taken in Catalonia as a sign that he was more concerned with his own regional power base in Andalucía. The continual presence of his vice-president, Narcis Serra, a Catalan and former mayor of Barcelona, the man who led the successful bid for the Games, does not seem to have offset the negative impression made. The assessment of the latter's role in the rest of Spain was also very low. In Catalonia, although he manages more accolades, coming fourth on the list in this respect, he still gets more negative ratings than anyone except González. Given his very prominent presence on the tribune and the part he played in securing the Games, one must assume his low rating is a function of the unpopularity of the government. It could also be associated with resentment in the rest of Spain against him as a Catalan. The tendency for the central government's financial contribution to be discounted, together with the unpopularity of González and Serra, mean that the central government lost the propaganda battle to the nationalists. It should be clear that this does not mean Spain was the loser. We noted earlier the unanimous positive evaluation of the king's role in the Games and the consensus on the good image Spain projected. Catalan antagonism here is directed at the Spanish government and its leader and not at the Spanish state.

If González and the central government are the losers, clearly there are two Catalan political rivals who are winners: Maragall and Pujol. Pujol vied for attention with Maragall, and very seriously challenged him, but eventually he was overshadowed by Maragall who, as mayor of the host city and president of the Organising Committee, occupied centre stage throughout. Table 11 confirms this. It shows he received most accolades in the rest of Spain and overwhelmingly so in Catalonia. Maragall emerged with his prestige enhanced: he gained the highest public opinion poll rating for his contribution to the Games, and acquired an international reputation. In Catalonia, and particularly in Barcelona, which contains the majority of the Catalan population, this was a vote of thanks for his role in the renewal and transformation of Barcelona that was accomplished with the help of the Games. Maragall and his party almost certainly strengthened their power in the city as a result. It was to help him retain power in the subsequent municipal elections in May 1995, when Barcelona was one of the few large socialist municipalities to remain in their hands. Both Maragall's and Pujol's parties lost seats on the City Council to the Partido Popular and Esquerra Republicana (*El País*, 30 May 1995).

Pujol won as well, and moreover he looks like being the bigger winner in the long run. In the rest of Spain he ranked third in terms of accolades received, although the ranking was tinged by a note of unpopularity. And in Catalonia, his home base, he was ranked third again, but with twice as many accolades. Pujol skilfully used the Games to put himself and Catalonia on the map and to reinforce his party's hegemony in Catalonia. In the 1993 election for the Spanish government, one year after the Olympics, González's Spanish Socialist Party lost its majority and needed Pujol's agreement to keep him in power. In the elections for the Catalan government in November 1995 Pujol and his party paid the price of supporting an unpopular Spanish Government and lost its absolute majority (*The Times*, 21 November 1995).

The *independistas* gained in the sense that they helped to achieve a substantial Catalanisation of the Games and they certainly projected themselves as having been successful. They did not achieve all their objectives: in particular, they did not obtain recognition of a separate Catalan National Olympic Committee (COC), an objective which was more central to them than to Pujol's more moderate nationalists. However, they did gain an enormous amount of publicity for their cause, especially through their vigorous pursuit of the 'Freedom for Catalonia' campaign. As we have seen, ERC went on to increase its representation in the Catalan parliament in the following elections, although this cannot be directly attributed to its stance on the Games. Also, they shared in the gain represented by the transformation of Barcelona and the economic gains Catalonia made. Whether they received full credit for their efforts is a moot point. It could be argued that Pujol and his party took most of the credit for the Catalanisation of the Games, having stolen much of the radicals' clothing by covertly merging his campaign with theirs.

Catalonia benefited in economic terms to the tune of ten times the amount of investment there would have been without the Games. Consequently, unemployment trends in the region were reversed in the period 1986–90 (Brunet, 1992). This was largely the result of the modernisation of the urban infrastructure of Barcelona that had been the prime reason for the city making a bid for the Games in the first place. Under the guidance of its chief urban theorist, the architect and historian Oriol Bohigas, who designed the Olympic village, the Town Hall's policy was to renew the urban infrastructure in a way that would restore the importance of the neighbourhood in city life. Whether the changes actually restored the *barrio* to its former place of importance is debatable, but undoubtedly the city was spectacularly transformed. The Games generated a total investment of from five to six and a half billion pounds, most of which went into the infrastructure of the city. Sixty per cent of this came from the public sector and 40 per cent from the private.

The city's road transport system was revolutionised: new ring roads, urban routes, traffic interchange systems and tunnels, and a computerised traffic management system, made it possible to travel around, and in and out of the city with more ease and speed than almost any comparable city in the world. The airport was extended and improved: Ricardo Bofill, Spain's most prestigious architect, was brought in to design the new main airport terminal, and Girona airport was also improved. A virtually new telecommunications system was installed, incorporating the very latest advanced technology, and providing the city with two new landmarks. Barcelona is squeezed between the Collserola range, that runs roughly south-west to north-east, and the coast, which runs parallel. Norman Foster's 800-feet Collserola telecommunications tower now looks down over the city from Tibidabo, the main peak. On the coast opposite, at the southern end of the city, Montjuic, the mountain serving as the city's major recreational area, provided the site for the Olympic stadium complex. Conspicuous at the centre of this complex stands Calatrava's gleaming white, futuristic telephone tower. The external façade of Domenech's main stadium on Montjuic, dating from the 1929 Exposition, was retained, and the rest was demolished and replaced by a new state-of-the-art stadium seating 75,000 people. Below, and linked by steps and plazas to the stadium, probably the most distinguished building associated with the Olympics, the Palau Sant Jordi (Palace of St George), was built as an indoor sports arena seating 17,000 people, designed by the Japanese architect, Arata Isozaki.

The city had been closed off from the sea by the old, derelict residential and industrial area running along the coast from Barceloneta towards the River Besos at the north-eastern extremity. This area was demolished, in order to open the city to the sea and to make way for building the Poble Nou Olympic area, where the Olympic village, given the utopian name of Nova Icaria, was located. It housed 15,000 athletes and was destined to be a private residential development after the Games ended. Two forty-two-storey towers, one a hotel, the other for offices, formed the gateway to the village. Opening the city to the sea created a five-kilometre-long waterfront area and a huge public recreation area, consisting of the Olympic port, immaculately clean new beaches, parks and gardens, a splendid esplanade, and numerous cafés and restaurants.

Other major Olympic areas were developed at Vall d'Hebron on the outer ring road, and another, adjacent to the Barcelona Football Club, Camp Nou, on the great Avinguda Diagonal that bisects the city from roughly west to east. A total of fourteen Olympic sub-sites were constructed elsewhere around Catalonia, necessitating further urban redevelopment and environmental changes. Several very large hotels were built, notably the Les Arcs tower at the Olympic village mentioned above, and many hotels were improved. The old port area was remodelled and metropolitan transport improved. These were only the most notable developments. There were scores of other renovations and additions to the city's facilities and public spaces. *In toto*, Barcelona was transformed into not only one of the most modern and attractive cities in Europe if not the world in cultural terms, but also into a potential magnet for inward investment in the future. This was a tremendous gain for Barcelona and a coup for Catalonia.

It is difficult, if not impossible, to envisage an equivalent stimulus to the Games that would have brought so much investment into the city and the region. Investment was mobilised on a global scale: exogenous capital flowed in from North America, Japan and the EEC, and national and local capital was galvanised. Modernisation of this major Mediterranean city and its hinterland was thus propelled by globalisation processes that had been triggered by the Olympics. As Spain, Catalonia and Barcelona sucked in capital they in turn were being sucked into globalising processes at the economic as well as the cultural level. While there were obvious benefits, the process also exposed the recipients to fluctuations in the global economy. Immediately after the Games, and to some extent even before they started, there was an economic downturn and talk of fewer visitors turning up than anticipated. What was also significant was the fact that the effects of the economic stimulus provided by the Games were concentrated in the city service sector, and not the industrial belt around Barcelona, where investment in new industries was needed to replace the older, declining industrial sector devastated by foreign imports in the 1980s (Kurth and Petras, 1993). The Spanish economy has been characterised as 'post-industrial' in the sense that the most dynamic sectors are the high service or financial sector, and the low service or tourist sector (Kurth and Petras, 1993). It does seem that the link between the Games and global economic processes reinforced this kind of pattern in the Spanish economy, and in Catalonia in particular.

It must be understood that COOB was not financially responsible for this massive investment programme. Its budget was separate from the companies that were set up to manage the infrastructural projects, many of which were joint public and private sector enterprises. COOB had its own budget specifically for running the Games, and since it achieved its aim to balance its budget (in fact it made a profit), in this restricted sense the Games as such were made to pay for themselves. Of course in terms of the investment in the urban infrastructure the Games did not pay for themselves at all. A great deal of public money went into urban redevelopment schemes and these added half a billion pounds to the Town Hall's deficit as a result. Fortunately for the latter, central government took responsibility for helping to pay off a considerable proportion of this debt – yet further evidence of its positive contribution to the Games.

The urban redevelopment discussed so far was part of a larger ongoing programme and the economic downturn brought into question whether the remaining targets could be achieved, and also whether the new facilities could be run without a substantial subsidy from the public purse.

Relations with Spain

By the end of the Games relations between Catalonia and Spain had on the whole worked out well; indeed, the outcome exceeded general expectations. In important respects, however, relations seem to have remained at an impasse as a result of the Games.

We have argued that the conflict over the Games was resolved amicably because all the protagonists perceived themselves to have made significant gains. While this is so, the data in tables 13–15 indicates deep-seated residual conflict between Catalonia and the rest of Spain. Tables 13 and 14 show that roughly 40 per cent of respondents in the rest of Spain strongly objected to the use of the Catalan language and political symbols, while an overwhelming majority of Catalan respondents strongly approved. True, those who objected are not an absolute majority in the rest of Spain, but they constituted a larger group than those who positively approve (28–29 per cent), and there was a sizeable proportion (18–20 per cent) in the middle who, presumably, might have gone either way. If we take voting choice into account, opposition to manifestations of Catalan identity was not confined to those voting for the PP, the party most sympathetic to centrism. It ranged across most of the political spectrum from left to right (Hargreaves and García Ferrando, 1997) and it points to strong resistance among the population in the rest of Spain to a greater degree of autonomy for Catalonia and to a continuing problem of national integration. It means the Catalan government's present policy of

Table 13 *Evaluation of the use of the Catalan language as an official language in the Games (%)*

	Total	Catalonia	Rest of Spain
Very good	11	45	4
Good	27	39	25
Average	16	7	18
Bad	22	4	26
Very bad	12	–	14
Indifferent	5	4	5
Don't know/no anwer	7	1	8
	(2,495)	(396)	(2,099)

Source: Hargreaves and García Ferrando (1997).

Table 14 *Evaluation of the use of the Catalan flag and the Catalan national anthem together with those of Spain during the Games (%)*

	Total	Catalonia	Rest of Spain
Very good	10	42	3
Good	27	40	25
Average	18	9	20
Bad	20	2	24
Very bad	12	2	14
Indifferent	5	3	5
Don't know/no anwer	8	2	9
	(2,495)	(396)	(2,099)

Source: Hargreaves and García Ferrando (1997).

exploiting the central government's weakness in order to increase its independence risks alienating the rest of Spain and opening up past wounds. Pujol is well aware of this resistance and is careful to emphasise constantly that his demands for more autonomy are within the existing Spanish constitution. On the other hand, in Catalonia there was strong support for Catalanising the Games, and that indicates there is strong support for more independence, enabling Pujol judiciously to play the nationalist card.

Table 15 confirms the existence of a stand-off, in a sense, between Catalonia and the rest of Spain. It shows that a greater proportion of respondents in the rest of Spain (39 per cent) see little or no improvement in attitudes to Catalonia as a result of the Games. Of the 35 per cent who

Table 15 *Opinion concerning the contribution of the Games to improving relations between Catalonia and the rest of Spain (%)*

	Rest of Spain		Catalonia	
	Great/ Average	Little/ Nothing	Great/ Average	Little/ Nothing
Improved attitudes towards Catalonia in the rest of Spain	35	39	49	37
Improved links between Catalonia and the rest of Spain	32	42	44	41

Source: García Ferrando and Hargreaves (1999).

see a great or average improvement, a minority fall into the former category, if this figure is broken down; and when considering whether links between the two have been improved, a still larger proportion, paint a negative picture (42 per cent). Clearly, some sectors of public opinion were not as open as the central authorities were to Catalanising the Games. In Catalonia the view is more optimistic about Spain's attitude towards them, but it is divided quite evenly on whether links have been improved. It would seem that the experience of the Games induced the Catalan public to open up somewhat more to the rest of Spain than the latter did to Catalonia. The difference reflected resentment in the rest of Spain at the extent to which Catalonia cashed in on the Games. Such an outcome calls into question whether the Games heralded a greater tolerance of different regional identities and interests in Spain as a whole.

8   Conclusion

If, as we have argued, Olympism is one aspect of an emergent global culture, the key issue is whether it is part of a profound process whereby national cultures are being winnowed out and, if so, under what conditions and to what extent this occurs. The other main issue raised by the Barcelona Olympics was the relationship between Spain, as the official host state to the Games, and Catalonia, a historic nation within the Spanish state, which was actually staging them. Would the Games further the national integration of Spain in a way that helped to undermine Catalan culture, identity and independence, or would they help to strengthen them? The Barcelona Games demonstrated unequivocally that far from any tendency for the Games to exert a homogenising effect, in fact the very opposite occurred. Catalan self-awareness was stimulated and a process of cultural and political mobilisation was activated in which Catalan nationalism was at the forefront. A vibrant sense of cultural and national identity exists in Catalonia, carried in its history and cultural traditions and reproduced daily in its social and political institutions. Globalisation and Españolisation processes were filtered through the national culture and sense of national identity, their meaning refracted through the prism of nationalism, and their impact monitored by individuals, organisations and political parties, who made every effort to turn the Games to the cultural, economic and political advantage of Catalonia.

This was not a one-way process. However much resistance there may have been among Catalans to the Games functioning as an assault on their national identity, once their representatives had opted to play the Olympic game and Barcelona had been fortunate enough to play host, the city and its hinterland were swept into the maelstrom of economic modernisation and subjected to external cultural and political influences which they had to come to terms with. That Catalonia succeeded in doing so without sacrificing its national identity says much about the character of its culture and about the capacity of national identities and nationalism to flourish, despite globalisation and the power of state-nations.

We have argued that the outcome of the Games was due to a combination of factors. The openness to Catalonia on the part of the rest of Spain and the central government regarding Catalonia's legitimate interests and sensibilities, meant that relatively early on the rest of Spain realistically accepted that the major benefactors would be Barcelona and Catalonia. Central government accordingly diverted the required resources and responded positively to Catalan pressure for concessions. The predominant form that this pressure took was that of inclusive nationalism, i.e. a form of nationalism that was prepared to accommodate pragmatically to Spain and which, therefore, did not threaten the integrity of the state. The majority of the population of Catalonia does not identify exclusively with Catalonia, nor want independence from Spain: a large proportion are happy to be both part of Spain and of Catalonia and see no contradiction in this. Strictly speaking the studies do not reveal what feeling part of both Spain and Catalonia means for the majority of respondents. No doubt for some Spain represents the Spanish state and Catalonia the nation. Others may see the two entities differently. Whatever the case may be, however, the main point stands that there is not necessarily any feeling of ambiguity or of being in a contradictory position when individuals feel part of both.

The majority of the nationalist population are inclusive nationalists: they want home rule while remaining part of Spain. The conduct and outcome of the struggle around these Games on the Catalan side was orchestrated by 'pactism', a feature of Catalan political culture running across the political spectrum from the socialists, communists and moderate nationalists to the *independista* factions. Unlike the Basque nationalists in ETA, or the Irish nationalists in the IRA, at present no section of the Catalan nationalist movement espouses armed struggle, although in the past a politically insignificant minority did so.

The combination of an inclusive nationalism, a policy of democratic non-violent independence struggle, and a 'pactist' political culture takes us a good way towards explaining why conflict was fought out largely in symbolic terms and why political and cultural symbols were so important. The way they were deployed was absolutely crucial in determining the outcome – they were the major weapons in the conflict and it is inconceivable that without such a deployment the protagonists could have mobilised the support they did. Symbols of the nation spoke to people in their innermost being. And their deployment was especially important in a political culture which has largely abolished violence as a solution to conflict and that operates on pactist, pragmatic lines. Within the national minority the issue to be decided was, above all, what constituted the meaning of the nation, and the nationalists in a masterly way manipulated the national symbols so that the dominant message they contained was a nationalist one. In overall terms, by the end of the Games Catalan identity had been more enhanced than Spanish identity. It would be a great mistake here to think that displaying the national flag, singing the national anthem, using the national language, putting on displays featuring the national dance and national sports, and so on, was mere play-acting and posturing, or somehow a substitute for real action. The deployment of national symbols around the Games provided a direct link to the funda-mental issue of Catalonia's autonomy and Spanish and Catalan identity. National symbols were ubiquitous: they pervaded every aspect of the context of the Games and of the Games themselves. That is why it is a mistake to focus on any one aspect, such as the victory ceremonies or the torch relay as most commentators do, to demonstrate a link between Olympism and nationalism. Paradoxically, the victory ceremonies were relatively unimportant in this case. The relevant Catalan symbols, the flag and the anthem, did not figure in these ceremonies and when the Spanish flag was raised and the anthem played to celebrate a Spanish victory, it was a celebration of the Spanish nation and Spanish identity – not a nationalist display of triumph.

Several contingent factors that impinged on the Games helped to bring about the amicable outcome and aided rather than impeded Spanish national integration. First the threat of terrorism did not materialise, as it could so easily have done. Why there was no attack by any group at all – and there were a number of them in the offing – was, it seems, a matter of sheer luck. Consequently, the atmosphere of the Games was relaxed and there were no tragedies to tarnish their memory. Second, the fact that the king is a sports enthusiast, and that his son's credentials as a top yachts-man qualified him to lead the Spanish team in the parade of the athletes, meant that the public could more strongly identify with them as symbols of the nation. Sporting prowess and enthusiasm for sport have nothing necessarily to do with monarchy, but they can help to make it more popular when incumbents also happen to be sportsmen. Third, the pres-ence of an IOC president who was also, coincidentally, a member of both the Spanish and Catalan elites smoothed the negotiations between the nationalists and the centre. Fourth, the exceptional personal qualities, especially the leadership and negotiating capacities of the two main polit-ical protagonists, Maragall and Pujol, were major factors in resolving conflict. Both men stand head and shoulders above any other figure in their respective parties and one wonders what might have occurred if lesser men had taken on their functions. Last, but by no means least,

Spain won an unprecedented number of medals – more than anyone could reasonably have expected; indeed, Spain was one of the most successful countries in the Games in this respect. Countries may prepare their teams as hard as they like, but the outcome of sports competitions is notoriously uncertain. So the fortune that smiled on Spain created a national euphoria. If Spain had failed to win medals and feelings of national humiliation had arisen, the tension between Catalonia and Spain might have exploded into open conflict.

The Catalanisation process was, of course, driven by politics, but it was underpinned by cultural nationalism – a rich cultural repertoire, of which the language is the key component. This is a culture confident of its capacity to defend itself and to survive. Demonstrably, Catalan nationalism is a form of ethnic nationalism, that is, the aim is to promote an ethnic rather than a civic identity. Getting the Games accentuated the competition between these two different forms of national identity. The political elite at the centre tried to promote a civic conception of the Spanish nation, a conception that sought to avoid any association with Spanish nationalism, as such, as a discredited thing of the past. That is to say, 'Españolisation' in this context was not a manifestation of Spanish nationalism (the term is commonly associated with it in the minds of Catalan nationalists), but was part of an attempt to integrate a multinational, multicultural Spain on the basis of a civic form of national identity, and one which eschews nationalism of whatever variety.

The Catalan socialists were caught between the two. Clearly, they cared more about the Catalan language and culture than their PSOE allies in government and the rest of the political elite at the centre, but not to the extent of working within the framework of an ethnic conception of the Catalan nation like the nationalists. The Catalan socialists' conception was predominantly civic, to which the ethnic elements, though significant, were subordinated. In deploying a predominantly civic conception they were more at one with the centre's promotion of a civic, multicultural Spain.

We have argued that there was no outright winner among the different protagonists in the conflict around the Games and that the fact that they all gained something is one of the main reasons for the successful resolution of the conflict. However, it may be that in terms of the competition between ethnic nationalism and civic nationalism there was a winner. The evidence suggests that the Games reinforced Catalan identity more than Spanish identity. For historical reasons Spanish identity has been weak, and the punitive efforts of the Franco regime to enforce it ultimately made it even weaker. Whether this is a matter of the nature of historical circumstances in a given case, or whether ethnically based forms of national identity possess certain advantages over civic forms of national identity, is an interesting question. The ethnic revival in the contemporary world perhaps provides some support for the latter view. Civic conceptions of the nation and national identity are based on abstract, universal, legal–rational conceptions of rights to belong to a territorial community, whereas ethnic conceptions of the nation make immediate, concrete, particularistic and highly emotive reference to the nation as a group. The latter, perhaps, has a propensity to provide individuals with a firmer sense of belonging and an identity capable of generating a stronger sense of commitment and loyalty to the nation. What was striking about the campaign to Catalanise the Games was how energetically it was pursued compared with the efforts of the centre and the Town Hall. The nationalists made the running and their opponents seemed for most of the time to be reacting rather than taking the initiative.

We also see here that the Games witnessed not simply a clash between Catalan ethnic nationalist identity and a civic conception of national identity, but a division within the nationalist community, between separatists and those who want to remain part of Spain, or in other words, a clash between exclusive and inclusive nationalism. Thus the Games brought up not only the question of Catalonia's relations with Spain, but they also touched on the question of the viability of the Spanish state in its present form. As a matter of fact, inclusive nationalism smothered exclusive nationalism in this case, as it has done in Catalonia ever since the first elections for the Catalan government after the democratic transition; and relations with Spain worked out satisfactorily as far as the majority of people were concerned. As we have argued, this was in no small way due to the phenomenon of dual identity. But what does this case tell us about how far a national minority's drive for autonomy can go without challenging the viability of the host state? The answer seems to be, at least where stable pluralist democracies are concerned, quite far, provided nothing untoward happens. Significantly, these Games revealed a substantial opposition among the Spanish population as a whole to the presence of the core Catalan symbols – the language, the flag and the anthem – in the Games, which suggests that beyond a certain point, perhaps not too far away in this case, even inclusive Catalan nationalism could challenge the viability of the Spanish state. Minority nationalisms are rarely satisfied with the gains they make, because the national minority can only be kept mobilised if the image of the host state as nationally oppressive can be sustained; and nationalist elites are in the business of sustaining that kind of image, or otherwise they are out of business (Hargreaves, 1998). The question is, can the inclusive nationalism that Pujol espouses be sustained without pushing beyond the limits which constitute the viability of the Spanish state; and at what point would inclusive nationalism then spill over into exclusive nationalism? Before the civil war those limits were reached rather easily, with tragic results. Perhaps the ambiguity of the Spanish constitution here is helpful, rather than the hindrance that the nationalists, in some ways, see to their ambitions. It recognises historical nationalities, but it also states the indivisibility of the Spanish nation; it acknowledges the richness of regional languages, but insists that Castilian is the patrimony of all Spaniards and the official language of Spain. In the new pluralist Spain there is much more room for manoeuvre, so perhaps Catalonia can keep pushing for more autonomy and the centre can keep finding ways of gratifying that urge without jeopardising the stability of the host state. This is what seems to have occurred on the occasion of the conflict over the Games. The fact that all the main protagonists made some significant gains was vitally important and this was linked to the pluralist system that constitutes the new *España de las Autonomías*. In a pluralist system, power is likely to work in an expansive, permissive manner rather than a restrictive one, enabling all sides in a major conflict to gain something worthwhile. In contrast, in a zero-sum game situation, power is a fixed quantum and any gains made by one party are necessarily at the expense of others. The existence of pluralism does not guarantee that there will not be losers, or that there will be no irreconcilable conflict – for one thing because contingency must enter the equation. With respect to the conflict around the Olympics, if it had constituted a zero-sum game situation, Catalan nationalism could have been an explosive, destabilising force.

On this occasion the outcome of the conflict surrounding the Games represented, not a reinforcement of Spanish hegemony, but a significant step in the delicate process of negotiating a greater degree of autonomy for Catalonia within the existing democratic constitution. Spanish prestige and Spanish identity were enhanced simultaneously, so there was no fundamental challenge to the integrity of the Spanish state. Here the predominance of dual rather than polarised national identities, and inclusive rather than exclusive nationalism, proved to be stabilising factors contributing to national integration. This is, perhaps, a timely reminder that a unitary, one-dimensional national identity is not a prerequisite for a viable state.

Bibliography

PRIMARY SOURCES

SPANISH/CATALAN PRESS

Avui, occasional (broadly Catalanist, Barcelona-based, Catalan-language newspaper)

El Observador, occasional (populist, Barcelona-based, Spanish-language newspaper, now defunct)

El País, February–July 1992 (a left-of-centre, liberal, Madrid-based, Spanish-language, national newspaper with a Barcelona edition oriented to its Catalan readership)

El Periodico, occasional (populist, Barcelona-based, Spanish-language newspaper)

La Vanguardia, Febuary–July 1992 (conservative, CiU-orientated, Barcelona-based, Spanish-language newspaper and leading organ of the Catalan press)

INTERVIEWS WITH KEY PERSONNEL IN THE FOLLOWING GOVERNMENTAL ORGANISATIONS

Organising Committee of the Barcelona '92 Olympic Games (COOB)
Generalitat de Catalunya (Catalan government)
Diputació de Barcelona (Barcelona provincial government)
Ajuntament de Barcelona (Barcelona Town Hall)
Consejo Superior de Deportes, Madrid (Spanish Sports Council)

INTERVIEWS WITH KEY PERSONNEL IN THE FOLLOWING POLITICAL ORGANISATIONS AND INTEREST GROUPS

Catalan Olympic Committee
Acció Olímpica
La Crida de la Solidaridat
Esquerra Republicana (ERC)

OTHER SOURCES

COOB, 1992a, *Pressbook for the Opening Ceremony*

166

COOB, 1992b, *Pressbook for the Closing Ceremony*

Centro de Investigaciones Sociológicas (CIS) 1992, 'Estudio 2018 Barometro', Madrid: CIS.

Hargreaves, J. E., 1994, *Final Report to the ESRC, Olympism and Nationalism*, Award Number R.-000.-23.-3970

Hargreaves, J. E., 1995, 'Staat und Nation: Politik auf drei ebenen bei den Olympischen Spielen in Barcelona', in Lüschen, G. und Rütten, A. eds., *Sportpolitik und Sportorganisation*, Stuttgart: Nagelschmidt Verlag.

Hargreaves, J. E., and García Ferrando, 1997, 'Public Opinion, National Integration and National Identity in Spain: the Case of the Barcelona Olympic Games', *Nations and Nationalism*, 3(1).

García Ferrando, M. and Hargreaves, J. E., 1999, 'La Paradoja Olímpica y el Nacionalismo: el caso de los Juegos Olímpicos de Barcelona', in Heinemann, K. and Schubert, M., *Sport und Gesellschaft*, Schorndorf: Hofmann.

SECONDARY SOURCES

Abe, I., Kiyohara, Y., Nayajima, K., 1992, 'Fascism, Sport and Society in Japan' *International Journal of the History of Sport*, 9 (1).

Anderson, B., 1983, *Imagined Communities*, London: Verso.

Antich, J., 1994, *El Virrey*, Barcelona: Editorial Planeta.

Appadurai, A., 1991, 'Decolonising the Production of Culture: Cricket in Contemporary India', in *Towards One World*, Seoul Olympiad Anniversary Conference, vol. I, Seoul: Poon Nam Publishing Company

Armstrong, J. A., 1982, *Nations Before Nationalism*, Chapel Hill: University of North Carolina Press.

Bairner, A. and Darby, P., 1999, 'Divided Sport in a Divided Society: Northern Ireland', in Sugden, J. and Bairner, A., eds., *Sport in Divided Societies*, Aachen Meyer and Meyer.

Balcells, A., 1996, *Catalan Nationalism*, London: Macmillan.

Barrera-González, A., 1995, *Language, Collective Identities and Nationalism in Catalonia and Spain in General*, Florence: European University Institute Working Paper No. 95/6.

Billig, M., 1995, *Banal Nationalism*, Sage: London.

Boix, J. and Espada, A., 1991, *El deporte del poder. Vida y milagro de Juan Antonio Samaranch*, Madrid: Ediciones Temas de Hoy.

Brennan, G., 1962, *The Spanish Labyrinth*, Cambridge: Cambridge University Press.

Breuilly, J., 1993, *Nationalism and the State*, Manchester: Manchester University Press.

Brown, D., 1999, 'Are There Good and Bad Nationalisms?', *Nations and Nationalism* 5 (2): 281–302

Brubaker, R., 1996, *Nationalism Reframed*, Cambridge: Cambridge University Press.

Brunet, F., 1992, *Economics of the Barcelona Olympic Games*, Barcelona: Centre d'Estudis Olímpics, Autonomous University of Barcelona.

Burns, J., 1999, *Barça: A People's Passion*, London: Bloomsberry.

Busquet, J., 1992, *Cobi Al Descobert*, Barcelona: Parsifal Edicions.

Cabana, F. *et al.*, 1998, *Catalunya i Espanya una relació economica i fiscal a revisar*, Barcelona: Proa la mirada.

Cardús, S., 1992, 'La estrategia de la condescendencia', *El País*, 24 August 1992.

Crexell, J., 1994, *Nacionalisme i Jocs Olímpics del 1992*, Barcelona: Columna.

Conversi, D., 1997, *The Basques, the Catalans and Spain*, London: Hurst and Co.

De Grazia, V., 1981, The Culture of Consent, Cambridge: Cambridge University Press.

Diez Medrano, J., 1995, *Divided Nations*, London: Cornell University Press.

Dixon, J. G., 1986, 'Prussia, Politics and Physical Education', in P. McIntosh *et al.*, eds., *Landmarks in the History of Physical Education*, London: Routledge.

Duke, V. and Crolley, L., *Football, Nationality and the State*, Harlow: Longman.

Durkheim, E., 1982, *The Elementary Forms of the Religious Life*, London: George Allen.

Eisen, G., 1984, 'The Voices of Sanity: American Diplomatic Reports from the 1936 Berlin Olympiad', *Journal of Sport History*, 11 (3).

Elliot, J., 1963, *The Revolt of the Catalans*, Cambridge: Cambridge University Press.

Estradé, A. and Treserra, M., 1990, *Catalunya Independent?*, Barcelona: Fundació Jaume Bofill.

European Commission, 1992, *Olympic Programme 1992*, Neuilly/Seine.

Ferrater i Mora, J., 1960, *Les formes de la vida catalana*, Barcelona: Selecta.

Finley, M. and Pleket, H., 1976, *The Olympic Games: The First Thousand Years*, London: Chatto and Windus.

Flaquer, L. 1996, 'Language and Identity in Barcelona: Catalan as a Tool or as a Symbol'?, paper presented to the conference on Paisagens Urbanas: Espaço e Poder nas Grandes Metrópoles, Universidade Estadual de Caminas, Brazil.

Flaquer, L. and Giner, S., 1991a, *El debat de la cultura catalana*, Barcelona: Centre d'Estudis de Temes Contemporans.

1991b, *La cultura catalana: propostres teòriques i metodològiques*, Barcelona: Centre d'Estudis de Temes Contemporans.

García Ferrando, M., 1990, *Los Hábitos deportivos de los Españoles*, Madrid: Consejo Superior de Deportes.

García Ferrando, M,. 1992, 'Including and Excluding Nationalisms: Dual Identity in Spain', paper presented at the First European Conference of Sociology, Section III/6 Regional, Ethnic and National Identities, University of Vienna, 26–29 August.

García Ferrando, M. *et al.*, 1994, *La conciencia nacional y regional en la España de las autonomías*, Madrid: Centro de Investigaciones Sociológicas.

Gellner, E, 1983, *Nations and Nationalism*, Oxford: Blackwell.

Giddens, A., 1990, *The Consequences of Modernity*, Cambridge: Polity Press.

Giner, S., 1986, '*Political Economy*, Cultural Legitimation and the State in Southern Europe' in O'Donnell, G., Schmitter, P. and Whitehead, L., eds., *Transitions from Authoritarian Rule in Southern Europe*, Baltimore, Md.: Johns Hopkins University Press.

1984, *The Social Structure of Catalonia*, London: Anglo-Catalan Society.

Goksøyr, M., 1996, 'Phrases and Functions of Nationalism: Norway's Utilisation of International Sport in the late Ninteenth and Early Twentieth Centuries', in Mangan, J., *Tribal Identities*, London: Cass.

Greenfeld, L., 1992, *Nationalism: Five Roads to Modernity*, London: Harvard University Press.

Gruneau, R. and Cantelon, H., 1988, 'Capitalism, Commercialism, and the Olympics', in Seagrave, J. and Chu, D., 1988, *The Olympic Games in Transition*, Champaign, Ill.: Human Kinetics Books.

Guelke, A., 1993, 'Sport and the End of Apartheid', in Allison, L., ed., *The Changing Politics of Sport*, Manchester: Manchester University Press.

Guelke, A. and Sugden, J., 1999, 'Sport and the "Normalising" of South Africa', in Sugden J. and Bairner, A., eds., *Sport in Divided Societies*, Aachen: Meyer and Meyer.

Guttman, A., 1984, *The Games Must Go On*, New York: Columbia University Press.

1992, *The Olympics: A History of the Modern Games*, Urbana, Ill.: University of Illinois Press.

1994, *Games and Empires*, New York: Columbia Press.

Hall, J., 1986, *The Congress of Catalan Traditional and Popular Culture*, Barcelona: Fundació Serveis de Cultura Popular.

Hargreaves, J., 1986, *Sport, Power and Culture*, Cambridge: Polity Press.

1992, 'Olympism and Nationalism: Some Preliminary Considerations', *International Review for the Sociology of Sport*, 27, (1).

1998, 'Reply to Keating on Stateless Nation-Building in Catalonia, Quebec and Scotland, Ethno-Nationalist Movements in Europe: A Debate', *Nations and Nationalism*, 4 (4), 569–574.

Harvey, J., 1999, 'Sport and Quebec Nationalism: Ethnic or Civic Identity?', in Sugden, J. and Bairner, A., *Sport in Divided Societies*, Aachen: Meyer and Meyer.

Hastings, A, 1997, *The Construction of Nationhood*, Cambridge: Cambridge University Press.

Hechter, M. and Levi, M., 1994, 'Ethno-Regional Movements in the West', in Hutchinson, J. and Smith, A. D., eds., *Nationalism*, Oxford: Oxford University Press.

Hill, C., 1992, *Olympic Politics*, Manchester: Manchester University Press.

Hirst, P. and Thompson, G., 1996, *Globalisation in Question*, Cambridge: Polity Press.

Hoberman, J., 1995, 'Toward a Theory of Olympic Internationalism', *Journal of Sport History*, 22 (1).

Hobsbawm, E., 1990, *Nations and Nationalism Since 1780*, Cambridge: Cambridge University Press.

Holt, R., 1995, 'Contrasting Nationalisms: Sport, Militarism and the Unitary State in Britain and France before 1914', *International Journal of the History of Sport*, 12 (2).

Houlihan, B., 1994, *Sport and International Politics*, London: Harvester Wheatsheaf.

1997, 'Sport, National Identity and Public Policy', *Nations and Nationalism*, 3 (1).

Hughes, R., 1992, *Barcelona*, London: Harvill.

James, C., 1976, *Beyind a Boundary*, London: Hutchinson.

Jarvie, G. and Walker, G., 1994, *Scottish Sport in the Making of the Nation*, Leicester: Leicester University Press.

Jennings, A., 1996, *The New Lords of the Rings*, London: Simon and Schuster.

Jennings, A. and Simson, V., 1991, *Lords of the Rings*, London: Simon and Schuster.

Junco, J., 1996, 'Spanish Nationalism in the Nineteenth Century', in Smith, A. and Mar Molinero, C., eds., *Nationalism and National Identity in the Iberian Peninsula*, Oxford: Berg.

Kanin, D., 1981, *The Political History of the Olympic Games*, Boulder: Westwood Press.

Killanin, Michael, Lord, 1983, *My Olympic Years*, London: Secker and Warburg.

Kim, J., 1989, *Impact of the Seoul Olympic Games on National Development*, Seoul: Korea Development Institute.

Kruger, A., 1996, 'Buying Victories is Positively Degrading: European Origins of Government Pursuit of National Prestige through Sport', in Mangan, J., ed, *Tribal Identities* London: Cass.

Kurth, J. and Petras, J., eds., 1993, *Mediterranean Paradoxes*, Oxford: Berg.

Lawrence, G. and Rowe, D., eds., 1986, *Power Play*, Sydney: Hale and Iremonger.

Laitin, D., 1989, 'Linguistic Revival: Politics and Culture in Catalonia', *Comparative Studies in Society and History*, 31, 2.

Linz, J., 1973, 'Early State-Building and Late Peripheral Nationalism Against the State: The Case of Spain', in Eisenstadt, S. N. and Rokkan, S., eds., *Building States and Nations*, vol. II, London: Sage.

Linz, J. and Stepan, A., 1996, *Problems of Democratic Transition and Consolidation*, London: Johns Hopkins University Press.

Llobera, J., 1983, 'The Idea of Volksgeist in the Formation of Catalan Nationalist Ideology', in *Ethnic and Racial Studies*, 6 (3) 333–50.

    1989, 'Catalan National Identity: The Dialectics of Past and Present', in M. MacDonald, *et al.*, eds., *History and Ethnicity*, London: Tavistock.

    1994, *The God of Modernity*, Oxford: Berg.

Llobera, J. forthcoming, 'The Force of Language and National Identity: The Western European Experience', in Barrera, A. and MacDonald, S., *The Politics of Language*, London: Routledge.

Lukes, S., 1975, 'Political Ritual and Social Integration', in *Sociology*, 9 (2).

MacAloon, J., 1981, *This Great Symbol: Pierre de Coubertin and the Origins of the Modern Olympic Games*, Chicago: Chicago University Press.

    1996, 'Humanism as Political Necessity?: Reflections on the Pathos of Anthropological Science in Olympic Contexts', *Quest*, 48, (1).

Mandell, R., 1971, *The Nazi Olympics*, New York: Macmillan.

Mann, M., 1993, 'Nation-States in Europe and Other Continents: Diversifying, Developing, Not Dying', *Daedalus*, 122 (3).

Miller, D., 1992, *The Olympic Revolution*, London; Pavilion.

Monnington, T., 1986, 'The Politics of Black African Sport', in Allison, A., *The Politics of Sport*, Manchester: Manchester University Press.

Moragas, M., 1992, *Los Juegos de la comunicación*, Madrid: Fundesco.

Moral, F., 1998, *Identidad regional y nacionalismo en el Estado de las Autonomias*, Madrid: CIS.

Nieguth, T., 1999, 'Beyond Dichotomy: concepts of the nation and the distribution of membership', *Nations and Nationalism*, 5 (2), 155–73.

Pallarés, F., 1994, 'Las elecciones autonómicas en España, 1980–1992', in P. de Castillo, ed., *Comportamiento político y electoral*, Madrid: CIS.

Perez Díaz, V., 1993, *The Return of Civil Society*, Cambridge, Mass.: Harvard University Press.

Preston, P., 1986, *The Triumph of Democracy in Spain*, London: Routledge.

1990, *The Politics of Revenge*, London: Unwin Hyman.

Puigjaner, J., 1992, *Everything About Catalonia*, Barcelona: Generalitat de Catalunya.

Pujadas, X. and Santacana, C., 1992, 'The Popular Olympic Games, Barcelona 1936: Olympians and Antifascists', *International Review for the Sociology of Sport*, 27 (2), 138–50.

Real, M., 1996, 'The Postmodern Olympics: Technology and the Commodification of the Olympic Movement', *Quest*, 48 (1).

Robertson, R., 1990, 'Mapping the Global Condition: Globalisation as a Central Concept', in Featherstone, M., ed., *Global Culture: Nationalism, Globalisation and Modernity*, London: Sage.

Shabad, G. and Gunther, R. 1982, 'Language, Nationalism and Political Conflict in Spain, *Comparative Politics*, 14, (4).

Shaw, D., 1987, *Fútbol y franquismo*, Madrid: Alianza Editiorial.

Smith, A. D., 1986, *The Ethnic Origins of Nations*, Oxford: Blackwell.

1990, 'Towards a Global Culture?', in Featherstone, M., ed., *Nationalism, Globalisation and Modernity*, London: Sage.

1991, *National Identity*, London: Penguin.

Sobrequés, J., 1982, *El pactisme a Catalunya*, Barcelona: Edicions 62.

Solé Tura, J., 1974, *Catalanismo y revolución burguesa*, Madrid: Cuadernos para el Diágolo.

Stuart, O., 1996, 'Players, Workers, Protesters: Social Change and Soccer in Colonial Zimbabwe', in MacClancy, J., ed., *Sport, Identity and Ethnicity*, Oxford: Berg.

Sugden, J. and Bairner, A., 1986, 'Sport in a Divided Society', in Allison, L. ed., *The Politics of Sport*, Manchester: Manchester University Press.

1993, National Identity, 'Community Relations and Sporting Life in Northern Ireland', in Allison, L., ed., *The Changing Politics of Sport*, Manchester: Manchester University Press.

Tejero, E., 1992, 'El Poblenou: El canvi urbanístic i la transformació social', in *Revista de Sociología*, 38, Universitat Autónoma de Barcelona.

Thomas, H., 1965, *The Spanish Civil War*, London: Penguin.

Tilly, C., 1975, *The Formation of National States in Western Europe*, Princeton: Princeton University Press.

Trias, J., 1992, 'Symbol and Logo of the Barcelona '92 Olympic Games', in *Olympic Games: Media and Cultural Exchanges*, Barcelona: Centre d'Estudis Olímpics.

Turner, V. W., 1970, 'Symbols in Ndembu Ritual', in Emmett, D. and

MacIntyre, A., *Sociological Theory and Philosophical Analysis*, London: Macmillan.

Vanreusal, B. *et al.*, 1999, 'Divided Sports in a Divided Belgium', in Sugden, J. and Bairner, A., eds., *Sport in Divided Societies*, Aachen: Meyer and Meyer.

Vázquez Montalbán, M., 1992, *Barcelonas*, London: Verso.

Vegara, J. and Salvador, N., 1992, *The Economic Impact of the Barcelona '92 Olympic Games*, Barcelona: Ajuntament de Barcelona.

Vicens Vives, J., 1954, *Notícia de Catalunya*, Barcelona: Destino.

Weber, M., 1948, 'Politics as a Vocation', in Gerth, H. and Wright Mills, C., eds., *From Max Weber*, London: Routledge.

Werbner, P., eds. '"Our Blood is Green": Cricket, Identity and Social Empowerment Among British Pakistanis', in MacClancy, J., ed., *Sport, Identity and Ethnicity*, Oxford: Berg.

Woolard, K., 1986, 'The Crisis in the Concept of Identity in Contemporary Catalonia, 1976–82', in McDonogh, G., *Conflict in Catalonia*, Gainesville: University of Florida Press.

1989, *Double Talk: Bilingualism and the Politics of Ethnicity in Catalonia*, Stamford, Calif.: Stanford University Press.

Index